Supervisory Skills

ALSO AVAILABLE IN THE BANKING CERTIFICATE SERIES:

PRELIMINARY SECTION

Banking: The Business
Geoffrey Lipscombe
ISBN 0 273 03192 9

Business Calculations for Bankers*
Helen Coult
ISBN 0 273 02884 7

Business Communication for Bankers
Gill Kelly
ISBN 0 273 03325 5

FINAL SECTION

Banking Operations – UK Lending and International Business*
Audrey Davies and Martin Kearns
ISBN 0 273 02879 0

Banking: the Legal Environment (2nd Edition)*
David Palfreman
ISBN 0 273 03701 3

Customer Services – Marketing and the Competitive Environment*
Phil Ford
ISBN 0 273 02883 9

Economics and the Banks' Role in the Economy (2nd Edition)*
Geoffrey Lipscombe
ISBN 0 273 03250 X

Introduction to Accounting
Karl Harper
ISBN 0 273 02880 4

PITMAN BOOKS FOR THE BANKING DIPLOMA (SERIES EDITOR: B J BEECHAM)

Management in Banking
Helen Coult
ISBN 0 273 03218 6

Accountancy
Peter MacNamara
ISBN 0 273 03216 X

The Monetary and Financial System
B J Beecham
ISBN 0 273 03245 3

Law Relating to Banking Services
Paul Raby
ISBN 0 273 03217 8

Published in association with the Chartered Institute of Bankers

SUPERVISORY SKILLS

SECOND EDITION

Brian Stone

Series Editor: David Palfreman

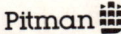

PITMAN PUBLISHING
128 Long Acre, London WC2E 9AN
A Division of Longman Group UK Limited

© B Stone 1988, 1991

First published in Great Britain 1988
Second edition published in 1991

British Library Cataloguing in Publication Data
Stone, Brian
 Supervisory skills. – 2nd ed. – (Banking
 certificate series)
 I. Title II. Series
 658.3

ISBN 0–273–03501–0

All rights reserved; no part of this publication may be reproduced, stored in a retrieval system, or transmitted in any form or by any means, electronic, mechanical, photocopying, recording, or otherwise without either the prior written permission of the Publishers or a licence permitting restricted copying in the United Kingdom issued by the Copyright Licensing Agency Ltd, 90 Tottenham Court Road, London W1P 9HE. This book may not be lent, resold, hired out or otherwise disposed of by way of trade in any form of binding or cover other than that in which it is published, without the prior consent of the Publishers.

Printed and bound in Great Britain

Contents

Preface   vii

Acknowledgements   ix

1 Organisations   1

Objectives – Introduction – History – Organisational functions – Alternative structures – Depicting organisations – Organisational roles – Objectives – Targets and behaviour – Specifications for good targets – Objectives and the supervisor – Summary – Self-assessment questions

2 The supervisor   19

Objectives – Introduction – What is a supervisor? – Early days – Learning the elements of the supervisor's role – The supervisor's boss – Supervisors and staff – People and production – Objectives and expectations – Relationships – Role separation – Summary – Self-assessment questions

3 Management techniques   36

Objectives – Introduction – Objective setting – Forecasting and planning – Organising – Problem-solving – Decision-making – Group decision-making – Delegation – Monitoring and control – Communication: a definition – The communications model – Originating messages – Encoding – Selection of medium – Receiving – The problems of decoding – Composition – Briefings and presentations – Information technology – Summary – Self-assessment questions

4 Managing the individual   66

Objectives – Introduction – Individual differences – The seven-point plan – Occasions for selection – Training responsibility – Training and learning – On- or off-the-job training? – Planning and controlling training – The supervisor as trainer – Motivation – The system and staff expectations – Internal motivation – Needs – Satisfaction – Satisfaction and motivation – Human interaction – Advice and counselling – Interviewing – Summary – Self-assessment questions

5 Managing the group   92

Objectives – Introduction – Groups: a definition – Why do groups form? – Social/affiliation needs – Formal and informal groups – Group boundaries – Group formation and development – Group norms – Enforcing the rules – Group communication – Leadership – Leadership qualities – Situational leadership – Leadership and management style –

Action-centred leadership – The overlaps – Group needs and leadership – Groups and teams – Management team roles – MBWA (Management by walking about) – Summary – Self-assessment questions

6 Managing yourself   115

Objectives – Introduction – Time management – Self knowledge – Assertiveness – Not my problem - your problem – Summary – Self-assessment questions

7 The rules and the law   135

Objectives – Introduction – The need for health and safety – Health and Safety at Work Act 1974 – Health and safety committees – Policy statements – Health, safety and the supervisor – Branch security in banks – Drills – Sickness procedures – Conditions of employment – The declaration of secrecy – Employment protection – Equal opportunity – The staff and money – Inspectors and auditors – Summary – Self-assessment questions

8 Procedures   156

Objectives – Introduction – Staff representation – Office representatives – Staff consultation and participation schemes – Quality circles – Performance appraisal – Grievance and discipline – Training procedures – Planning for training – After training – Professional qualifications – Mobility and changes of location – Other procedures – Summary – Self-assessment questions

9 Benefits   179

Objectives – Introduction – The rewards package – Wages and salaries – Job evaluation – The grading system – Manager's salaries – Salaries and the supervisor – Overtime – Financially beneficial schemes – Car, car loan and leasing schemes – Location allowance – Holidays as a benefit – Working conditions – Use of the company 'product' – House purchase loans – Other loans – Bank accounts – Pensions – Benefits and the supervisor – Summary – Self-assessment questions

Appendix   200
Index   213

Preface

This book has been written as a textbook for the Supervisory Skills paper of the Chartered Institute of Bankers' Banking Certificate. When the syllabus for this paper was designed, the intention was to aim it at people in supervisory positions who would take the Banking Certificate examinations for one or more of a number of reasons: they may wish to give themselves a qualification which would permit them to enter for the higher level Banking Diploma and the Associateship of the Chartered Institute of Bankers; they may wish to gain a qualification which would indicate their proficiency at supervisor level, and leave it at that; or they may wish to study simply to learn more about their profession and their work.

When you read this volume you will find that it is written with all of these purposes in mind, but of all of them, the last named has been the main thrust: it is for supervisors who genuinely want to improve their supervisory skills – but then, after all, the examinations would be quite meaningless if they too did not have exactly the same purpose. The book follows the syllabus of the Institute's Supervisory Skills closely (which is hardly surprising since the syllabus was composed by the same author). It has a strong flavour of the systematic, containing lists and tables and diagrams and schemes of learning, where possible, to provide useful study tools.

These lists and tables also help supervisors to take a systematic look at their working environment, and the personalities, behaviours and motivations of the people who work for them. They will also point out in a methodical way the rights and wrongs of what the supervisor is already doing, possibly more intuitively than thoughtfully. This is because of a strong belief that whatever is done consciously, as a manager, is going to be more effective in the long run than what is done instinctively: a good supervisor never does anything accidentally.

Both for work improvements and for examination preparation, there are activities placed throughout the text, such as to write something down, go and get a copy of a document available to bank supervisors, give special thought to a topic, relate what you have read to your own work situation, etc. This is not done in any conversational sense: they are deliberately placed, or timed, to enhance your learning experience.

It is also obvious that in this subject you clarify the ideas in your mind by noting their relationship with your real world of work. You may, by the way, find that examples you come up with actually disprove or deny what is said in this text. That should be no problem: no examiner will refuse a well-argued, well-backed refutation of the textbook argument if it is sensibly put and properly and thoughtfully illustrated – which is another good reason for thinking the ideas through when requested to do so in this book.

Especially in the later chapters, it is suggested that you get hold of your own organisation's documentation, such as recruitment and appraisal forms, or statements of policy, or training requisition forms and feedback forms, or digests of procedures. You must understand that this is no idle or even just helpful suggestion: it is imperative that you obtain these documents.

In fact, if tutors are following the Institute and the Chief Examiner's suggestions, either in correspondence or in face-to-face courses, you will find that you are requested to bring and compare your bank's forms with those of your classmates, or to base your correspondence answer on a good knowledge and a working familiarity with your bank's various forms. This is provided always that you are confident that you are not in breach of your principles of confidentiality, and you can always check this with your bank's personnel or training departments. If you are reading this book for the purpose of improving your view of supervisory skills, and hopefully, your performance, it is equally important for you to know your own bank's specific practices in the areas in which such a book as this can only deal with generalities and good practices.

At this point it is worth mentioning that the book can be used by those who do not work in a bank but in a similar, structured organisation, in which they are the supervisors of clerical staff. Certainly in the first six chapters, you can almost always substitute the word 'organisation' for the word 'bank' and not change the meaning. On the rare occasions where there are technical banking phrases or names for, say, sections or departments, these are easily understood. Even for the later sections, there are parallel or other procedures and benefits available to staff, and the principle of learning by obtaining the organisation's documentation and studying it still applies. Where examples are given they are largely set in a bank, but this is for dramatic purposes only: you will find very similar characters and plots in an office in the Civil Service, or college, or employment agency, or insurance company!

Now as to the content of the book itself: each chapter begins with a set of objectives for the chapter, and you are well advised to think of the meaning of each of these carefully before you start. There follows a short introduction, which expands on the objectives so as to clarify any problems. Then there is the text followed by a summary of the chapter and finally a set of questions. These are not, nor are they intended to be, examination questions; they simply recall to your mind some of the major points in the text, and help you to cement your learning by reminding you of them.

People have asked whether these is a danger of overlap between the knowledge needed for the CIB Supervisory Skills paper at the Banking Certificate level, and the Management in Banking paper at Diploma level. The answer is that obviously there is overlap, but it is no danger. The subject is the management of people and the custodianship of organisational rules; the principles are the same at whatever management level. The direct responsibilities differ, and in this book we have tried to aim carefully and constantly at the supervisor's, the first level of management's situation in the organisation.

Acknowledgments

This book was written with the help of a lot of people, and I can only mention the more significant ones.

I worked in management training for about eleven years for Williams & Glyn's Bank, now Royal Bank of Scotland, and all of my former friends there, especially at supervisory level, have contributed to my writing this book and aiming it at the right level.

The encouragement of my friend and colleague Chris Bagley at Manchester Polytechnic helped me to keep going in writing and revising the book.

My Deputy Chief Examiner in Supervisory Skills for the Chartered Institute of Bankers, Tricia Goodyear, has kept me on the track of technical accuracy when I sail close to the wind of the specifics of banking practice, with the permission and help of her employers, the Royal Bank of Scotland.

My academic colleague David Palfreman has given invaluable support, advice and help as an experienced writer of technical books, as well as in contributing hugely to the production of this volume.

At the Chartered Institute of Bankers, the cooperation of Ruth Palmer has helped me sustain my interest in banking management at the supervisory level; thanks also to Justyn Young, who involved me with the development of some computer-assisted learning in this subject.

I am indebted to the late Alan Siddall, once Assistant General Manager of Williams & Glyn's Bank. He proposed me for fellowship of the Institute, and set me a great example in energy and appetite for life.

Brian Stone
Manchester Polytechnic
Business Studies Department

1 Organisations

OBJECTIVES

When you have read this chapter, you should be able to:
- **Recount the recent history of thinking about organisations, and the reasons for modern ideas about them;**
- **Relate the importance of this thinking to your organisation and its various functions;**
- **Understand how important it is that organisational structure matches what the organisation has to do;**
- **Understand the variety of an organisation's functions and how they relate with each other;**
- **Depict an organisation in more than one way, and show what your diagram actually means to convey;**
- **Convey sensible ideas about organisational objectives, and their importance to the behaviour of employees;**
- **Relate these ideas to your own organisation, its objectives and how these are conveyed to staff;**
- **Think clearly about levels of objectives, down to the operational targets visible to supervisory staff;**
- **Consider how such targets are made known to you and your staff;**
- **Carefully examine the role of the supervisor with relation to organisational objectives.**

■ INTRODUCTION

We all work in organisations, but the only occasions on which we devote time to thinking about the organisation as such are in casual conversation or when preparing for examinations! We even take the word 'organisation' for granted, and most people could define it only with some difficulty.

Let us take a simple working definition which will help us to structure the discussion you will find in this chapter:

A group of *roles* arranged in a *structure* to pursue a set of *objectives*.

Each of the emphasised words is important. To start with, why 'roles'? Why not 'people'? The answer is that it will help us to understand the structure and functions of modern organisations if we realise that there are many ways in which organisations remain the same regardless of which person occupies which role. In other words, we can and shall start by looking at organisations in terms of 'The Chief Executive' rather than, say, 'Mr Paul Heath'; or 'The Manager, Cleethorpes Branch' rather than 'Miss Sarah Doyle'.

What is more, the organisational role we take, and our perception of the nature of that role, is one of the strongest influences on what we actually do in our working life, and even on how we identify ourselves, to ourselves and to others. Consider, for example, how you answer when strangers ask you in social conversation: 'And what do you do?'

Structure is also important. What people do in organisations – this is particularly important for anyone in a supervisory position – has a great deal to do with how they see the structure. It powerfully affects what they think it is legitimate to do, and the way in which they respond to orders, discipline and direction. It is also a vital determinant of how the organisation reacts to its environment, that is, markets, social environment, new advances in technology, labour/employment position, competition and so on.

For this reason we shall spend some time looking at how we depict organisations, graphically and in words, because the better supervisors understand exactly their place in it, the better they can use the elements of the organisation's structure to further its objectives (the essence of their role, as we shall see later in this book).

Objectives are almost literally the reason for the existence of the organisation; and yet as we develop the theme, and your thinking about them, you may be surprised at how difficult they are to pin down in practice. Objectives should be clear statements about what the organisation and the various parts of it, down to the individual worker, are supposed to achieve. It is a fault of very many organisations in the world we live in, however, that most people are more concerned with what they are supposed to *do*, rather than what they are supposed to *achieve*. It is in fact the organisation's fault rather than the workers': if you cannot find clear statements about aims, you make sure you don't get anything wrong instead of showing initiative! Performance must be better where there are clear statements about objectives, everyday-practical as well as philosophical.

As representative of the organisation to the staff, among other things, it is an important part of the supervisor's role to seek out, interpret and convey both the overall objectives and the operational aims and targets to the people working for them. Think how much more effective your staff would be if they could clearly see what they are aiming for, and if all their efforts were properly aimed at visible, achievable, agreed targets.

In summary, in this chapter we will look at what organisations are, how people react to the place they find themselves in organisations, and in which direction they direct their efforts.

■ HISTORY

Thinking about organisations has been going on a long time: the Roman army was not organised without a fair amount of theory! Yet recent thought concerning people in organisations, and organisations in society, dates back to the end of the nineteenth century when the industrial and commercial world was completing its change from small, owner-run units to the larger industrial and commercial organisations resulting from the Industrial Revolution. Banks were not exempt from this move: financing the new enterprises had even earlier become too much for the smaller banking operations, and these had already had to combine to cope with the larger sums and longer terms demanded by the new commercial companies.

Weber

These phenomena attracted the attention of theoreticians and practising efficiency experts alike. The theory element interested social scientists, concerned with the human aspects of organisations. One such was the German social scientist, Max Weber.

What Weber sought were principles which would describe perfect models of kinds of organisation; he called these *ideal types*. He discovered three ideal types, based on the nature of leadership in the organisation. These were:

1 *charismatic:* organisations whose structure was based on the leader's strength and personality, e.g. Genghis Khan;
2 *traditional:* organisations where succession to leadership was based on clear tradition such as sons succeeding parents, e.g. as in the American 'Dynasty' soap-series;
3 *legal-rational:* organisations characterised by impersonal rules and specifications concerning the posts occupied rather than the people occupying them.

The last-named has become known as the *bureaucratic* type of organisation. According to Weber, what makes an organisation bureaucratic, is that it has:

- written specifications for every position;
- top-to-bottom hierarchy of lines of authority and responsibility;
- succession to and occupation of jobs by qualified, trained personnel;
- continuity and impersonality, i.e. no task dependent on the personality;
- a bureau which contains a written record of every move, i.e. the central files.

The word 'bureaucratic' actually means that the office rules, and the above list shows why.

ACTIVITY 1.1
(a) Give one or more of your own examples of charismatic, traditional, bureaucratic leadership, from history, current affairs, or your own experience.
(b) Ask yourself: closest to which of these ideal types do banks come? Do they have elements of all three? In what way do they differ?

Classical theory

As the twentieth century and its organisations became more sophisticated, a school of organisational thinkers emerged, whose main aim was to prescribe corrective principles for companies as well as to describe them for interest. These were called the *Classical School*, and included such names as Urwick, Fayol, and Gilbreth. They emerged with a more elaborate set of central elements for good organisation, some of them following along the lines set out by Weber, such as:

- *continuity:* posts continue even when the person moves on;
- *specialisation:* jobs are subdivided into tasks, and the job-holder is trained specially to do them;
- *scalar principle:* there is a hierarchy of command, straight from top to bottom;
- *unity of command:* only one boss for each person to report to;
- *parity principle:* responsibility is matched by authority;
- *unity of direction:* one set of objectives, and all aim at it;
- *span of control:* nobody has too many people reporting to them;
- *corporate interest:* individual interests subordinate to those of the organisation.

How, if at all, do you think banks adhere to these principles. Stop for a moment and think through a specific example in your own experience of the operation of each principle, or an example of where there has been a clear breach. The statement of these principles here should focus your attention on organisations and their nature. Later we will look at the supervisor's part in maintaining efficiency of the organisation's operations.

Systems thinking and contingency

Not too long after people had tried to suggest 'best' ways for organisations to structure themselves, came the thought that an overall principle you should apply was embodied in the phrase 'it all depends...'. In technical language, this was called *contingency theory*. For our purposes, we will link this up with a way of thinking which became popular after World War II and gave rise to new sciences such as computing and cybernetics, called *systems thinking*. It also has repercussions for organisational theory, as we will see.

In essence, systems thinking suggests you take any 'working thing', e.g. an organism or an organisation or a machine, and note that you can draw a diagram of its essential operation and show that all 'working things' have certain elements in common: they have a *boundary* round them, defined wherever the drawer wants to say what is in and what is out in the *environment*. Things go into the system, called *inputs,* in the form of energy, information or material (or any combination); things come out, called *outputs,* also in the form of energy, information or material; and inside the system *conversions* take place. Most living systems have 'holes' so that they can react with the environment; therefore these systems are called *open systems*. Some of what the system puts out goes back in; this is called *feedback*. A systems diagram is shown in Fig. 1.1.

Please note that in such systems as organisations, the conversions would not just involve technical or machine operations, but also social or people operations; for this reason this kind of system is called a *socio-technical system*. One other feature of systems thinking is that it points out that tampering with any element, either outside or inside the system, alters the operation of any other element.

ACTIVITY 1.2

(a) Just to get this clear in your mind, stop and apply the diagram to, say, your hand (a boundary of skin except at the wrist, where you have drawn the imaginary line that completes it; inputs of nourishment, warmth, information; conversions as the energy

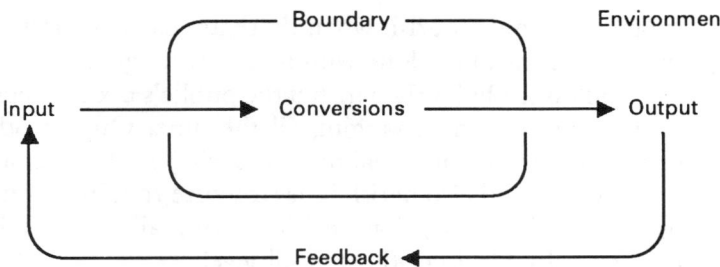

Fig 1.1

is converted to movement; outputs of information and energy – such as a slap – and feedback of the sensation of impact of that slap!).

(b) Now jump to another extreme, and apply it to your branch or office, but look simply at information inputs, their conversion, the information outputs, and feedback. Consider what happens when you alter the social or technical conversions (change the staff, cause conflict and a different relationship between them, alter the structure of expertise; or introduce new computer terminals or other information technology). Does the change in any element not alter the operations of most of the others?

Contingency theory

What is thus the best structure of the socio-technical conversions of an organisation – or how it is set up to perform its tasks? 'It all depends': but on what? Two researchers called Burns and Stalker answered this after they had looked at companies in Scotland, and discovered that companies facing different markets were more or less successful depending on their structure. They noted that there were a number of different kinds of environment faced by organisations, but if you arranged these environments you would find two extreme types:

1 the *stable*, predictable, unchanging market with regular features which remain the same for long periods; and
2 the *volatile*, unpredictable, shifting market in which demand altered almost from day to day.

Now classical theory has described a bureaucratic type of organisation which could be described as machine-like, and you can see how such an organisation would fit in well with the first, stable kind of environment, with regular procedures for predictable occurrences, everything in triplicate and little active decision-making needed at lower levels at least. Burns and Stalker called this a *mechanistic* type of organisation.

But what if the environment was volatile, changing, unstable? Such a mechanistic structure would not bend, would have no flexibility, could not change quickly to adapt to new demands. What you would need is not a machine-like but a creature-like organisation, reacting sensitively and quickly, making major decisions on the ground floor, no great number of fixed procedures, agile in thought. This was called an *organic* organisation.

Neither is better than the other as 'it all depends' is contingent on the right environment. Mechanistic (bureaucratic, machine-like) organisations like the

Inland Revenue flourish when there are clear, written rules about what goes in, what needs to be done with it, and what goes out year on year. However, it would quite obviously perish if the public's tax problems were totally unique to each person and changing all the time. On the other hand, an organic organisation (flexible, shallow hierarchy) such as a small chain of fashion boutiques would also perish if its structure required every move to be referred up a long hierarchy for decision, with all communication recorded and impersonal job descriptions at all levels.

Would it ring any bells if it were suggested that banks have moved from being largely mechanistic organisations in the early 70s, when the economic environment was much more stable, into (admittedly with a struggle) a more volatile environment and that they are battling to introduce more organic reactions to changing demands – and having difficulty structuring themselves to do so?

The truly effective organisation would structure itself so that it had departments/divisions/branches which were themselves structured contingent on their environment, e.g. marketing organic, savings mechanistic, tailored loans organic, car loans mechanistic and so on. All you would need is different sorts of people with different inclinations and skills in each, and managers at higher levels forming *linking pins* who would ensure that the activities of the one type harmonised with the activities of the other.

Before you leave this topic, give a little thought, however, to the problems of recruitment, promotion, transfer and job satisfaction this could cause in a large organisation.

■ ORGANISATIONAL FUNCTIONS

ACTIVITY 1.3

To help you to relate this section to your own working environment, and to help you see the relevance of it, set this book down for a moment and get hold of an organisation chart for your bank. (You will need this chart later on and it is vital to your revision.) You might find one in the Annual Report and Accounts. If you can not find it there, ask your manager where you can find it. If you and your managers fail to find such a diagram, ask yourself – write it down, even – what this says about communication in your bank!

Organisations can structure themselves in a variety of ways. Let us start by asking what functions are businesses normally described as having. We will find that traditionally they have five functional areas:

Production/operations

This includes the provision of a service. This function is responsible for liaison with marketing to discover what the market wants, and getting the material, storing then converting it, maintaining quality, warehousing and packing, or in the case of a service, making sure that what the organisation promises as a service is available to the customers and that it is of the type and quality they require.

Finance

This function is responsible for discerning how much money is needed to finance the business, for administering, controlling and accounting for the use and disbursement of this money; for providing information, including forecasts, to authorised receivers, and making authorised payments on behalf of the company.

Marketing

This function is responsible for finding out the demand for the output, its extent and its detailed specification; for liaising with designers concerning the nature of the product or service and with production concerning amount and quality provided; for advertising, often via liaison with agencies, for package design, distribution, and sales; and sometimes also for public relations.

Personnel

On the basis of the human resources needed, as specified in the Manpower Plan, personnel advertise for, select and recruit staff. They set up systems and facilities for training, act as central clearing house for the deployment, transfer and promotion of staff, check working conditions, deal centrally with grievance and discipline matters, with dismissal and redundancy; and represent the organisation in industrial relations matters.

Administration

This function includes 'everything else', i.e. administrative systems, files, computers, cleaning, maintenance, property, dispatch, messengers, internal-mail and telephone information-flows and the like.

■ ALTERNATIVE STRUCTURES

If life were simple, organisations could just structure themselves in those functions, and indeed some do.

There are other ways of structuring organisations:

1 by *product line:* Boots Co plc might have a baby, a cosmetics, a pharmaceuticals and a household division;
2 by *region or district:* Sainsbury's could have a South West, a North West, a Wales and a West Country Division;
3 by *customer type:* a computer company such as NCR might have a commercial customer, Government, small firms, and retail divisions.

Then, of course, there are combinations of these. Your bank chart will probably show 'product lines' or groups of them under perhaps, insurance services or trustee division or even more generally under such a name as 'related services'. It should also have some element of the regional, even if under the production or line-division heading, e.g. if you have a domestic banking division you may well find senior managerial functions in charge of a geographical area. Within your central lending function (called advances department perhaps?) there could be division by customer or size of loan, like a large advances department. Then there is structure by alphabet, e.g. many banks and departments and branches have their A–F and G–N and S–Z sections.

Try to locate some of these elements on your bank's charts.

■ DEPICTING ORGANISATIONS

ACTIVITY 1.4

(a) Having obtained a copy of your organisation's chart simply copy it by hand. In this way you will gain an understanding and insight into the nature of the organisation. Doing this will also help you if you ever have to reproduce it in, say, an examination, or to describe your organisation to outsiders or a new member of staff.

(b) Consider whether you can recognise the organisational functions (production/operations etc.) marked at high levels on your organisation's chart. (Finance will be referred to by a different name, e.g. Treasurer, Comptroller or Accountant.)

Your chart will probably be of a type called hierarchical or traditional; but there are other ways of describing organisations, such as the concentric or the matrix, or even in words. Let us examine these different types before we go on to discuss why we are doing this at all.

Traditional charts

These indicate hierarchical levels from top to bottom. You *would* probably believe how sensitive people are to where they are horizontally with relation to others in a chart – they even use a ruler to line up whether they are up or down on others on the chart! The actual intention is to an extent to show who reports to whom, who has command or authority over whom, who is senior to whom and in what line; so the measurement of where you stand is not such a joke. It does not make much difference if the chart is drawn 'sideways', as it sometimes is, with the most senior on the left and the most numerous on the right: the ruler is still applied, and the importance is just the same.

Note that there may be two 'things' set down at each point, i.e. certainly the name of a role and possibly also the name of a person who currently fills that role. At this stage you need only fill in the names of the roles.

As you drew your chart, did you reflect on what the lines, especially the vertical ones actually mean? There are a number of alternative possibilities:

1 *Communication?* Not really, because while the relationships normally imply the use of communication, if you were drawing a chart of just who communicates with whom you would have a lot more horizontal and diagonal lines too; also trainers, say, would be pretty central.

2 *Power?* Well, the person who has the hand on the plug of the computer has a lot of power; as does the senior convener of shop stewards, or the car-park gate key-holder, or the personnel clerk with access to your personal records! If it were just power, it would certainly be oddly distorted.

3 *Interaction?* It is implied but is not what the line means. Plenty of people work with others but with no hierarchical line joining them.
4 *Authority?* This could be it. The vertical line could mean has direct-line authority over, or is the boss of, or in the other direction, reports directly to, takes first-priority orders from.

Note the phrases 'direct' or 'first-priority'; because you will also take orders from, or report to, others above you on the chart, subject to these direct or priority relationships (and sometimes causing role conflict, as we shall see).

As another exercise, draw up the chart for your own office or branch. Observe and contemplate again what the lines mean. Then add dotted lines meaning 'communicates quite regularly about work-subjects' wherever they are appropriate – there will be a lot of them.

Concentric charts

While these can be interesting to study, they do little more or less than traditional charts. They consist of a series of concentric circles, one inside the other, with the most senior people at the centre and levels reporting to each other radiating outwards. While at first glance they may seem a little more democratic than the traditional chart, they are not. They could be more useful if the circles were attached at the centre like a hub and you could rotate the outer rings to try out different combinations.

But they illustrate that there is more than one way of depicting an organisation, however it is actually structured.

Matrix organisations

This is genuinely a different way of depicting organisations, but is it useful? There is an enormous amount of debate about this.

It is important to note the distinction between line and staff. Line management was responsible for the business of the organisation, producing the goods or providing the service; and the staff management and departments serviced the line departments. Thus the manager of Kenilworth Branch of the bank is a line manager, and the property department manager responsible for the Midland Region who handles Kenilworth's building and equipment matters is a staff manager.

Do not confuse this use of the term 'staff' with the more traditional use to mean personnel. Staff in this context mean what we sometimes call service departments who *work across* the organisation, providing their service to all who need it. This is a point worth making here because you can often tell who has studied this subject and who has not by their understanding and use of the terms line and staff in this context.

Is it the term 'work across' as used in the previous paragraph which is the point about matrix depictions of organisations? If you draw the lines of an organisation vertically, and the staff horizontally, so that you have a matrix of boxes, then you can fill in the name of the person in property department that deals with Kenilworth, and all the other branches in the Midland Region, as shown below (only note, in advance, what the chart for the entire of the branch network for, say, Barclays Bank will look like!).

Midland Region	Kenilworth	Wolverhampton	Coventry	Stratford
Property	Mr Warwick	Mr Dougan	Ms Godiva	Miss Hamlett
Personnel	Miss Talbot	Mr Molyneux	Mr Spence	Ms Capulet
Marketing	Mr Stanley	Miss Gold	Mr Send	Mr Hathaway
Computers	Ms Segrave	Ms Wander	Miss Michael	Mr Royall

The problem arises if you want to show levels of authority or seniority on either axis of the chart: how do you get Miss Hamlett's boss, Mr Falstaff, on this chart? You will need another dimension, and another if you note that Personnel and also Service Computers provide their expertise to Marketing and so on.

The matrix picture can show who is on whose team, and the level of detail can clarify the relationships. In certain organisations where there are project teams it can also legitimise the use of Person 'A' from Team 'A' where s/he is usually based, by Team 'B' on their project where his/her expertise is useful, because Person 'A' appears in the box where Team 'A' crosses with Team 'B'. But whether it would ever be useful in a bank is a question you may like to ask yourself. Should you ever be discussing organisational charts or structure, however, give a mention to the matrix.

■ ORGANISATIONAL ROLES

Having located them in the organisational picture, what are these roles, as distinct from the people who fill them? They are, essentially, the job specification, as defined formally, or the requirements emanating from all those who make demands on them if you look at it less formally. Roles are defined as a set of duties, responsibilities, customs, i.e. having an associated set of norms about dress, language, demeanour, attitude and behaviour, attached to a position in an organisation.

Role requirements

Roles have a powerful influence on behaviour: whatever role you are currently taking determines how you dress, speak, move. For example, as a male bank employee you must wear a jacket of a conventional shape of a material identical with your trousers (regardless of whether it is as smart or expensive or fashionable or even as clean as a cashmere blazer you own which is worn with contrasting trousers).

If you are a female banker it is unlikely that you will wear trousers at all, however smart and whatever relation the material bears to the jacket. As a female college student, however, you may well wear trousers. If any of you were in the role of football supporter, you would probably wear jeans and a sweater and rigidly prescribed colours on your scarf.

Bank managers do not run. Lecture audiences do not stand up and stretch. Solicitors do not whistle. In other roles the same people might very easily do all these things, quite comfortably and without too much conscious thought about whether they were appropriate or not. In fact, we do not normally select behaviour appropriate to a role, we simply assume the role requirements of a recognisable social situation.

Learning new roles

How can we slip easily into a role if we have never been in it before? What if we do not know the right behaviour?

If you have never been in a workplace before how do you know what to do, how to dress, how to relate, how to judge timing, what to call people, when to arrive and leave, and what to say? Pause for a moment and remember when you yourself were in that situation. Supervisors have to help people to acquire new work roles by assisting the learning process in ways which reduce confusion.

Note that we are not just talking about the specifications and duties of the job, but of the role. The best bosses understand that we want to learn not just how to do the work but how to identify with being a banker at one level or another. By the way, the same goes for the supervisors themselves: is it as easy to become a supervisor as it is to learn how to do the work of supervision? Is it the same thing?

Clearly not, and equally clearly no book can prescribe how to teach new roles. Two points to bear in mind for supervisors, however: first, that taking up a new role is not automatic and instant but a learning process; and second, it is quicker when the process becomes a little more conscious and sympathetic attention is paid to it by both learner and superiors.

Role conflict

Sometimes more than one role seems equally appropriate and we have difficulty in choosing. For example, if I am a lecturer whose relative is a student, who must be failed because they are not up to the mark, then as a lecturer I must fail the student, but as a relative I want the best in life for them. Bank managers are sometimes faced with refusing finance to the companies of the people they play golf with: if they take the bank manager role, they may lose the friendship role; and if they were to take the friend role they would jeopardise their bank role. What happens if I am a supervisor with a terminally lazy subordinate who happens also to be my very good friend? All of these are *role conflict* situations.

Compromise, a weak solution to either side, is not viable. There are two alternatives: *opt out* or *compartmentalise*. Opting out can be quite legitimate: having determined that any solution would bring costs for you, but not for anyone else in the role situation, you can delegate the decision to them. Lending bankers will (and in most banks are instructed to) ask their superior manager to take major decisions about their friend-customers.

Compartmentalising means putting yourself firmly in the compartment of one or the other role and simply not allowing the other to intrude. Weigh the decision and the role to adopt becomes quite unequivocally one or the other. At this point you will find yourself displaying *role signs,* using the phraseology of the role you have adopted, sitting in that role's chair, even wearing the more extremely conventional clothes. One senior executive, having discussed this with the author, was intrigued to observe about himself that he had for years worn a particular especially sombre suit when having to dismiss someone.

■ OBJECTIVES

We now come to an extremely important aspect of organisations, one which is only being slowly developed in British industry and commerce, namely, those objectives which, as mentioned in the introduction to this chapter, were what the organisation was set up to pursue. To arrive at the supervisor's duty with relation to objectives, we shall first discuss, briefly, overall organisational objectives, look at how these are operationalised, or made to be applicable to everyday work, make observations on how they are communicated, and then see how supervisors can use objectives to improve the performance of their staff. We shall use the terms objectives or aims or targets interchangeably, rather than enter into semantic discussion of how precisely they differ: they shall all mean *what we are supposed to achieve,* or statements thereof.

Objectives statements

It seems blindingly obvious that we have work objectives and that they are what we pursue. How else could we know in which direction to bend our efforts? But when we look more closely, or particularly when we seek statements of organisational objectives, things seem a little more problematical.

If it were not a trick question, we could now ask you to give us a statement of your organisation's objectives. If you answered straight away you would most probably be giving your personal supposition of what they are, rather than relaying an official statement; or you would be making a bald broad statement so wide as to be meaningless in terms of actual organisational behaviour. This seems a little rude, so, to explain, we must first look at the sources of information about company aims available to supervisors.

However unreasonably it sounds, it is conventionally extremely difficult to obtain a statement of company aims. To start with, where would you look? We are inclined here to leave half-a-page blank to represent the silence that question would provoke if asked orally. In fact, some broad statement might be found as a passing remark in the Annual Report; some even broader statement could be looked up in the Memo and Articles (when did anyone last read those as a guide to performance?); frequent inspirational talks include the claim that 'we are, after all, all aiming for the same objectives' without telling us what they are.

ACTIVITY 1.5

Many banks engage in customer care programmes; and a useful thing about these is that they have had to condense and distil a statement of corporate objectives for staff to aim at. This is sometimes called a 'mission statement' and you may find this easier to obtain than a more lofty statement of corporate objectives.

(a) Obtain a copy or photocopy of your organisation's mission statement' or the similar document used to express customer care.
(b) Write the main points in the form of notes so as to be able to remember the main elements for a possible exam answer. Include these with your notes or with your revision file.

Some organisations make meaningful overall statements; some install *Management by Objectives* schemes in which people are assessed by their prowess in reaching goals they have helped to set, and to do this the goals must be clear and written down. In some cases the nearest you get is the corporate plan or budgets, which we will now discuss.

Corporate Plan

Earlier we suggested that any simple overall statement of objectives would be less than meaningful in indicating how people in organisations would behave. For instance, if you said that the objective of your bank is to make a profit, why do they not sell all the branches? They would make an enormous profit. You would say, no, 'to make a continuing profit'; and we would ask, maximum, minimum or sufficient, and you would say 'to make a maximum continuing profit'. So why not close and re-open as a bookmaking business (they are more profitable than banks) so you would add 'by providing banking services' and we would ask, ethical or dishonest? And you would add ... and so on as we ask about competition and the customer and the law and the staff and society and the centre and the regions, until you were specific enough for the statement to be meaningful – but no longer short.

The closest modern organisations come to a full statement of objectives, or at least specific intentions to which the staff are guided to contribute, is by compiling the *Corporate Plan*, a lengthy, complete and complex document, adjusted periodically to keep up-to-date on current forward plans. There is only one problem as far as supervisors are concerned: they do not usually see it! However, managers often have targets set as a result of the Corporate Plan, and they even get to see it or extracts from it.

To set your own view of your bank's objectives in perspective, and this is meant perfectly seriously because you can use your resultant experience in discussion with management or staff or in examinations, ask your manager to tell you what he or she has seen of the Corporate Plan and record the response verbatim.

Budgets

Budgets are, at least, statements of objectives, and *Budget statements* are received by the farthest-flung branches of well-controlled organisations. Banks in the main have well-developed budgetary control schemes with supporting documentation.

They are regularly produced (usually computer-printed) statements of:

1 the limits of cost within which the management have *planned* to stay;
2 updated figures of the *actual* income and expenditure;
3 the difference *(variance)* between 1 and 2, absolute and percentage.

In sensible systems the managers responsible for a specific budget have contributed by consultation in the first place to the planned figures, and there is a reporting procedure so that they can explain variances in the actual figures and make requests for alterations or extra facilities to comply with the next rounds of budgetary demands.

Budgets tend to be negative as they set the limits within which you are expected to stay. However, some budgets also set sales or profit or cost-reduction targets, and therefore indicate means to achieving something.

How much control do supervisors have over budget-determined activities? The best chance they have of gaining control is to know what the budget statement says, and to have determined how much of it they can use for targeting their staff activities.

Ask your management to explain the statement, its measurement of variance, and the reporting procedure. You might then stand a chance of being involved in the process. If you are already involved in such consultation, consider what motivational effect this has on you as a junior manager, and whether you can and are permitted to carry any of this on to your own staff.

■ TARGETS AND BEHAVIOUR

Why have we gone on at such length about objectives? Because while it is true to say that supervisors have a good deal of negative responsibility − making sure that nothing goes wrong, that we are no worse off, that we make no mistakes, that nobody is failing to pull their weight − the best ones take positive responsibility for improvement and achievement.

People tend to behave in a goal-orientated manner, i.e. they tend to want to aim at targets. However difficult it might be to obtain statements about company objectives, they all have them, even if only implied, and they naturally want their staff to aim at those rather than others; thus operational objectives should be in line with company objectives and approved by the company.

People also like to be involved in the setting of objectives in the first place since it is perfectly axiomatic that they will be more committed to any realistic target they have helped to agree than any they have handed down to them without consultation.

Next, if they cannot clearly see targets that their organisation set but fail to communicate, they will make suppositions of what those are and aim for them instead, or else they will behave − well, aimlessly.

People also do not react well to targets, even where visible, that they consider to be unrealistic or out of reach. They may try once or twice, but the certain knowledge of repeated failure to reach impossible targets again leads to setting of their own targets, or aimlessness. Conversely, the organisation can set targets which are too easy and present no challenge. For a short time people will then set themselves higher targets than demanded, and there is plenty of evidence that where there is worker control of output, that control is exercised to keep production up as often as to keep it down: people do have a sense of a fair day's work. Eventually, however, a series of low targets simply become meaningless.

Finally, unless there is adequate reward, i.e. something in it for people who make extra effort to hit targets, they will declare even realistic, achievable targets simply not worth the effort of reaching. They will in that case also set their own targets at levels where they do feel adequately rewarded. Reaching targets is rewarding in itself, but organisational recognition is essential, even where all it consists of is the thanks and acknowledgement of the management, including at supervisor level.

■ SPECIFICATIONS FOR GOOD TARGETS

So if there are to be targets at all, what are the specifications? You may deduce from the above that they must be:

1 approved and derived from higher level targets;
2 agreed by those involved in reaching them;
3 visible and communicated to all participants;
4 realistic and sensibly within reach;
5 challenging enough to make the effort worthwhile;
6 rewarded in addition to the in-built satisfaction.

If you can see a clear statement of such targets, and you and your staff have the means to carry out the job, you can at least perform no worse and you are actually likely to perform much better, simply because your efforts will be clearly directed.

■ OBJECTIVES AND THE SUPERVISOR

ACTIVITY 1.6

(a) Relating all this to you, name one objective which you are supposed to achieve, however minor the target, right down to getting your workspace tidy by Friday, for example.
(b) Now name the particular branch or office objective which in achieving *your* objective you would help to achieve.

How can good supervisors ensure that their own performance, and how they are seen by their subordinates, are in line with the company's objectives?

First, they should attempt to get a grasp of the organisational objectives, or at least the branch derivative thereof. What does the budget statement say about what the branch should be striving for, both in terms of cost limitation and in terms of positive contribution?

Second, they can agree their own section's objectives in a series of initial interviews with their superior officers. If you have been reading this chapter carefully you will know the difference between the content of the job (what you have to do) and the objectives of the job (what you have to achieve), and the latter are less often stated and not as easy to state.

As part of this process supervisors can set up or agree a series of periodic reviews at which they and their bosses can check out progress towards, shortfall from or exceeding of targets, and adjust them for the next period. The sections' targets can be aligned at that time with the branch budgets, and so it would be a good idea to have those periodic reviews roughly simultaneously with the announcement of the budgetary statement.

Next, the supervisor will want to communicate the targets to the staff. This of course also means agreeing them, so that after the supervisor has agreed them with the boss, communication should be done first in discussion with the staff, and then by keeping those targets constantly visible. Regular review meetings are a good idea; but in the meantime it is useful to see a target to shoot at it; therefore display targets and draw lines showing progress.

The supervisor will then want to acknowledge the achievements and spur staff on if the targets are not met. We shall discuss this and other matters of the relationship with staff as we proceed in this volume, having laid the foundation by attempting to clarify, and given you means of extending this clarification of, the organisational setting in which you are expected to work effectively.

■ SUMMARY

In this chapter we have discussed the following aspects of organisations:

1. The history of organisational thinking:

    (a) Weber's theories of bureaucracy;
    (b) Classical Theory;
    (c) Systems thinking and contingency;
       through to where organisations were seen to need structures which enable them to react to what happens in their environment.

2. The functions of organisations, as traditionally divided:

    (a) Production/operations: the provision of goods or services;
    (b) Finance: the flow through, and administration, of funds;
    (c) Marketing: discovering demand; design, packaging, advertising, promotion, sales;
    (d) Personnel: recruitment, selection, deployment, development and training of staff; grievance, discipline and industrial relations policies and practices;

(e) Administration: 'everything else' – computers, cleaning and maintenance, dispatch, porterage, telephones, tea and biscuits!

Depicting organisations, by traditional chart or by concentric pictures, by matrix or in words; and how you can clarify your organisation to yourself by drawing it.

4 Organisational roles and their influence on our behaviour: how we learn them and how we cope with conflict between those we have at various times – and simultaneously.

5 Objectives: the vital function that objectives have:

   (a) the overall organisational objectives;
   (b) the budget; and the supervisor's role;
   (c) the targets for supervisory groups and individuals.

6 Objectives and their communication to staff, both effectively and less effectively carried out in organisations.

7 The effect of objectives on behaviour, encouraging people to direct their energies and effort.

8 Specifications for effective use of objectives or targets, and the supervisor's responsibility in ensuring that they are:

   (a) known;
   (b) agreed;
   (c) clear;
   (d) communicated;
   (e) aimed at by the staff.

■ SELF-ASSESSMENT QUESTIONS

Try to answer these questions to remind you of the content of this chapter:

1 How would you define 'organisation'? How does your definition fit your own organisation?

2 Name the three types of organisation described by Max Weber. Explain what the names mean.

3 State three of the characteristics which describe the bureaucratic kind of organisation.

4 Name four or five of the principles of good organisation according to the classical theory.

5 Draw a simple open system, and label all its characteristics. Can you relate it in your mind to, say, a football team?

6 What words are used to describe the extreme kinds of environment which could be faced by an organisation, and to which they must adapt to be successful?

7 What are the words used to describe the two extreme forms of organisation which most effectively adapt to their environment; and what do the words mean?

8 What are generally agreed to be the five main functions of commercial organisations? How does your bank ensure that those functions are fulfilled?

9 Draw a chart of your organisation. Try to get the levels right. Write down what the lines on your chart actually mean.

10 What is the difference between line and staff?

11 What is role conflict? In what ways do people cope with it?

12 In the simplest possible terms, what is an objective?

13 Try to think of any one clear statement of an objective, or set of objectives you have officially had drawn to your attention at work. What exactly did it ask you to achieve?

14 What is a corporate plan?

15 How close can you get to seeing any part of your organisation's corporate plan (answer this by asking your management)?

16 What does variance mean?

17 Write down the titles of the areas for which you have personal official budgetary responsibility, for saving targeted cost or making targeted income.

18 What are the specifications for a set of organisational targets to be really effective?

19 In what ways should supervisors behave to ensure that targets in their responsibility are met by their staff?

20 Write down three ways in which your organisation complies with Weber's idea of bureaucracy.

2 The supervisor

OBJECTIVES

When you have read this chapter you should be able to:
- **Define the role of the supervisor;**
- **Relate that role to the organisation's management at higher levels and understand the need for team operations;**
- **Relate the supervisor's relationships with immediate subordinates, and with colleagues at the same level;**
- **State the various functions of the supervisor in the role of junior manager;**
- **Reconcile the complex relationship between management and technical responsibilities of the supervisor, and**
- **Recognise the supervisory element of senior clerical workers, either formally recognised by the management or not;**
- **Understand the various ways of relating effectively with subordinate staff, and styles of management;**
- **Balance the needs of organisation and staff, of concern for production and concern for people;**
- **Understand the qualities, skills and abilities necessary to perform supervisory functions effectively;**
- **Plan for self-development in those abilities.**

■ INTRODUCTION

People who are promoted into supervisory positions will recount a variety of experiences concerning how they were introduced to and trained for the uniquely supervisory aspects of their work, varying from absolutely nothing at all, through the short inspirational speech of the personnel department or new books, to sensible training for the new responsibilities, position and duties. Very often they find themselves in the position of someone who has achieved prowess, distinction and skill in playing football, and then, on the basis of that, is selected to play water polo for England but nobody asks them if they can swim, or suggests any training other than plunging in and having a go!

In this chapter, we shall start by looking closely at the role of the supervisor, and in particular the supervisory/management aspects. The word 'aspects' is used, because the supervisory job which is all supervision is extremely rare; usually there is a major technical element to the work, and the supervision is added to it – the water polo player has to play football as well!

It is important for those in the supervisor's role to understand its relationships with other roles. To begin with, it is frequently described as the first line of junior management, which it is, and in this way it has a lot in common with managerial practices and principles throughout the organisation; and, as we have seen Chapter 1, there is responsibility to the organisation for its objectives, which is certainly a management responsibility. This responsibility is to immediate superiors; therefore, both because of the overall managerial responsibility, and the importance of the way you work with your boss, we shall be looking at your *superiors*.

Next, we shall devote our attention to the possibly more important relationship between supervisors and those over whom they have control at work. In so far as you are judged at all in the purely supervisory aspects of your work, it will be on how you obtain the best possible work from your staff for your organisation. There is certainly no question that such is the way in which those staff will judge you first and foremost; and the fact that you may be technically superb, or have other qualities which are admirable, will always be less important than how you are as a manager of people, as far as they are concerned.

We shall also examine in this chapter how supervisors can develop their working relationships with staff, covering here among other topics the distinction between liking bosses and respecting them. There are various ways of working with the people whom you supervise (generally called 'management styles' in textbooks). For instance, you can just give incontrovertible orders without regard to staff welfare; you can take actions without consultation, and give such orders but this time for the good of staff; you can ask staff opinions and then make your own decisions, possibly taking them into account; or you can share decisions equally with staff; or combine these, or use one style or another on different occasions. We shall look at *subordinates*.

It is not just how the staff relate to the supervisor that counts in their assessment by their managers, but also to what extent the work also gets done, and how well. Concern for production, or the quality of the provision of customer service, has to be balanced with concern for the staff. Indeed each is intricately dependent on the other, and we shall examine this interdependency.

There are many ways in which effective supervisors can develop their supervisory expertise, and one of those ways is to share problems, leaning and techniques with others at the same or similar levels. The relationships between such people are not always clear in organisations, but they can be important to supervisors. We shall look at relationships with *colleagues*.

Finally, we shall examine how supervisors can use a clear view and a systematic understanding of their organisational role to plan and develop their supervisory/management performance.

■ WHAT IS A SUPERVISOR?

Literally a 'super-visor' is a person who looks at things from above, i.e. an overseer. That is its most simple definition. At the other end of the definition scale, you could say that this entire volume defines the role.

There is a lot of debate in textbooks and in the workplace about what is meant by 'supervisor'. Some would say that they are the link between the management and the workforce, but this implies that there are two kinds of people, or at least two kinds of status, namely, management and workforce. That division is a little old fashioned, and in any case is a good deal less appropriate in banks than many other places (where trade union membership, for example, goes well up into managerial levels). Are the managers not part of the workforce? Is the supervisor not part of the management?

Of course there are certain organisations that do make that clear distinction; and in a way, banks are among those organisations. Because of the job-evaluation/grading system (which we elaborate on in Chapter 8) there are distinct bands of employment classification in banks: the clerical and senior clerical levels; the assistant manager, which is the base of the manager level bands; and above this senior manager and executive levels.

Officially, then, titles including the word 'manager' appear above senior clerical levels. However, it is customary to refer to the supervisor as the first line of management. That distinction poses some questions, but they are not terribly important; it must be fairly accurate and most supervisors like the idea.

Though occasionally supervisors have responsibility only for non-staff resources or materials, supervisors are more normally, and will certainly be defined throughout this volume, as:

People at or below the top senior clerical levels who have responsibility for the work of staff and associated resources.

The title of supervisor is usually applied to such people. Note that there are those who are supervisors by this definition but who do not have the word supervisor in their title. As a matter of fact traditionally nobody in banks below official level has a title as such at all! Rather more seriously, there are those who have supervisory responsibilities by the above definition, but receive little or no recognition for that fact. A sound job-evaluation scheme, well operated by local management, should see it that this is a rare phenomenon.

■ EARLY DAYS

Never is the British tradition – or cult – of the amateur more clearly on show when we talk about management, and in particular on first appointment. Supervisors really are expected to be born with the ability to manage, and the idea that management is a set of professional skills is slightly foreign to the British. As a matter of fact the supervisory element in one's work is something of a side issue, since it is almost invariably extra to the technical job which is the main part of the work. In an otherwise excellent early management film on the work of supervisors, the commentator suggested that you cut down on work that is not truly supervision, but have you ever come across a job that is mainly or essentially supervisory?

To be perfectly frank, there are many areas of industry and commerce in which even where the job has the title of manager included, the occupant can get away with engaging in very little management, as such. We have hardly any methods of judging the quality of management in any objective manner, and inspectors and internal auditors include the matter as an appendix or side-issue after a comprehensive examination of all the operations of an office.

This odd philosophy is really evident when you are first appointed into a supervisory situation, unless you are fortunate in your bosses. All the technical duties will be explained, and any previous job you have had will have prepared you for a good deal of it. But it could be the first time you have had charge of the work of staff. If you are lucky you may get a short course in supervisory skills or the like, but usually after you have been in the job for some time.

So how can newly appointed supervisors sort out how to begin the supervisory part of their work? We can go back to the functions of the organisation for this, but it should be noted here – and we may repeat this time and again throughout – that the *management element of the supervisor's work takes time,* and time should be set aside for it. Chapter 1 covered the various functions an organisation must contain, i.e. Production/operations, Finance, Marketing, Personnel and Administration; we shall see that this is also a way in which supervisors can classify elements of their role.

■ LEARNING THE ELEMENTS OF THE SUPERVISOR'S ROLE

It does no harm as people set out to be supervisors to keep a file or a notebook to store facts. Once again, only the true amateur thinks it is somehow clever or macho to store everything in their memory but it can lose information, and it can also overload! Budding professional supervisors, as they set out, sit down and make notes about the following:

Production/operations

This is the technical element, as we have said, usually the major part of the work. A good deal of the ensuing chapters will deal with keeping this in order.

Finance

Supervisors should determine the extent to which they are responsible for the finance, especially for loss. Is any part of the branch budget in their control? Could it be? Would it be useful if it were, under the close eye of the management, of course? How much information is there about this financial responsibility? Do you have it in writing? Do you need any training, or technical information or instructions as to how to handle it? Where can you get it from?

Marketing

Using this to represent relationships with people outside the group, in the office, in the organisation, outside the organisation: how much responsibility do you have for any of this? What information do you need to do this liaison? What resources are available? What leeway do you have to leave the premises or use the communication resources? And what actual marketing responsibility do you have, for selling to the public? And what targets?

Personnel

This is the central part of the role, and not one we can cover in detail here. But who are your staff? Should you know/can you fill in, in your notebook, their full names, nicknames, length of service, experience, training, grades, skills, expertises, job-inclinations, relationships, salaries, holiday entitlements, birthdays, appraisal/increment dates, discipline records, current work and how long they've done the job? What are your responsibilities for health and safety? What are the rules and local customs, for discipline, for example?

Administration

What other supervisory duties are there? What do phrases like 'Oh, by the way the banking hall is yours – keep it looking good' entail? And what other 'Oh, by the ways' are there? What about information flows, i.e. whom must you tell about what, in what form and how regularly? Who moves the information, posts the letters, contacts Dispatch? What are your responsibilities concerning the premises, fixtures and fittings, furniture? Do you have other rules and regulations responsibilities? Who is responsible for payments such as overtime?

Can you legitimately delegate any of your work if you are absent or if eventually you feel such delegation would have a training or a motivational effect? Exactly whom do you report to on each of the above matters, as there may be more than one manager responsible for each area of your work? These are just some of the details which it is sensible for supervisors to learn in the early few weeks.

ACTIVITY 2.1

Before you move on, let's make sure you fully understand the genuine importance of all the above to the practising supervisor. Write down examples of the way a supervisor (yourself or your own) performs the five functions outlined above. We'll give you an one example of what we mean.

Production/Operations
- Setting deadlines for work

Finance
- Consulting office budgets

Marketing
- Responding to requests from outside the office

Personnel
- Sorting out lunch rotas

Administration
- Filling in returns for Head Office

■ THE SUPERVISOR'S BOSS

As to whom supervisors report we will now take a focused look at bosses. A good relationship with a boss can be the difference between a good supervisory performance and a poor one. When we later discuss delegation, we will see that the best ones strike a balance between being involved in their subordinates' work, and leaving them to get on with it. The boss is a manager, and as such is traditionally seen as having a number of functions, to a greater or lesser degree.

An American researcher, Henry Mintzberg, looked at senior executives in organisations, and how they actually spent their time. He discovered that they occupied ten different *managerial roles*, divided into three groups:

1 *Interpersonal roles:*

(a) figurehead: entertaining visitors, attending social events, making speeches;
(b) leader: motivating staff, maintaining morale, resolving internal staff problems;
(c) liaison: establishing and being in networks outside the group for its benefit;

2 *Informational roles:*

(a) monitor: gathering information, monitoring progress;
(b) disseminator: passing information into and out of the group, clarifying and interpreting;
(c) spokesman: acting as expert on group activities to people outside the group;

3 *Decisional roles:*

(a) entrepreneur: initiating business projects, seeking and exploiting opportunities for the group;
(b) disturbance handler: monitoring and handling unusual situations which disturb the normal work;
(c) resource allocator: ensuring the effective allocation and use of organisational resources;
(d) negotiator: representing and obtaining the best possible deal for the group in negotiations.

These roles are pretty complex and do apply to senior managers, but in many ways the bank branch manager takes some or all of these roles, and depends on staff to see to it that each is carried out effectively. Stop a moment and see if you can think of occasions on which the most senior manager in your office spends time in each one of the above roles.

Managers are seen by most analysts to have six main *functions,* and it is in these that supervisors are first-line assistants. For this reason it is worth your paying particular attention to these, and to the parts of this book where we elaborate on them. This is first because supervisors really ought to understand the managers' functions to work effectively with them, and second because supervisors really are managers themselves and therefore, to one degree or another, also have the functions which are explained below.

Setting objectives

We discussed this at length in Chapter 1. Note herewith that it is the managers' responsibility; they really are the ones seen by the staff either to set or not to set, or rather agree, targets. How the organisation treats their managers is not very relevant to their staff.

The supervisor, too, should take responsibility for drawing targets out of the manager, and applying them down the line, even if the manager has difficulty in getting targets from above.

Forecasting

Whatever functions they may have in current activity, forward thinking also resides in the manager's domain. Forecasting is trying to foresee future events, estimating forward trends, getting and disseminating a picture of the business future. This is done by having a good grasp of current events, trends and situations.

As assistants, supervisors play a role in helping to provide that information, deliberately or in the course of their everyday work. They should also be taking the responsibility of forward thinking in their own capacity as manager of their group, and forecasting to avoid predictable pitfalls.

Planning

Forecasting and planning will be covered in more detail in the next chapter. Planning is designing actions to cope with forecast events. It is a central managerial function which takes time which should be allowed for (though it rarely is!). A good plan should have an element of flexibility and have contingencies built in.

Once again, supervisors can help managers to plan, but they also have their own managerial planning function. They need to give advance thought to what will happen in the short, medium and longer term and how to influence events for the sake of the organisation's objectives.

Organising/co-ordinating

Managers plan actions for the future; they organise and co-ordinate present actions, allocate resources, distribute skills and deploy staff in the most effective manner, and solve problems on-the-spot. They also make sure that things run smoothly and that the activities of one section or person do not disrupt those of others, either within or outside the group.

It is here, of course, that supervisors most neatly combine the indirect responsibility, to help the manager, with their own direct responsibility, since immediate or short-term allocation and problem-solving are central to their functions.

Motivation

If you also count de-motivation, there is nothing in a manager's relationship with staff that does not involve motivation. In organisations which depend on staff commitment, managers who cannot motivate are bound to fail eventually. Anyone in power can order you to do things but a good motivator inspires you to want to do them, and encourages, guides and counsels, and gives you such opportunities as are available to fulfil yourself.

This applies no less to supervisors in their own right. If you have staff working for you, take note of that phrase *working for you* and see that this working relationship is vital. Chapter 5 is essentially devoted to this matter.

Control

Last but quite obviously not least, managers set up systems based on forecasts, plans, and co-ordinated current activities. They monitor what is actually happening and have mechanisms for stopping the ineffective or disruptive, for encouraging the advantageous, and for guiding and adjusting progress. This includes discipline from the mildest corrective word to the heaviest procedure.

Supervisors are both instruments of managerial control and operators in their own right of the reins on the work of their group.

Note how under each heading there is reference both to the managers' functions and the supervisors' support function, and also allusion to the supervisors' own managerial function. Give some thought to examples of how you help your managers in their work and to how you, yourself, function as a manager.

A good working relationship between supervisor and manager is essential for the efficient approach to organisational objectives. We can reflect on this further after we have looked at supervisors' relationships with their staff.

ACTIVITY 2.2

Expand the chart below and complete it with an examples of observable actions you and your manager take in carrying out each of the functions. (It's always useful to have thought through examples before you enter the examination room; and we say 'observable' because that causes you to be specific rather than vague.)

	Yourself	Your manager
Setting objectives		
Forecasting		
Planning		
Organising/coordinating		
Motivating		
Controlling		

■ SUPERVISORS AND STAFF

Unless you are able to work well with your staff, and your staff work effectively with you, you cannot be a good supervisor. Your task is not just to direct and control your staff: it is to obtain the most effective work from them, and you can only succeed in this if you have a good working relationship with them.

This will depend to a large extent on what is referred to as your management style, which we will now examine.

Management style

Much has been written about management style, the way in which managers relate with their workforce. A great deal of research has been done into which range of management styles is appropriate. This concerns the way in which managers involve their staff in decision-making, and the trust and reliance placed on their judgement, as well as an implied view of the roles of manager and subordinate and how the former get the latter to do their job properly.

While the range is a continuum, points on it are particularly worthy of attention. Among the foremost writers on this subject were Tannenbaum and Schmidt, in the early 70s, and four of the points on their continuum of management styles were:

Autocratic

What is the autocratic manager's philosophy? It is simply that you will do exactly as you are told, or I will punish you. It is not your place to make suggestions or take decisions; that is my role. The only location of power is where I am, or where I put it subject to my own power.

Benevolent autocratic

And what of the benevolent autocratic manager? In this case too you will do exactly as you are told, but it will be for your benefit as well as for mine, and if you do what you are told you will be rewarded. The organisation will look after you and your family if you do a good job. We shall not, of course, require your help in decision-making or your suggestions for improvement: why trouble yourselves? And, if I do have to punish you, that too will be for your own good.

Consultative

In the case of the consultative manager, I will ask you for your views when there are significant decisions to be made (and I will decide whether they are significant, though most of them will be). I shall seek your suggestions, and do this seriously, even systematically. I shall then take the responsibility of making the decision myself, though I will genuinely take your views into account.

Participative

As a participative manager, I make no decisions by myself: we make all decisions as a group and create the new schemes of action. In fact participation is a mild word for it: total involvement would be more appropriate. I do have a role as manager, which is, once the decision is made by the group, to plan and effect its implementation.

Two slightly later writers also used four points on the range to analyse management style, and they used more basic terms, namely, tells, sells, participates and delegates.

As you see, these do not differ much from the Tannenbaum and Schmidt range:

1 the manager who *tells* subordinates what to do gives them nothing in the way of leeway and must control them by power of punishment and reward;
2 the manager who *sells* feels that the responsibility lies with management, but that the staff must be persuaded rather than ordered, and would concentrate on reward, reserving punishment as a legitimate tool but in the background;
3 the manager who permits *participation* in decision-making (and note the slightly different place where this word comes in this range) *lets* the staff take a part in the management;
4 and finally the manager who *delegates* gives the responsibility for decisive work to the staff, who get involved in implementation.

Rensis Likert, yet another American – they have treated management as a profession for longer than the British have – characterised whole organisations as having a range of management styles, which were also arranged along a continuum, but since the range of organisational features in each style-type were so complex, one word would not adequately characterise them and he called them system 1, system 2, system 3 and system 4, with 1 being the autocratic type and 4 the participative.

Likert found in his research that organisations with system 4 type/participative styles were the most financially successful in America. Soon afterwards, similar research was done by the Ashridge Management College researchers in Britain, and system 3/consultative styles correlated with more successful companies here.

Your style

You should at this point be asking yourself how you can describe your own management style. Remember that whatever it is, it could be altered if in considered judgement it needed to be. Realise that while one true judge of how you relate with staff is *yourself*, and another your *bosses*, an excellent set of judges will surely be your *staff*. The author has often surmised that wherever a manager or supervisor, or even an organisation, would put themselves on these ranges, their staff would probably put them somewhere slightly to the authoritative end.

ACTIVITY 2.3

There are four steps you can take to approximate to a true description of your style:
1 To what extent do you believe you should be involved in your boss's decisions?
2 To what extent do you believe your staff should be involved in the decisions you have to make?
3 Think of an example of when you last made quite an important decision, and declare honestly the extent to which you actually involved your staff's suggestions and ideas in the making of that decision.
4 (You really want to know what your style is?) Tell your staff about the range of styles from *Tells* through *Sells* and *Participates* to *Delegates*, and ask them to say – written on a piece of paper anonymously! – which best describes your normal procedure.

■ PEOPLE AND PRODUCTION

Having looked at how managers at any level can choose to relate with their staff, we should not forget that they are also concerned importantly with production, or the provision of a service, i.e. with getting the job done. Not that these matters are separate: you cannot get the job done without allowing people some satisfaction from their work, nor can you keep the people working if the work is not achieving anything for the organisation, especially in the long run.

Two consultants called Black and Mouton developed a model for diagnosing management style, which they used as a basis for training schemes which they would introduce into organisations after the diagnosis. It concerned the weight of concentration that managers devoted to production and to their staff, and the balance between them. Black and Mouton put these on a two-dimensional chart, or, as it is known, on the *managerial grid*. They characterised points on that grid to indicate types of management style, giving them quite colourful names, and managers could be placed on the grid (*see* Fig. 2.1).

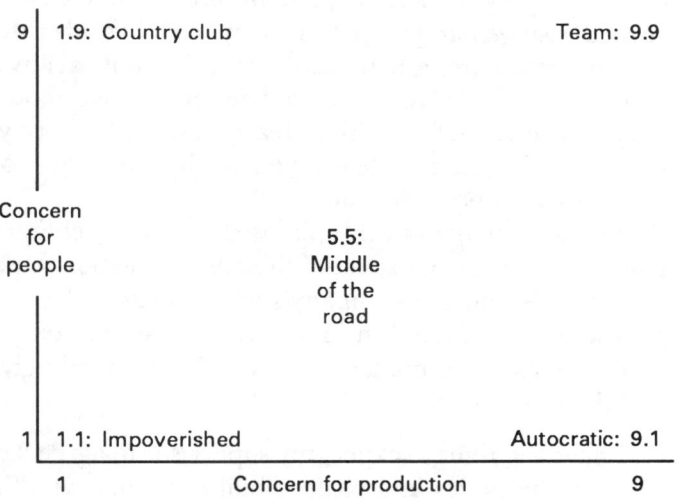

Fig 2.1

Notice that there is no zero: nobody can be totally unconcerned with people, but they can get down to the minimum concern necessary to get any work done at all, and similarly nobody can be totally unconcerned with production.

Blake and Mouton frequently found managers around the 5.5 middle-of-the-road style, and tailor-made ways of moving towards 9.9. This, however, rather assumes that this is the 'best' style; but there are circumstances where it may not be, where for example the work concerns production and the manager has hardly any contact with people, or where personnel welfare is the particular concern of the manager.

Rather more recently, a certain WJ Reddin added one dimension and one new concept to the idea of relating production and people. The dimension was the third one of *effectiveness*. How effective the balance is between production and people depends on the job. So you can be 9.9 when the job actually needs you to be 9.1, and you are therefore less effective. The additional concept was, therefore, flexibility of style, or *style-flex*, which is that managers should adapt their overall style of balancing work and staff relationships to the actual scene in which they are set.

At the supervisory level nobody expects you to be an expert in the theory of management style; but they do expect a conscious awareness of yourself and your image as a first-line manager. The managerial grid should at least draw your attention the fact that the supervisor as manager has a complex task outside their technical work to which time and attention needs to be devoted.

We shall now go on to use all of the foregoing to look at what staff can legitimately expect of you in your role as their immediate supervisor, in our industrial civilisation and in your organisation which is part of it.

■ OBJECTIVES AND EXPECTATIONS

At one time it was very fashionable, and in some places it still is, to introduce schemes called *management by objectives*. You may consider that it is a poor reflection on our commerce and industry that this should at any time have been considered revolutionary, given what has been said above about objectives, but it served its purpose and left us with a clearly-stated philosophy. The problem with it was, and still is, that while the philosophy works, just occasionally the formal schemes based on it do not.

We will use the statement of this philosophy here to characterise what the subordinate at any level can expect of the boss, if the boss is paying attention to the subordinate's and the company's work needs.

This philosophy is reflected in four demands: set me targets, allocate me resources, review my performance and reward me accordingly. Let us look at these in a little more detail:

1 Targets: I have the right to expect my supervisor to agree 'key results areas' in which I have the duties and responsibilities to achieve things; and to set standards for my performance in the shorter term and targets to be aimed for in the longer term, e.g. 'how much work, at what quality, at what cost, with what timing deadlines'; and jointly to anticipate difficulties and their effect on reaching targets and advance methods for handling those as the work progresses.

2 Resources: I have a right to demand the correct resources, otherwise the targets are meaningless. These resources may be staff, finance, materials, equipment or office space and the like.

Furthermore, I should be informed about my training and my access to the supervisor for help and guidance, and access to other departments and sections of the organisation.

3 Review: Nobody can constantly accurately review their own performance: I need my supervisor to keep me in touch with how I am going. This needs

to be in the form of regular review periods set in advance, and agreement to occasional interim reviews where either of us thinks it is necessary. I also need to feel I can at any time point out difficulties, in advance of a formal review, which are impeding my progress towards targets or causing artificial enhancement of my performance.

4 Finally, reward me adequately for my performance. In most cases I accept that in clerical, career-based employment the reward cannot be instant. But I can expect my supervisor to be recommending me for the maximum that the organisation allows for excellent performance, whatever that is in the existing system. I can also expect acknowledgement from my supervisor, and that my achievements are drawn to the attention of higher levels of management.

You see that this philosophy neatly defines the role of the supervisor in terms of how they should be seen by staff. It by no means defines relationships which are typical, either between staff and supervisor or between supervisor and manager, but the whole of the above is couched in terms of expectation, and, let us be frank, of the highest expectation. But unless you know what the best is, how can you aim for it?

ACTIVITY 2.4

Taking any specific objective for which you are responsible, comment frankly but objectively under each of the following headings how your bosses have managed these objectives with you.

(a) Agree my targets with me;
(b) Give me the appropriate resources;
(c) Tell me how I am doing;
(d) Reward me when I meet my targets.

Please note that we have not spoken about being popular with the staff. We will conclude this chapter by looking at popularity and respect.

■ RELATIONSHIPS

One of the biggest problems supervisors meet is when they are first promoted, because to be really effective they must alter their relationships with those who were previously their equals, even friends. Being liked and accepted is very important to people, and the newly-promoted supervisor is faced with the possibility of having to compromise former relationships.

It is for this reason that organisations, banks included, very frequently promote people away from their current work location. The problem revolves around the reconciliation between two valued roles, that of boss and that of friend, and can give rise to role conflict as discussed in the previous chapter.

'Like or 'respect'?

Even when promoted away from the original workplace, the supervisor can be faced with the conflict between the perfectly natural human desire to be *liked,* and the ambitious hope that people will react to them as boss, in fact with *respect.*

Of course these two attitudes towards someone are not mutually exclusive. Just for clarity you could put them on a matrix, describing how the staff feel about the supervisor (*see* Fig. 2.2).

	Like	Don't like
Respect	A	B
Don't respect	C	D

Fig 2.2

Where would you like to be as supervisor?

We can certainly eliminate D, because not many people opt for being disliked and not respected. We can also go for A as an ideal, because we will take for granted that the good supervisor will want to combine liking and respect.

What about B and C? Ask yourself: given an absolute choice (though things are admittedly rarely absolute), would you prefer a 'C' boss who was a lovely person, whom you really liked and regarded as a friend, but for whom as a boss you had no respect. On the other hand, in the extreme again, would you prefer as a boss a 'B' person, someone whom you did respect, had the necessary strength, made effective decisions, achieved group objectives, but was on the other hand not someone you liked or would want to spend social time with, or invite to your parties?

Most people would rank order the supervisor they want as 'A', 'B', 'C', and then 'D'. It is respect that you go for, and oddly enough, liking very often follows. It can be useful, too, because if you actually like your supervisor you are more likely to make extra effort or do the odd 'favour', at unusual times when these are necessary and outside the normal work requirement.

Getting respect

How do you get respect? Easy to write down here, less easy to do. But there are two major principles; be good at what you do, and pay respect to others for what they do.

1 A good supervisor is what an operative wants, not a super-good operative. The supervisor needs to know what the operative's job involves and what it produces, not be expert in doing it.

2 Staff are seekers of the respect of their supervisors. They not only want to respect them, they also want to be respected for what they do. It is not a sign of weakness but of strength for the supervisor to make staff believe that those staff do their work better than the supervisor could do it. The supervisor still controls and deploys the work. When managers dispute this, the retort is to ask them how, then, do they relate to the work of their typists? Have they, and do they frequently display, superior typing skills?

In summary, then, to gain respect as a supervisor you improve your supervisory performance, and furthermore, you must simply pay respect.

■ ROLE SEPARATION

This chapter is entitled 'The Supervisor', and has been a description of, and a series of prescriptions for, a role. Little if anything has been said about personality or personal characteristics; and a very wide range of different kinds of people can and do fit the role requirements.

People are able to, and must in life, adopt a number of different roles, depending on the situation they find themselves in. When a person encounters problems, these are often caused by confusion or conflict about which role they are in.

Supervisors only strike this kind of difficulty when, for example, they confuse friendship with organisational level, or when they bring 'home' roles into the workplace. Traditionally, men have had an easier time than women in separating – or rather being allowed to separate – home and work roles. The best supervisors of either gender will be those who pay attention to the performance in the supervisor role, deliberately separated from any others they may quite legitimately occupy in other role situations.

■ SUMMARY

In this chapter we have discussed the following aspects of the role of the supervisor:

1. What is a supervisor? The definition, as first line of management; a person at senior clerical level with responsibility for staff and associated resources.

2. Learning the supervisor role: the traditional lack of extensive training, and the non-observance of the principle that supervisory work takes time; but also the attitude of the responsible supervisor, to set time aside and force the learning of managerial principles into the schedule.

3. The critical evaluation of the supervisor's own job under the functional headings of the organisation:

    (a) Production/Operations or Service;
    (b) Finance and Accounting;
    (c) Marketing and Selling;
    (d) Personnel and Development;
    (e) Administration.

4. Managerial roles: the various ways managers are supposed to spend their time and how these can be classified; and the relationship between boss and supervisor.

5. Managerial functions, with relation to what bosses do, what the supervisor can do to help, and the supervisor's own managerial functions, in

(a) setting objectives;
(b) forecasting, delineating the future;
(c) planning, actions to cope with the future;
(d) organising, and co-ordinating staff effort;
(e) motivating, getting staff to want to co-operate;
(f) controlling, setting critical events and checking on them.

6 Managerial styles, different ways in which the supervisor can relate with staff; these have traditionally been seen to be:

(a) autocratic: Do as you are told;
(b) benevolent autocratic: Please – do as you are told;
(c) consultative: Tell me your views, then I shall decide;
(d) participative: We all decide: I implement.

7 Relating with people and the balance between this and getting work done: the managerial grid; and adding appropriateness or effectiveness to this model; and style flexibility, adapting how you act to the demands of your managerial job.

8 Expectations of staff concerning how the supervisor should treat them, and the formal demands of management by objectives adapted to help you examine the supervisor's role:

(a) Tell me what my targets are and agree to them with me;
(b) Allocate to me resources to hit those targets;
(c) Tell me how I am doing, and how I can adjust;
(d) Reward me for my performance relating to my achievement.

9 The relationship between liking and respect, and the supervisor's difficulty in balancing these, and their relative importance.

SELF-ASSESSMENT QUESTIONS

Try to answer these questions to remind you of the content of this chapter:

1 How do you personally define the word 'supervisor'?

2 Recall when you were first promoted to the supervisor role. Write down a brief historical (not 'hysterical') diary of the experience.

3 How could your induction into the supervisor's role have been improved?

4 Call to mind the five functions of the organisation, and write down at least one activity the supervisor can do in each.

5 Name some of the managerial roles referred to by Mintzberg. In what way does your manager fill those roles?

6 Name at least four of the six main managerial functions.

7 What is the difference between forecasting and planning? Write down your answer and compare it with what has been said in this chapter?

8 What is the relationship between planning and organising?

9 Define control (write your answer down).

10 What are the four points usually referred to on the range of management styles?

11 What is the difference between a consultative and a participative management style?

12 Describe your immediate superior's management style in the above terms, with examples of how they behave to illustrate your belief.

13 Honestly, how would you expect your staff to describe your management style? Write down examples to illustrate your belief.

14 What are the two axes or dimensions of the managerial grid?

15 What is the Country Club style of management, and why is it so called?

16 What is style-flex? Why is it a good idea?

17 In management-by-objectives formal schemes, and in the philosophy of MbO, what are the four demands the staff are entitled to make of their organisation and their superiors?

18 What are key results areas?

19 Write down a few sentences concerning the relationship between being liked by your staff, and being respected by them.

20 In what ways can a supervisor gain the staff's respect?

3 Management techniques

OBJECTIVES

When you have read this chapter you will be familiar with some techniques of the following management functions:
- **Objective-setting: laying out operational targets for your staff;**
- **Planning: the use of forecasting, setting short, medium and longer term schedules, considering priorities;**
- **Organising: allocation of resources available, and implementing immediately necessary actions;**
- **Problem-solving: recognising problems, defining them, gathering data, analysing the data and looking for sensible solutions;**
- **Decision-making: methodical action considering alternative actions;**
- **Delegation and the ways of using the qualities, talents, skills and time of others in the organisation;**
- **Monitoring: keeping a systematic eye on what is happening both inside and outside the group, sensing changes;**
- **Control: designing, implementing and controlling schedules for the completion of tasks;**
- **Communication: generally receiving and transmitting the organisation's messages and your own;**
- **Briefing: specifically ensuring that staff understand exactly what they are to do.**

■ INTRODUCTION

Simply understanding the role and responsibilities of any managerial position, including that of the supervisor, is not enough. To manage effectively, you need routine ways of thinking and doing, methods for getting things done; in fact you need *techniques*.

In this chapter, we shall look at the bare bones of some of the techniques used by good managers. Hopefully this process of looking at and learning these will prove useful to the practising supervisor, and also will help you to perform well in examinations. In fact, unless analysing the techniques also helps to perform them properly, the link between the theory of examinations and the practices of the workplace does not hold, and the examinations and the associated qualifications become meaningless.

All of the topics we shall cover in this chapter have at least one thing in common: they are characterised by *lists*. In most cases the fact that various stages or elements or parts of the technique can be listed under headings is an indication of the logical and structured nature of the supervisor's managerial tasks. It also helps to memorise them, and as a reminder, not only for examination purpose, but again, to help you to remember how to systematise your work process.

We shall look at the steps to be taken to set *objectives,* not distinguishing between such words as objectives, aims, targets, and the like, but how the supervisor learns what they are, makes realistic sense of them for themselves, and communicates them to subordinates. We shall then look at *planning,* i.e. forecasting future events, examining and arranging priorities, and setting schedules of future work for all who concern the supervisor.

The topic of *organising* comes immediately thereafter, because having planned, the next task is to set those plans in motion, allocating resources and making sure that they are deployed to pursue the objectives according to the plans.

The linked management techniques will follow, *problem-solving* and *decision-making*. These are linked because they have a good deal in common. In both cases the initial situation calls for careful supervisory action preceded by planning and thinking; both have to do with setting out alternatives, and selecting from those as a result of applying criteria for effectiveness, communication and implementation.

However hard it is to admit it, or to release any part of one's own work, the manager at any level cannot do all the work: at some point *delegation* must enter their lives! We shall distinguish between giving people responsibility for the work they currently do, which is the first level of delegation, and dividing off part of your own work and passing that on to subordinates, delegation in its truest sense. We shall look at doing this well, never mind doing it at all.

Once responsibility has been allocated, the work must be *monitored* and *controlled,* that is, supervisors must do what their title literally means (supervisor comes from the Latin for over-looker) and keep a vigilant and careful eye on what is actually going on in the workplace. Simultaneously they must control all these activities, neither by excessive interface in others' work nor by abdication of all responsibility to others, but by setting control events and monitoring progress.

Finally and very importantly, supervisors must develop skills in *communication,* because none of the foregoing is of any real use unless the results of managerial deliberations become known to those whom they affect. Supervisors should understand the communication process, to begin with, and then set out a series of skills related to the various parts of that process. We shall look at formulating messages, sending them via a variety of organisational media, receiving and decoding them – listening – and passing them on.

Passing on messages has a specific name: briefing. This particular supervisory technique will occupy a separate and final part of this chapter.

■ OBJECTIVE SETTING

Much has been said about objectives in terms of their place in the philosophy of organisations and in the role of the supervisor. But what of the practical way in which they should be set/agreed with staff? There are a number of steps through which the supervisor should go to make objectives operational, which are:

1 to agree key results areas with superiors;
2 to obtain and agree section objectives, including deadlines, from superiors;
3 to allocate and agree key results areas with subordinates;
4 to agree objectives with subordinates; and,
5 to draw up an action-plan to achieve the objectives.

Remember that operational objectives have to be on the one hand reachable and on the other challenging, otherwise they are of little use. It would not be possible to go into detail for all supervisory situations; so to illustrate just how a supervisor can work through these stages let us take as an example the branch counter supervisor who is in charge of cashiers, and who has some responsibility in supporting the manager's business development activity. Let us also suppose that that activity includes targets for increasing personal loan business. Now let us look at the stages to develop section objectives:

1 The key results area in this case is sales support: cashiers, and their supervisors, are usually responsible for sales support (not sales, because Personal Loan Sales is lending, and this is usually, though not always, a technical management function); and for instance a key results area could be the effective distribution of leaflets. The section, under its supervisor, has to obtain, check storage, re-stock and check up-to-dateness of all promotional material.
2 The section/supervisor's objectives in this key area could be couched in terms of turnover; to distribute a certain number of leaflets over a certain period and to re-stock accordingly.
3 Parts of this key results area can be delegated to subordinates in terms of obtaining leaflets from the centre, counting stock and ordering replacement, keeping the held stock in good condition, keeping the cashier points and displays stocked with an adequate daily supply.
4 The operational objectives would be in terms of number of leaflets given out to genuine personal loan candidates, which would, if couched in those terms, not just be a paper chase but would depend on trusting the cashiers' judgement, over a given series of periods.
5 The action plan is something to which we will undoubtedly return in this and other chapters. It is simply a piece of paper drawn up, in this case, in four columns, as shown below.

What	How	Whom	By when
Is to be done: the 'title'	It is to be done: the methods	To involve	Specific dates

This action plan is drawn up in consultation with staff.

ACTIVITY 3.1

Taking the headings in the diagram above, draw up an action plan for at least one item which is within your own responsibility.

■ FORECASTING AND PLANNING

Little of what has gone before can be done without planning. In fact in many ways objective setting can actually be equated with planning, which we have previously defined as 'designing activities to cope with future events'. We have also lined up planning with forecasting, which is trying to foresee future events, estimating forward trends, and getting a picture of the organisational or business future. To do both of these activities requires the ability to develop vision, and what the good manager at any level does is to take a 'helicopter view'.

The *helicopter view* requires you to imagine that you and your team are a helicopter crew whose task is, as it were, to hack your way and create a path through a thick jungle. While quite obviously you must all spend a good deal of the time actually cutting through the undergrowth, you must all – or at the very least the captain must – get in the helicopter every now and then and rise above the jungle, to see where the path is going, to check on direction, see if there are any clearings you can make for and see what other crews are doing. Then you have to get back down and go on hacking!

This applies to both forecasting and planning, so let us look at them in turn.

Forecasting

How can supervisors forecast what is going to happen? To start with they can divide the future up into *short term, medium term* and *long term*. Short term simply means the immediately foreseeable future, a day to a week or so. Medium term could be described as within a slightly longer period, before which things can be changed; and long term means really the future, perhaps six months or longer, before which major changes in direction could be implemented. Across these supervisors can look at trends in the key results areas, partly by closely examining, analysing and extrapolating past trends. Should they again wish to draw up operating charts, a form for forecasting likely future trends and events could look as follows on page 50.

Forecasting has the positive purpose of being the groundwork for planning. It also serves the negative purpose of allowing the supervisor to foresee, and to warn others of, pitfalls. Unfortunately there is less visible credit in avoiding pitfalls than in getting people out of them, however more sensible it is!

ACTIVITY 3.2

Forecast an event in your life and in your bank and write down what will happen in the short- medium- and long-term. (We have suggested one example in each.)

(a) *Self*
- *Short*   Decision about holiday destination in the next week or so

- *Medium*   Complete 6-month holiday savings plan
- *Long*   See every country in Europe

(b) *Bank*

- *Short*   Complete minor redecoration
- *Medium*   Major decorative refurbishment
- *Long*   Larger scale expansion of office

Planning

If we define planning as designing future actions to cope with forecast situations, then we have already suggested how the supervisor can do this with an action plan. The main danger is inflexibility, wherein the plan becomes too rigid to cope with unexpected changes in actual situation. There is also the danger of being discouraged from planning because events change so quickly that the plans frequently become less meaningful. However, to fail to plan because of this is like saying 'We won't lay railway tracks between Manchester and London because there may be signal failures'.

Like many other management activities, planning takes time, and you must make time to plan. The most ludicrous thing you will ever hear a manager say is 'I haven't got time to plan'. This is rather like saying 'We haven't got time to get organised because there's such chaos around here'.

In summary: managers must break into the cycle and make time to plan; they must do the planning; the plans must be flexible enough to handle changes in situation and they must be reviewed in the light both of actual events and of altering forecasts.

ACTIVITY 3.3

Just to show the difference between forecasting and planning, 'design a future action' to implement the forecasts in activity 3.2.

■ ORGANISING

Organising is about ensuring that all is happening as it should at present and in the immediate future. It consists of two main activities, namely, the allocation and re-allocation of present resources, and the exercise of vigilance to keep things going well.

To organise effectively on a continuing basis, the supervisor must first of all 'get organised', which means sorting out faulty or inefficient current systems. To play a familiar tune, this takes time, and while the supervisor has other work to do, it is this among other tasks which gives rise to the advice that the supervisor must obtain the boss's approval for devoting time to supervision.

We are talking about the allocation of present resources to maintain the flow of work, and to do this, the supervisor must know what resources are available at all times, and especially at the start of the day. It is at this time that the supervisor should be setting aside time to think about what needs to be done and what has to be arranged to get it done.

Next, supervisors must develop the characteristic of being vigilant, keeping an eye on everything that is going on. To an extent what they will be doing is 'management by exception' because all they will need to notice will be exceptions to routine events. Make no mistake, this set of activities is central to the supervisor's role: you need only remember again the literal translation of supervisor (over-looker) to be reminded of that.

Having allocated present resources, the supervisor must now communicate and control, both of which will be dealt with later in this chapter.

■ PROBLEM-SOLVING

In real life most problems are solved instantaneously, because the human mind is an extremely powerful object and is capable of almost unbelievably rapid thought. In many cases applying this speed of action is reasonably sensible, because the problem to be solved needs to be solved quickly.

But the mental process does itself follow a logical process, however quickly; and there are problems which will be better solved if time is taken and the problem approached step-by-step. There are pitfalls associated with solving longer-term problems with instant solutions. In these cases, and even in the urgent cases, you can improve your problem-solving capabilities by understanding, and sometimes applying, the entire logical progress.

This process is a series of steps, and an informal description of them would run as follows:

1. *Recognise* the existence of a problem.
2. *Set criteria* for a good solution.
3. *Gather facts* and opinions.
4. *Analyse* facts and opinions.
5. Set out and consider *alternative solutions*.
6. *Calculate* the expected value of outcomes.
7. *Select* a solution.
8. *Implement* the solution.

Let's expand on these steps a little. First you recognise the existence of the problem, then consider criteria for a good solution. Next, the facts are gathered and analysed. A number of possible solutions occur to you, and by calculating the probable outcome of each and applying your judgement as to a good solution, you select the best, or the only, solution. All this can indeed happen very fast, and sometimes it needs to.

Take for example a driving situation: the problem is that a child has run into the road in front of your car. You recognise the problem, and you know that good solutions preserve the child's safety, your own and others', and your car's. Almost subconsciously you take in all the facts of the scene, not just where the child is but the bus stop on your left and the fairly distant oncoming lorry and its speed, and so on. Do you brake, turn, carry on, sound horn, jump out? The emergency stop is the only solution which fits the criteria, so you slam on brakes then clutch.

Compare the two previous paragraphs. One is the 'theoretical' skeleton of the other.

Now let us put some flesh on the bones of the skeleton so as to understand the whole body better.

1 *Recognise* the existence of the problem, by vigilance or using the helicopter view or by listening to others who alert you to a problem. Good problem solvers are those who are open to this recognition, not only of their own, but of others' problems.

By the way, beware of the phrase 'no problem' when counselling staff about personal difficulties. What you normally mean is 'that is a problem for you, but I can see a way to help you to solve it'. 'No problem' belittles the person. We will return to this in the next chapter.

2 *Criteria* should be set for good solutions, and indeed separately for the best solution. By this we mean that you should think through in advance of coming to grips with how to solve the problem, what you are seeking as features of a good solution. Good solutions must include those features. Sometimes this does mean the quickest available satisfactory solution; but if this process is being done more deliberately, there is no harm in setting time aside to consider excellence, the *best* instead of just satisfactory.

3 The *facts* should now be gathered. To do this in the best possible manner it should be done without prejudice (pre-judgement), just collecting data without making any judgements as to its value, truth or bias.

This is not easy to do, because even when you are thinking deliberately your mind will sift and judge its information. But it is a feature of effective problem solvers that they are neutral as to the early facts gathered so that they are presented at all. Anyone who suspects bias in the problem solver could withhold facts from them altogether.

4 *Analysis* of the facts, after the collection, will reveal which are important, which are substantial, which are biased, and which are more accurate than others. Note that facts will include opinions and it is at this stage that analysis can be coloured by your views of where the opinions come from.

Only in the most complex problems do we need to apply, say, mathematical techniques, and these are usually discussed in the somewhat similar process of decision-making, which we will deal with next in this chapter.

The result of analysis should be a clear view of all aspects of the problem situation.

5 *Alternatives* in the way of solutions can now be considered in the light of the facts. Once again, the criteria should be 'pended' while a free-ranging uncritical gathering of all the possible solutions is done, because by constantly applying the criteria at this stage you can prejudice the appearance of a really creative solution.

Here you can accept the contributions of others, provided that you give this uncritical receptive impression. Ridicule or even mild disapproval of any sort of suggested solutions inhibits the giving of further suggestions.

6 Now you can *calculate the value* of the most likely solutions, having eliminated

those which will not work. This calculation in most cases is not simply mathematical, although there is a sort of formula which says that what you are seeking is the expected value, which is the utility or value of each solution multiplied by how probable it is that it will happen. So if your solution is calculated at £100 but is only 40% probable to work, it has less expected value than a solution worth £50 which is 90% sure.

To make this really impressive, remember your school maths:

Solution 'A': £100 x 0.4 = £40
Solution 'B': £50 x 0.9 = £45

7 You may now *select your solution* by applying your criteria. In the above example, the criterion could have been 'highest expected value' (but it was carefully worded so that it could also have been 'lowest expected value': it could have been 'cost'!). Carrying on the maths:

Select Solution 'B': £45 > £40

8 Problem solved? Now *implement the solution*. It is intellectually difficult to know whether implementation is really part of the problem-solving process: 'I've solved it – you get on with it'.

ACTIVITY 3.4

Go back to the list of elements of the decision-making process above and carefully apply each one to a problem you have recently encountered at work. (This activity could be very useful to you in an examination because well-thought through specific personal examples are always welcomed and given good credit by the examiners.)

As supervisor there is no difficulty: you usually have to get something done, and problems are usually solved with that sole purpose.

It is probably for this reason that the next process we look at is, at least in a book about supervisory skills, a remarkably similar one. It is the process of decision making.

■ DECISION-MAKING

In fact, in adult/work life problems are usually solved in order to make decisions as to action; and decisions are usually made to solve problems. It is therefore hardly remarkable that the processes are similar, and can be seen to be parallel in many ways. You may be studying this for examination purposes, and decision-making sometimes comes up, and often as part of a case-study type of question. Whether for this or any other purpose, remember in looking at decision-making that the more deliberately it is done, the more effective it is likely to be. We can take the same step-by-step approach to decision-making as we did for problem-solving, but more briefly, because they have so much in common. We shall be looking at group decision-making a little differently after the description of steps in decision-making.

What happens (again often almost instantaneously) in making a decision? You discern the fact that a decision has to be made, and set out criteria for choice. You get hold of and analyse facts and opinions, set forth alternatives, calculate the utility of each alternative, forecast outcomes and side-effects of each course of action, select the action, implement and monitor it.

For example, Saturday evening is approaching and we must decide what we shall do: go to the cinema or revise for examinations? A good decision will be what will benefit our lives in the longer term. The situation is that exams are six weeks away and we have not really got out teeth into the revision; but we have had a really hard week at work and we have already planned to work all Saturday afternoon. The range of alternatives is work or film. As to utility, revising may net us an extra mark or two at the exams; the cinema will permit our brain to rest and recuperate. Applying the criteria, rest on Saturday evening will permit really energetic revision on Sunday. The cost – a mark or two lost with no Saturday evening revision – will be recouped by refreshed Sunday work. Decision: go to the cinema. Action: book the seats.

Briefly in more detail, the decision-making process is as follows:

1 *Need* for a decision discerned, or brought to attention by others;
2 *Criteria* set up for what would constitute a good decision; in the case of the supervisor, for the organisation;
3 *Facts and opinions* should be gathered so that the decision is made in the full light thereof;
4 *Analysis* should be done of those facts, checking their accuracy and relevance, working out figures, applying statistical techniques and the like;
5 The *alternatives* from which the decision is to be chosen should be clearly set forward;
6 The *utility or value* of each alternative is to be calculated with relation to the criteria; and multiplied by its probability;
7 *Side-issue outcomes* of the alternative courses of action should be thought through to the conclusion;
8 The *decision* should be made, firmly;
9 It should be *communicated* to all those involved;
10 *Action* should be taken to put the decided-upon course of action into operation.

ACTIVITY 3.5

As an exercise, apply these steps deliberately to the decision as to whether to go abroad or stay in your home country for next year's holiday, given that you do not want to spend an extraordinary amount of money.

■ GROUP DECISION-MAKING

We have already discussed the relationship between your management style and the amount of decision-making you delegate to your group, in the normal way of your work. You can also look at differing decisions and allow differing involvement in individual decisions. For example, you can:

1 make the decision yourself;
2 ask for information from selected individuals in the group and then make the decision yourself;
3 ask the opinion of individuals, without getting them together in the group, and make the decision yourself;
4 ask the opinion of the group as a whole and make the decision yourself;
5 ask the opinion of the group as a whole and implement whatever decision they come up with.

Your selection of one of these courses of action would depend on:

(a) how 'logically better' one solution is to the organisation and its objectives than any other. If there is no question, you don't need so much involvement of the staff in the decision.
(b) how much you need the staff's commitment to the decided course of action: the more you need it, the more they need to be involved.
(c) how much power you have: will what you say go, regardless of whether they are committed?
(d) how far you can trust them to want to pursue the organisation's goals rather than their own: the more you can trust them, the more you can leave it to them.
(e) how much harmony there is in the group, and how likely they are to agree with each other: again, the more there is, the more you can leave it to them.

These distinctions were made by two researchers called Vroom and Yetton, and there is a complex model for choice; but they are set forth here once again to suggest that the good supervisor will be seeking a systematic approach to management, and in this case to decision-making, either to improve performance at work or to structure a good examination answer.

■ DELEGATION

You will never hear a manager talking about management without using the word 'delegation'. They will all claim to do it, and they will believe that there is a special virtue in it, which will be heard in the tone of their voice!

Unfortunately, far too many managers fail to understand delegation, never mind practise it; and in any case the best judges of how much and how well managers delegate are their staff.

In this section we shall start by defining delegation; then we will discuss two kinds of delegation, which we will call simple delegation and complex delegation; we shall enumerate the reasons to delegate at all, and go on to talk about the benefits and the risks in delegating work; and we shall then look at ways to plan to delegate sensibly, and to keep control of delegated work.

Delegation is *giving people work and the responsibility for that work and the authority to carry it out.*

Strictly speaking, true delegation is giving to your subordinate some of your own work, together with the responsibility. We shall refer to this as complex delegation, for reasons which will become apparent. Just doing what is defined above when the work is supposed to be done by the delegatee we will call simple delegation.

Of course delegating is not that simple. For example, how can you give responsibility away? If your subordinate makes a terrible mess of delegated work, are you not still responsible? The answer is that you are; but you can use the analogy of *leasing* here: just as if you own a house and lease it to someone, you retain the ownership but you give the occupation to someone else. They have to keep the property in good repair, and even have agreements to indemnify you against loss. You still have responsibilities as lessor, and the ultimate ownership is still yours.

Delegated responsibility is also an agreement, between the person who 'occupies' the responsibility and the person who still owns it, with mutually agreed rights and duties. For the agreement to work harmoniously it must be drawn up with care in the first place and the relationship must be carefully attended to throughout.

There was also mention of authority. Perhaps you will remember the classical parity principle, which is that responsibility should be matched by authority. It is no good giving me the responsibility to do work unless you also give me the power to access the resources necessary, e.g. there is no good you going on holiday and asking me to write to Miss Sara Jane Jay about her overdraft unless you authorise me to sign the letter; or telling me to look after the training of Andrea and Joanne unless I can also order them to do this or that piece of clerical work for their learning experience.

Let us now go on to look at the more straightforward relationship between the supervisor, the work and responsibility by looking at simple then complex delegation.

Simple delegation

One of the remarkable features of much of our industry and commerce is confusion about how much of a job the job holder is responsible for. You might like to ask yourself, what of your work you are in fact responsible for. There will be areas you know you are responsible for; there will be work that you do which you know you are not responsible for (your boss is); and finally you will be quite unsure of certain vague areas. In fact there is only one way of knowing what you are responsible for, i.e. someone must tell you.

Being responsible for a job makes a very big difference to how you feel about it, how you feel about yourself, and how you do the job. Take for example sixteen-year-old Lizzie Whittaker, a school-leaver filing clerk. Lizzie files letters and vouchers and memos for three months, and she does it accurately and well. Not only does her supervisor acknowledge her good work; but one day Lizzie is told that, because of her efficiency, as of today she is completely responsible for the filing cabinet. Should there be mistakes, she will take the blame; but where the efficiency contributes to the work of the office or the customers' goodwill, she will also take credit.

This is hardly being promoted to Chief Executive, but think of the effect on Lizzie. The least that will happen is that when she gets home she will tell Mr and Mrs Whittaker! She will start taking extra pride in her work precisely because it is that; her work. All that has changed is that she knows – because she has been told – that she is *responsible* for it.

Think carefully about this, and your own experience. When you are delegating in the sense of allocating work with the responsibility attached, you must make the latter clear; and it is this that distinguishes delegation from simple allocation, and it does have a remarkable effect on those receiving it.

ACTIVITY 3.6
Ask your current staff to write down in half-a-page *what they do*, and then ask them to write down how much of that they are *responsible for*. Look at where there is any difference between the lists, and see if you can extend the responsibility, within, of course, the rules of the organisation and your own good judgement.

Remember also that any responsibility you delegate you still retain the ownership of, and leasing it must not be done heedlessly, as we shall see.

Complex delegation
True (or complex) delegation has an extra element, i.e. the work passed on to the subordinate is in fact part of the superior's own work. Examination takes place of the work of the superior to find out what part of it must be retained, and part of it is passed down to subordinates with the main purpose of freeing the superior for higher level work, including that which is delegated to that person from the next level up in the organisation.

Doing this has all the problems of simple delegation but one or two added complications. To begin with, has one the authority to pass one's own work down at all? Then surely the leasing problem is even worse: if they mess it up, how do you justify passing it down? Surely if you want a job done well, especially your own job, you must do it yourself. And would you have promoted above your subordinate to do your job if they were as capable of doing it as you are?

So why do it at all? Let us go on to explore this and list the reasons.

Reasons to delegate
The reasons are largely fourfold: for the delegators, to reduce workload and to free them to take the opportunity to try higher level work; for the delegatee, to obtain practical training and experience and to enjoy the motivation associated with doing work of evident importance.

Reducing the workload
This is vital in most organisations, because jobs seem to be designed so as to make it impossible to complete all tasks. This is especially the case where people believe that the management element of, say, the supervisor's job hardly takes any time!

If you can pass on some of the lower level technical work you can have time to do all the things we have been suggesting that the supervisor has to take time to do, including simply to think about managing the group.

Higher level work

Higher level work, including that of the boss, comes within reach if you have passed on the lower end of your own job. The best way to learn how to do the next job up is to try it; and if delegation is truly being practised through the organisation, you need the time to handle the challenging work from above.

You may even need to prove in advance that you have that time available, otherwise the work may not be offered, and you can do this by showing that you have systematically delegated to your own staff.

Training and experience

Gaining training and experience through higher level work is incomparable. In 'apprenticeship'–type occupations (banking is one of these) learning is very often by doing; and while it is not actually true to say that there is no substitute for experience (there are other kinds of learning, as we shall see in the next chapter), experience is a lively training tool.

In fact grading systems acknowledge that to be promoted to a grade above you can qualify by spending a substantial proportion of your time in doing the work of that grade.

Motivation

This element is enormous. Referring once again to the example of Lizzie the filing-clerk, see how giving her responsibility would motivate her to work better. Think of how much you would want to do higher level work if your boss emphasised the trust in you that offering the work carried with it.

We shall spend a good deal of time in the next chapter on motivation: much of it will demonstrate how important it is to have parts of your work in which you can achieve, and be recognised for achievement. Delegating part of your work to your subordinates, with its attendant responsibility, authority and trust, has this achievement factor built in.

The benefits of delegation

These are of course implied in the above. If delegation is practised throughout, then all staff have time to do their own work better, and feel responsible for it, but also have some higher level work which is interesting, all are qualifying themselves for higher grades, and the organisation is obviously also feeling the benefit.

You should realise that though the work which you might delegate is 'lower-level' as far as you are concerned, to the subordinate it is naturally 'higher-level'; and while it might be work that you surreptitiously would be happy to be rid of, they may find it fascinating! Where this is the case the benefits of delegation are doubled. Consider tasks that your boss complains about having to do, that you would quite like to do: think of an example of this.

The only danger is that you might confuse delegation with dumping, which is simply getting rid of the boring stuff and letting your staff suffer it. This is clearly one of the risks attached to delegation, which we will now examine.

Delegation – the risks

If delegation is so valuable, why doesn't everybody do it all the time? It is because of the risks attached, genuine and perceived. Here are some of the expressions of these risks:

- What if they do a bad job, even cost the company money, for which I would be responsible?
- What if they are better than I am at my work?
- What if they don't like or won't accept what I ask them to do?
- Am I really getting rid of boring stuff for my own sake?
- Am I just getting rid of my responsibility because I don't like it?
- I have to fill my time to justify my salary: will I be left with nothing to do?

Let's look at these in turn.

1 *What if they do a bad job?* Well, they will, won't they – the first time, as you probably did. But you don't just delegate and leave them to it, you watch them the first few times, which is time-consuming but worth the investment in the long run. Eventually you do have to leave them, and that sense of risk is inherent in trusting people.

A closely associated problem is that you really like doing something you should pass on! This is less of a risk than a sacrifice, and for the sake of the organisation and your longer-term satisfaction you have to check that you are not keeping work just because you enjoy it.

2 *What if they are better than I am at my work?* This could show that they, and not I, should be supervisor. Of course it does not, and you still, as supervisor, control their effort. A general has to be a good soldier, but can, and has the responsibility to, command better soldiers than he is; you can actually take delight in your subordinate doing part of your job better than you: it only becomes problematical when they are doing all of your job better than you! So do not delegate all of your job.

3 *What if they don't like or won't accept what I ask them to do?* You should have consulted them in advance; but at least find out why they are reluctant. Not confident of their ability? Reassure/train them. Wrong grade? Mention qualifying for the next grade. Won't like it? They must repeat that later when and after they have tried it. Don't see the benefit? Tell them about the pleasures of achievement, show how the section/team will benefit, show them how it will free you to pay more attention to the well-being of the team.

Finally if they will not accept it in the spirit of delegation, you do have the final sanction: you are the supervisor and you can use your organisational power to order it. You might only do this if you know that once they try the particular work they will like it; you won't want to throw it about, but never forget that you do have the power.

4 *Am I really getting rid of boring stuff for my own sake?* This is called 'dumping', and you should examine your motives carefully. However, it is true to say, as we have already said, that what you find boring they may regard as new, fresh, interesting, challenging as you did when you first did it.

You may even find that you are doing some work which has stuck to you through promotion, and which your subordinates actually should be doing rather than yourself. You can certainly start by passing that down to where it belongs!

5 *Am I just getting rid of my responsibility because I don't like it?* This is called abdication, and you could ask yourself whether you are really in the right job if this occurs to you at all. Time to obtain counselling yourself! Of course there are responsibilities with which we are all uncomfortable, and truly these can be delegated, provided that this discomfort is not the only reason; and once again, others may be delighted to have these particular responsibilities delegated to them.

6 *I have to fill my time to justify my salary: will I be left with nothing to do?* Not if you are reading this book! Here it is again: management takes time, and you will never be short of high-level things to do if you spend time on your managerial duties, i.e. setting objectives, forecasting, planning, organising, motivating, controlling, devising new schemes for more effective section performance.

Also you will be freer to accept any of your boss's work which they may delegate to you, especially if you draw your better time-situation to their attention.

Planning and controlling delegation

Like any other supervisory activity, delegation must be properly planned and controlled: not only done, but done well.

In brief, the steps you must follow are:

- Plan carefully;
- Examine the work you are doing and decide what to pass on;
- Look at your subordinates and their workload;
- Audit their talents, skills and inclinations;
- Brief and orient them;
- Arrange for and effect training;
- Engage in the act of delegation;
- Watch, review and control.

Let's consider this list in detail.

1 *Plan:* don't plunge. Action-plan: think carefully about how you want the process to go in the short, medium and longer term, what you want done, how to do it, whom you will involve and by when.

2 What *work* will you delegate? Look at what you are doing and what you would be better off not doing (including any that really actually belongs to those below). This is the time-consuming work which impedes your getting on with the work at the top end of your job, but has enough substance to make it worth the subordinate's acceptance, as they see it.

3 The subordinates' *workload* should be examined. They will be busy: everyone at the lower end always is. This does not necessarily mean that they cannot find time for work they will find challenging; most people can. A balance has

to be struck between this philosophy and truly overloading, for instance moving them out into excessive overtime demands.

4 Their *skills* and talents should be audited: what can they do or could they do with training? What training have they had that is not being used? Note also that we suggest auditing their inclinations: what do they seem to like doing, enjoy, find fulfilling?

5 When all this is sorted out, you must *brief* and *orient* them, that is, tell them what you want them to do, and why, and what benefits they will receive, and the whole delegation background, remembering to pass on the responsibility that goes with the work. Briefing as such must be planned, and we shall discuss briefing towards the end of this chapter.

6 *Training*, either formal or informal, must be arranged and implemented under your supervisory eye. In fact, training others on the job is in itself something which is frequently delegated.

7 Simply *start them off* with the work that you have delegated.

8 You must maintain the whole process under *control*, setting time aside to monitor what is happening, catching the odd brick as it falls, particularly in the early period setting up reviews, and consulting constantly with the individuals concerned as to their progress and growing confidence.

ACTIVITY 3.7

Consider the above list. If you have staff to whom you can delegate work, think of one piece of work you can delegate and take it through the list, and actually delegate that piece of work to them!

If you are not in a position to do this, think of a piece of work your supervisor does and imagine how they should go through the list to delegate the work to you.

■ MONITORING AND CONTROL

We said at the outset of the chapter that we would cover these topics, and indeed we already have, in terms of the ongoing supervisory work. But there are separate points to be made under each of these subheadings.

Monitoring

By this is not merely meant the vigilance necessary to keep an eye on what is happening inside the group, which is, of course, absolutely necessary to perform the supervisor's tasks. All the information the supervisor can get is important to feed into the problem-solving and decision-making activities, not to mention the finger on the pulse of ongoing plans.

But to be a good overall manager, the supervisor should also monitor the environment. You cannot be a good manager, at whatever level, in a bank without understanding the environments to which the bank must react, e.g. the business or the marketing or the political environments.

To do this you should set time aside to keep in touch with current affairs, and especially local ones. You could see if your management would be happy to have you select business reading from the local papers for them to take further developments, both positive and negative, in your customer's (or prospective customers') businesses, new industrial or commercial building developments, special forthcoming local events and the like.

If you are in a specialist department, additionally you ought to want to monitor the trade press for new developments, regulations, equipment, ideas and marketing devices, and you can add support to your bosses, and interest your staff, by keeping in touch in this way.

Such information should not just be selected and passed on to the management, but also shared with the staff, if there is any likelihood that it will provide them with opportunities for visibly effective work in the business development line, or could affect the branch/office in other ways. This is, by the way, a work function and should be done in work time. Quite a challenge to see if you can get permission to do so, though!

Control

We have discussed the matter of setting review periods and dates for the control of plans, and we shall develop ideas concerning the control of people via discipline in the next chapter. Here we shall make a point or two about the control of time.

A senior bank inspector once pointed out that he had observed that all the good officials in the branches he visited always had their diaries to hand, never out of reach. The diary is genuinely the principal tool-of-the-trade of the effective manager at any, including the supervisory, level.

The good supervisor never hesitates to pause to put things in the diary, never forgets to enter dates and times and names, even if it means halting a conversation, even with a customer – after all, if I am a customer talking to you about the need to meet you again, and you stop to write my name and a date and a time in your diary, is that not more reassuring than watching you attempt to memorise details you may forget? The same goes for an entry during a conversation with a member of your staff.

In that diary, there will also be a things-to-do list. This will list all items to be dealt with, and these will be crossed off as they are completed. It will be reviewed in its entirety every day, at the start and/or the end of the day, and all uncompleted items will be carried forward. It takes self-discipline and honesty with yourself to keep this up; but it makes you a much better supervisor if you maintain control in this way over your work.

Finally, time needs to be controlled as well as diaried. If you set time aside to 'manage', you must be fairly ruthless in keeping that time to yourself, and not being interrupted, and not abandoning it to things you find more attractive to do!

■ COMMUNICATION: A DEFINITION

Depending on what you mean by communication, the subject can take up anything from a section in a chapter to a four-year honours degree to cover!

Here we will limit ourselves to looking at what we mean by communication, for purposes of supervisory techniques, and we shall take a look at methods of communication and their value for getting work done.

We shall pay particular attention to skills in the receiving of communication (or listening) because they are skills at which most of us are not as adept as we would like to be, or even as we think we are; but if you can develop skills in receiving information you can undoubtedly improve your managerial performance.

Indeed it is in the effective reception of communication that the term is defined. It makes little difference how wonderfully you send messages, and couched in whatever brilliant language: it is simply not communicated unless it is received and understood.

In fact that well-known communicator, the actor Peter Ustinov, said: *'Communication is the art of being understood'*. It is really nothing else. We will say this now and we will say it again later: if you are not understood, you must take responsibility for that. The only word in the above quotation which we could call into question is the word 'art': you may have to be born with the talent for art, but you can develop for yourself skills, as long as you understand the elements of those skills in communication.

■ THE COMMUNICATIONS MODEL

Communications can be summarised in a familiar model, which is shown in Fig. 3.1, in its most straightforward form (remember that it is a *message* which moves across the diagram, from left to right).

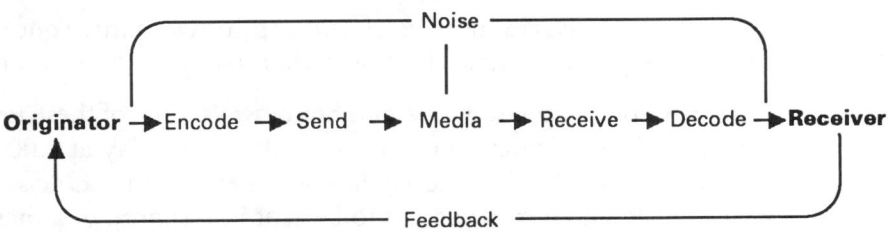

Fig 3.1

The message and its meaning are conceived by the originator, who encodes it, or puts it in the appropriate language and phraseology. Having selected the method whereby it will be sent, i.e. the medium (plural, media), the originator sends it. It is then physically received (read, heard, seen) and decoded (interpreted, understood) at the destination, which becomes that truly when the message is received and understood. There should follow feedback, method of acknowledging the receipt and understanding of the message and its meaning, back from the receiver to the originator.

There is one other word on the diagram, namely *noise*, which is anything which impedes the free passage of the message, and usually occurs between send and receive but can come anywhere.

Now take an example. Let us suppose that Kirsty's boss wants her to work late on an important project. This is the *message*. He will be out when she returns from lunch, so he decides on the *medium* of a handwritten note. Carefully wording it, he *encodes* it in the most polite and most persuasive terms. He sends it by leaving it on her desk, where it encounters *noise* in the form of twenty other papers requiring Kirsty's attention when she returns.

She finds the note (it is *received*) and she *decodes* it, interpreting the content as it was intended, and the tone as the boss's usual smooth-talking cover-up for his inefficiency. The message negotiates a little more *noise* in Kirsty's irritation, but the message has arrived at its destination. The boss will receive feedback in Kirsty's very terse note of agreement!

In what way is this theoretical model useful? Well, as all such models do, it sets out an overview of the whole process of communication. More importantly, it will give us an agenda for the discussion of the various particular skills you should develop to be a really competent communicator.

In brief, necessary communication skills lie in the ability to discern the need for a message, to consider carefully its content, to select the language and terminology accurately, to select the most efficient medium, avoiding noise throughout; and there are also important skills in being a receiver and being open to communication, in penetrating the meaning of messages when decoding them, and in feeding information back to the originator. We will look at these in turn as we move across the diagram in Fig. 3.1.

■ ORIGINATING MESSAGES

Originating messages must be considered in two parts: conceiving the need for a message in the first place, and then composing its content.

1 *Need* becomes apparent in a number of ways. One of these is routine, when, for example, the communicator knows that every day at 2.00 pm a message has to be sent to Head Office via the computer terminal. Or else the need arises as feedback, and a message has to be sent in response to a message received. Or it could arise out of the supervisor's vigilance, noting that someone needs to know something they don't know.

Not noticing the need for communication is one of the ways of defining the poor communicator, e.g. have you ever heard, things like 'They never tell us anything – doesn't realise we need to know, or want to know', or , 'I don't tell them because I didn't think they wanted to know'.

2 *Composition* is not just a school subject, although a good deal more of school education was devoted to it than you may think. There is one school rule that the good communicator abides by, i.e. messages should have a beginning, a middle and an end! The order of the elements of the message, the relative weight of importance, and length, and stress, are all vital: so vital that we shall deal with composition quite separately as a full section of this chapter. You

may like to refer to it now, or carry on with this one for the time being.

A necessary message badly composed can also be the mark of a poor communicator. Simply putting the wrong element before another can distort the relative importance and twist the meaning so as to call forth a completely wrong interpretation and wrong resulting actions from the receiver.

■ ENCODING

Encoding means simply selecting the correct language and putting the message in terms of that language. That seems easy enough: English looks like a good idea, doesn't it? You are hardly going to address your manager by saying 'Bonjour, madame. Je me permets de vous offrir mes compliments'.

Well, of course it is not as simple as that. It is equally unlikely that you are going to come into the office this morning and greet the manager with 'Hail to thee, blithe spirit, bird thou never wert ...'.

Not that she would not understand that: but this is an excellent example of the effect of noise, because her reception of that message would be affected by her (noisy) thoughts summarised mildly in the phrase 'Jim and Jane have been drinking gin again' which instantly occurs to her. It is actually even more complicated, because within modern English we can select different types of language, such as:

(a) formal written: 'We have pleasure in wishing you a good evening';
(b) formal spoken: 'A very good evening to you, Miss Hallett';
(c) informal written: 'Have a really good time tomorrow evening';
(d) informal spoken: 'Good evening';
(e) technical: 'Teleologically, we entertain neuronic impulses stimulating us to invite hedonistic responses in you after the crepuscular period';
(f) jargon: 'Break a leg' (wishes for an effective performance traditionally given by one actor to another).

Then there are also languages which, for the sake of this subject, we can give our own names to, such as:

- extreme familiar (male);
- extreme familiar (female);
- baby talk;
- grovelling/deferential;
- affectionate;
- extreme affectionate.

All of these also have a written and spoken version.

ACTIVITY 3.8

(a) Add at least one type of language we have not mentioned here.
(b) Encode 'Wishes for a pleasant evening' in that language and in each of the additional languages mentioned in the list above this activity!

You should see, then, how carefully language should be chosen in encoding. What is phenomenal is that we normally select our language style sensibly without conscious thought, and stay fairly consistently within them. For example, we do not think 'from the range available to me today I now select 'equal-level-colleague' because I'm Jeremy the Section 'A' supervisor talking to Lindsay the Section 'B' supervisor'. But this language could contain, to put it politely, words of emphatic strength which are subconsciously edited out when using the 'talking-to-Manager' language, and would certainly never appear in the written language, even when Jeremy is leaving a note for Lindsay!

In all of this, two guiding principles stand out for encoding. First, the words selected to carry messages should be selected in terms of *how the destination person(s) will understand the message, most clearly and noise-free* and second, *what the wording of the message will say to the destination person(s) about the originator(s)*.

While we habitually select such words, it is again the mark of the poor communicator to get these wrong, and of the skilled (as opposed to simply talented) communicator to pay deliberate attention to encoding at least for the more important messages.

■ SELECTION OF MEDIUM

Selecting the right medium is almost equally important as selecting the right language. We have already alluded to it above in referring to written and spoken languages. For the purposes of this chapter we shall discuss three classes of media: spoken, written and visual.

Spoken media

These can be divided into one-to-one and one-to-group, and also into immediate or distant.

The one-to-one immediate spoken medium can be conversation or interview, depending on the formality. We shall be looking at both of these, and in particular techniques of the interview, in the next chapter.

In communications terms, we can say that the advantages of these media are that they are direct, that response and feedback are easy, that testing correct encoding and decoding are also easy. However, one-to-one spoken communication can be costly or difficult or even inconvenient to set up; it can give rise to pressure or embarrassment, can be 'transient' which means not recorded and therefore not accurately remembered.

The one-to-many medium is usually only immediate rather than distant, and could be a short business presentation, like a sales pitch, or a briefing or a lecture. The advantages are that it is immediate and has impact, and is more economical than one-to-one; but once again it is impermanent, and normally unrecorded; and there are multiple opportunities for misunderstandings. There is still some opportunity for immediate response and feedback, but less than in one-to-one situations. It is normally called 'public speaking' or 'making presentations'. It too takes special skills and a section will be devoted to it later in this chapter.

Written media

These can be divided into internal and external, and formal and informal.

Internal formal written media are normally such missives as the memorandum or circular or sets of instructions or procedures in the form of manuals. They are intended to be written in precise and unambiguous terms, and their purpose is to provide a recorded message. For this reason, they are usually copied and a copy is stored by the sender. Indeed there are times when that copy is the main reason for the communication: the sender needs proof of sending.

The advantages are that they are permanent, can be referred to repeatedly because they are unchanging in form, and can be passed on in their same form from one person to another. They can protect the sender against accusations of failure to send. They often require more careful composition and encoding than oral/casual communication media. Their disadvantages are that they can be misleading or technically difficult, that the feedback is not immediate and understanding only indirectly checked, it can be interpreted in different ways by different people and may not reach the hands of the intended destination.

External formal written media are mainly letters, but also circulars, mailshots, other advertising, statements, invoices, orders and the like. They share all the advantages and disadvantages of the internal kind, but the difficulties are made more problematic by the fact that checking and adjustment is not so easy where there is confusion or the need to elaborate on the content.

We have no intention of giving instructions here as to how to write letters. While the assumption that any bank supervisor can write good letters may be false, by the time you have reached the supervisor's chair you should have absorbed the principles; or else you may not be the person who puts the letter in correct form. Do remember, however, to delegate responsibility for correct form and layout to the person whose professional skill it is, for example a secretary.

Informal written media tend to be internal only; 'the informal internal written medium' is a nice technical phrase for the handwritten note! (business people don't tend to send these outside the organisation). Please do consider the fact that there is a place for a friendly and well-worded note in the workplace, to convey information or to ask for a favour in the absence of the recipient, and it can be an effective tool in the hands of the good supervisor. It has the advantages of friendliness and informality, and can be worded in more personal terms than the memorandum. Therein lie the disadvantages too, of course: it can strike the wrong, or a false, note of informality where it would be inappropriate; and of course it tends not to be copied for reference by the sender. The best way of judging the use of the handwritten note is to put yourself in the shoes of the destination person and ask whether you would be happy to receive it.

Visual communications media

These are usually posters or notices; but we cannot these days ignore a number of technological additions to the communicator's armoury such as video/TV and facsimile machines. These will be touched upon later in this chapter.

Confucius actually said: *'I hear and I forget; I see and I remember'*. (He also said 'I do and I understand' – but we have discussed that under 'Delegation'!)

The advantages of visual media is that they are fresh and immediate, and you can build in dramatic impact for an effect you cannot always achieve in speech or writing. Also, because it is less usual, visual communication is novel and interesting, if well done. Diagrams and pictures of methods of working often help enormously in technical training, such as recognising documents of specific types. On the other hand, it can be naive and simplistic, insulting the intelligence of the destination people, and being inappropriate or flippant if not carefully chosen for its purpose.

ACTIVITY 3.9

(a) In writing explain to a new member of staff how to operate an office drinks-vending machine.

(b) Draw a flow-chart to achieve the same objective.

Which one of these do you think will be the more effective?

Notice that selections of language and media are closely related. Saying things in a certain way depends to a large extent on how you are going to send the message, and how you send the message also depends to a large extent on what you are going to say. Content of it depends on the effect you wish to have, i.e. your objectives, at the receiving end.

■ RECEIVING

Most people, when they talk of being a good communicator, usually mean good at formulating and sending messages. But the truly good communicator also has skills in receiving and decoding. Being receptive to messages means being sensitive to the fact that others want to communicate with you, and being open to that communication.

In this brief section we are referring only to being ready and expert in physically receiving information. One way of being receptive to oral communication is by keeping your door always open, not only in the symbolic phrase, but, if you have an office, literally wedging the door open. How many of the bosses you have had have told you that 'my door is always open' if you have problems or want to ask questions? Probably all of them. But of how many was it true, especially in a literal sense? If there are in fact no physical barriers to my talking to you I am more likely to approach you. And if it is your practice to keep your door open, then I know that if it is closed then you are out or you wish not to be disturbed.

To be receptive to written communication means that you must read it, and this takes time, which should be planned and set aside for the purpose. Some written communication cannot be read on receipt, because it is too long or too complex. An assessment of this can be made by scanning the document, its introduction, its headings, its conclusion, and any summary which might accompany it. It should not then just be pended, nor dropped in the bag to be taken home. It should be diaried, i.e. a convenient date and time set to read it and note its contents.

Please note that your brain, though an instrument of amazing capacity, cannot absorb everything that impinges on it, nor can it take in too much at once. You should arrange to store some of the information in notebooks such as the loose-leaf variety, or your diary, or files; and you should be firm in ordering the input, by having appointments systems, and not just getting your staff to 'see you later' but at a specific series of times.

Once again, note the fact that the term 'good communicators' include those who seem always available when you want to tell them something.

■ THE PROBLEMS OF DECODING

Being open to communication might suffice; the problems are that you also need listening skills, and that there are barriers to receiving messages.

Listening to the beginning of messages is difficult, because so much information is normally going in simultaneously. When you meet someone, for example, and are introduced, how difficult it is to remember their name! This is mostly because it is the first thing you are told, while you are also busy sizing them up, noting their appearance, clothes, attractiveness, accent, grooming and other details. You are, in fact, subject to a lot of *noise*.

The barriers to communication are as follows:

- noise;
- technical problems;
- technical mistakes;
- language;
- personal barriers.

Let's consider these in more detail.

1 Noise: the distraction from a properly-sent message because other things are simultaneously attracting the attention of the receiver, like how amazingly like your cousin Sarah the speaker is, especially when she smiles, etc.

2 Technical problems in the proper functioning of the communication: phone out of order, strike in the post office, fire in the dispatch department.

3 Technical mistakes in sending: wrong medium, message sent to the wrong person, not redirected, lost in transmission.

4 Language problems: the use by the originator of a language the destination person or group cannot understand, or might misunderstand, by reason of, say:

(a) foreign language;
(b) regional accent or dialect;

(c) technical language or jargon;
(d) unfamiliar typeface or writing or symbols;
(e) too complex, intellectually.

5 Personal barriers:

(a) on the part of the originator (don't really want you to know, don't think you want to know, am afraid of telling you, will look foolish if I tell you);
(b) on the part of the destination person (like to keep myself to myself, don't like to hear bad news, not interested).

Finally, we tend to listen to messages in the context of how we see the world: we have stereotypes about what kind of people do what, what men and women do, what people of a certain age do or don't do, what the British and French and Germans are like, and what they are likely to say.

ACTIVITY 3.10
We doubt whether communication between the bank and you has always been perfect! Taking the above list of barriers to communication, give an example of how each barrier may have caused you or the bank a communication problem.

Apart from simply increasing people's awareness of barriers, listening skills can also be improved with the resolved intention to listen carefully to what is being said instead of (or only coloured by) how it is being said.

■ COMPOSITION

Two processes are important in the composition of effective messages, apart from the selection of language. One is collecting and getting down all the information necessary, and the second is getting the order right.

Effective composition is often inhibited, strangely enough, by the fact that we tend to do things in order, such as making rough notes starting at the top of a page and working down. Then we cross bits out, and scribble inserts, and put in asterisks to refer to what we want to include at the bottom of the page, then add arrows and circles, and end up in a mess!

But during the composition stage, we would be better off if we could think across as well as down a page; there are at least two ways of doing this. One is called *column technique*, in which you draw up your page with, say, six to ten columns down it, put your headings at the top of each, and work down as far as you can under one heading, then move sideways to work in another, then back and forth across the page, putting in keywords to represent the points you want to make under each heading. Eventually you end up with a single page full of reasonably well ordered notes, logically gathered.

Another similar technique, which has no name, suggests that you draw your page up in the same number of boxes as you have headings. Suppose you wanted to write a memo about car-loans – you may think of eight headings, and so your page might have eight boxes (*see* Fig. 3.2).

Make	Age	Cost	Deposit
Source of funds	Repayments	Profit	Targets

Fig 3.2

You can now put keywords into each box, ranging in any order you like over the page. Both this and the column technique have the advantage of not inhibiting you by order or space. They are also quite fun to do and easy to return to after having to break off to do something else. Why don't you try filling some points in on the above diagram, and compare this method of composition with traditional note-making?

Naturally you now have to translate the composed notes into a more conventional acceptable form. What order you decide to put them in will give you no difficulty in selecting from your notes.

But on what principles do you decide the order of communication? Well, here are some, and you may like to add some for yourself.

1 First, people don't like to be put off by difficulties, so it's *easy to difficult*;
2 Then if there is something very urgent to be done, and your document is reasonably lengthy, they may not get to the urgent part, so it's *urgent to less urgent*;
3 People are not too happy with the bad news even if you have to convey it, so it's *good news to bad news*;
4 People like to get familiar with the whole content so they can prepare themselves for the body of the message, so it's *introduction to body*;
5 And finally, people like to end on an up-note, or a summary of all that has gone before, so it's *body to conclusion*.

■ BRIEFINGS AND PRESENTATIONS

Briefing is one of the central tasks of the supervisor and consists of presenting something to an audience (possibly of one). The best are carefully planned and executed. For perfection, the steps would be as follows:

1. grasp your own brief: understanding all the details of the task to be briefed;
2. set objectives in terms of understanding and feedback from the team;
3. select team to be briefed, i.e. those who need to know;
4. plan briefing session: composing, structuring and writing notes;
5. assemble material such as handouts, illustrations or brochures, in advance of session;
6. give briefing, in understandable terms, with motivation elements to ensure co-operation;
7. encourage feedback for complete understanding; be open to the simplest of questions, and say so;

8 require read-back ('tell me what I've brief you to do') to check and confirm understanding;
9 initiate action: remind people of the first steps and encourage them to get on with the task;
10 monitor progress of project and keep it on course. If necessary, add supplementary briefings.

■ INFORMATION TECHNOLOGY

As a supervisor in a modern organisation, you need to keep up with new technological methods of communication. A flavour of some of these can be given here; but advancement is so rapid that between the composition of this book and your buying it, you will doubtless be able to add to the list. In any case it is not necessarily complete; try and add to it from your own experience or observation:

Communication in individual work

Wordprocessors mean fast inputting, accurate, easily edited, stored information.
Electronic diaries in the form of small hand-computers make for more efficiency.
Desk terminals will keep you up-to-date, present information efficiently and allow rapid calculation.

Person-to-person information technology

Telephone technology is improving, with hand sets with memories, redialling facilities and so on.
Portable telephone network systems can be used anywhere.
Radiopaging and messaging are used to contact people away from the office.

Person-to-group communication

Photocopying in colour and *pagemaking computer software*, with better cut-paste and collation features, make documentation really impressive.
Video tape recording allows messages to be sent, with impact, cost-effectively; no need for sender to be present.
Closed circuit TV allows personal interaction at a distance.
Conference telephones (some even with visuals via CCTV) allow meetings between people in different parts of the country.

Office-to-office communication

Large computers with multiple terminals are carrying more and more information (perhaps you've noticed in the branch!).
Telex systems are faster, quieter, and more widespread than ever.
Wordprocessors can be linked, and networks are now possible over telephone land-lines: you type in yours, the words appear on mine.
Facsimile machines for transmitting documents are now very sophisticated.
Finally, the amount of information on teletext on TV, e.g. Oracle, Ceefax

and Prestel and associated networks, has grown enormously. No doubt it will continue to grow as communication becomes the essence of efficiency. How else could we have had a Big Bang, banking deregulation?

■ SUMMARY

In this chapter we have discussed the following aspects of the techniques of management:

1 Practical aspects of setting and agreeing and communicating objectives to staff, and action-planning their achievement.

2 Forecasting future scenarios and events in your own supervisory province, and planning actions to take care of those events.

3 Organising: 'getting organised' in the first place, then being vigilant about everything that happens to modify how you want things done.

4 Solving problems: we have looked at this in an idealistic way, delineating all the steps which your mind goes through almost instantaneously:

(a) recognising existence of problem;
(b) setting criteria for good solution;
(c) gathering the facts and opinions;
(d) analysing those facts;
(e) setting out and considering alternative solutions;
(f) calculating the expected value of solutions;
(g) selecting the solution by reference to your criteria;
(h) implementing the solution.

5 We have performed a similar analysis of decision-making:

(a) recognising the need for a decision;
(b) setting criteria for good decision;
(c) gathering the facts and opinions;
(d) analysing those facts;
(e) setting out and considering alternative courses of action;
(f) calculating the expected value of outcomes;
(g) considering side-effects of outcomes;
(h) making decisions, by reference to your criteria; communicating, and taking action.

6 Group decision-making has been seen slightly differently: the question is the extent to which staff should be involved in decisions, which depends on style and on the nature of the decision.

7 Delegation: we have distinguished between simple delegation of responsibility for tasks and functions already undertaken, and complex delegation of part of the supervisor's own tasks.
    We have looked at the reasons to delegate and its benefits (shifting the load, freeing for higher-level tasks, motivation and training); and we have looked at the risks (staff making mistakes, being better than the supervisor,

rebellion, dumping, abdication, and leaving the supervisor with nothing to do).

We have also looked at planning and controlling delegated work.

8 Monitoring activities and controlling them: the supervisor's (literal) role in overseeing the work.

9 We have looked at length at communication: its very nature, and the communication model:

(a) originating messages, having perceived the need;
(b) encoding them, putting them in the right 'language';
(c) selecting the medium, and the advantages of different media;
(d) receiving, how to be receptive and listen;
(e) decoding, making efforts to understand across barriers.

10 We have taken special note of techniques of composition, getting everything you want to communicate into some sort of pattern.

11 Briefings and presentations have been touched upon.

12 Finally, we have looked at the rapidly advancing technological methods of conveying information as part of our look at communication.

■ SELF-ASSESSMENT QUESTIONS

Try to answer these questions to remind you of the content of this chapter:

1 Under what headings would you create an action plan?

2 What does it mean to take a helicopter view? Think of an example at work when it would be a good idea.

3 Why is it not sensible to say 'I haven't got time to plan'? How do you overcome the problem implied in the statement?

4 What are the steps to be taken to solve a problem? Apply those steps to any problem you have in improving your working conditions.

5 What is *expected value* and how is it calculated?

6 What are the steps to be taken to make a decision? Apply those steps to whether to buy a British or a foreign car, on general principle.

7 On what sort of criteria should you consider involving your staff in a decision?

8 What is delegation? Write your definition down.

9 How can you cope with the idea that in delegation you give away the responsibility in one sense, but still keep it in another?

10 What is the difference between simple and complex delegation?

11 Give some good reasons for delegating part of your work.

12 What do people believe to be the main risks involved in delegation? Comment on each of these supposed risks in reality.

13 What is the difference between delegation and dumping?

14 What should supervisors take into account when planning to delegate tasks to their subordinates?

15 Get hold of a copy of today's local or national paper and select at least one item which should be of interest (a) to your management and (b) to your staff.

16 Construct, right now, a things-to-do list for tomorrow, or if you have one, check it out; and resolve to operate very deliberately with it tomorrow.

17 Define 'communication'.

18 Draw the communication model, and describe in a few words each element of it.

19 Name several organisational media of communication, and state one advantage and one drawback of each.

20 What are the principal barriers to communication? Think of and write down an example of each from your own experience.

4 Managing the individual

OBJECTIVES

When you have read this chapter you should understand:
- Individual differences, and the variety of human backgrounds, experiences and characters;
- How to select the right person for the job, matching individual with functions and tasks;
- Specific aspects of selection: recruitment, transfer, and selection for training and development;
- The supervisor's responsibility for training and development, and where else responsibilities lie;
- On-the-job training and the supervisor's tasks;
- Off-the-job training: the courses and other material available, the integration of such training in the workplace;
- Organisational arrangements to motivate staff;
- The internal motivation of individuals, and the drive to satisfy needs; consistency with satisfying organisational needs;
- Interpersonal control: effective advising, counselling and discipline of supervised staff;
- Techniques of interviewing: business interactions with people internal and external to the group.

■ INTRODUCTION

As soon as you become aware of the people around you in life, you realise, on the one hand, that there are, some regularities in human behaviour amounting almost to rules, and on the other, that everyone is different and has individual characteristics. This intriguing, even paradoxical pair of observations dominates all our relationships, including that of supervisor-subordinate.

In this chapter we will deal first with some of the influences which shape people's *personalities*, and give them the knowledge, experience, abilities, inclinations and characteristics which suit them for one kind of work or another. Note that included here is the word 'inclination'; you need hardly to be a trained supervisor to have observed that people often do better at jobs they like doing!

We shall then go on to look at *selection*, because the supervisor is often involved in it, both formally and informally. Staff are formally selected by the organisation for transfer or promotion, or membership of special teams or working parties, or for technical training or management development; and the immediate supervisor, of the supervisor, is or should be involved in this process, directly or by being consulted. Supervisors will frequently select staff for individual tasks or for continuing responsibility under their own authority too (informally), from making the tea to moving from their usual machine to relieving counter-staff for a lunch-hour spell. Selection is a process which can be more or less systematically done.

Only rarely will the selected candidate not need *training* or *development*, and there are a number of locations of responsibility for training. For example, the organisation has a responsibility, in that it has objectives which will not be fulfilled unless its staff is competent; the division or department has responsibilities derived directly from that; the training department has responsibilities to provide the facilities and expertise needed to carry out training; and the immediate managers, including the supervisor, has operational responsibility to ensure that training, both on-the-job and off-the-job, gets done, and is monitored for its effectiveness.

Trained staff are only fully effective if they have opportunity, and perhaps equally important, if they have *motivation*. While this is a topic which could quite justifiably occupy an entire chapter in a book on supervisory skills, here we have only the opportunity to set it in the context of managing the individual – which, after all, is at least its most appropriate setting. Motivation can mean two things: first, the systems set up in the organisation for motivating people which is effective as judged by the organisation and sufficiently rewarding to them to re-motivate them.

Secondly, we can study the internal needs and drives which spur us to want to do things, including those things the organisation wants us to do. How easy it is to say the only reason I come to work is for the money; and while the vast majority of us could not possibly come if we were not paid, there is more to it than that, otherwise money would be the only criterion for the selection of a job. It is, of course, truly basic, but once we have enough to pay our bills, we look for other – additional, not alternative – sources of satisfaction at work.

There are parts of the supervisor's role which call for the construction and maintenance of relationships between the supervisor and largely individual members of staff. Particular attention should be paid to what we could describe as *interpersonal control*, i.e. times at which supervisors have a clear responsibility for handling conflict or grievance, or must advise or counsel staff; or when they are confronted with the application of formal or informal discipline – it is never easy and should not be thought so.

Finally we shall look at 'business interactions with people internal and external to the work-group', or to put it more simply, at *interviewing*, a special and professional management person-to-person technique.

■ INDIVIDUAL DIFFERENCES

Everybody is different! We could leave this section at that point; and indeed much of what we shall say here is an elaboration of that statement.

To begin with, the phrase 'everybody's different' can be expanded to mean that each of us has a different personality, and this makes things much more complex, because we now have to define what we mean by 'personality'. We shall do that in a very straightforward manner, then we shall look at a way of categorising personalities, before we look at how organisations categorise personality for recruitment and selection purposes.

What is personality?

We are in danger of entering the extremely complex field of psychology at this point, and we must not lose sight of the practical reasons why we want to look at personality, which is from the supervisor's point of view. In fact there are two basic viewpoints of interest: 'how I see my own personality', and 'how others see me'. To be absolutely precise, there is also 'how I think others see me', but for purposes of this section we shall simply stick to 'me from my viewpoint' and 'me from others' viewpoint'.

You could say that *my personality is a set of statements about how I usually am and how I usually behave, or how I can be predicted to behave in certain situations.*

But who is doing the describing/predicting, you or others? You know that there are aspects of your personality such that you could say 'I would never enjoy a party like that', and others will respond 'Really? I wouldn't have believed it, I'd have thought it was just your kind of thing'.

There is a difference, and it is sometimes described as the difference between the 'I' and the 'me'. How I think I behave, what I am like, what I think I would do in this or that situation, where I am coming from; this is the 'I'. The 'me' is what others think of me, how they think I am, what they think moves or influences me and their feelings towards me. The least thinking supervisors can do is to be aware of the differences as far as they themselves are concerned, and to move from awareness of their staff's 'me' towards a better knowledge of their 'I'.

Categories of personality

Ever since people have noticed the differences between each other there have been attempts to characterise, such as by Zodiac or sun-sign, or Earth, Water, Air and Fire types, or the mediaeval Humours, types dominated by the bodily fluids of blood, phlegm, black bile and yellow bile (whatever those might be!).

More recently, and possibly more relevantly, a psychologist called Eysenck suggested that there were two main sets of categories: introvert-extravert, which does not mean what it usually does (reserved-outgoing), but means usually looks inwards for views of themselves and how they really are, or usually looks outwards and wanting to know what others think of them. Then there is stable-unstable, which again does not mean quiet or likely to go off the rails, but means emotionally unchanging and relatively constant, or, very changeable and moody.

You can put these on a four quadrant diagram, with extrovert-introvert on one axis and stable-unstable on the other. There are questionnaires, too complex to reproduce here, to find out what quadrant you spend your time in. Here we can just show the diagram (in Fig. 4.1), and you can make some surmises about where you would be on it. Start from the centre and guess how far out along each axis you would be.

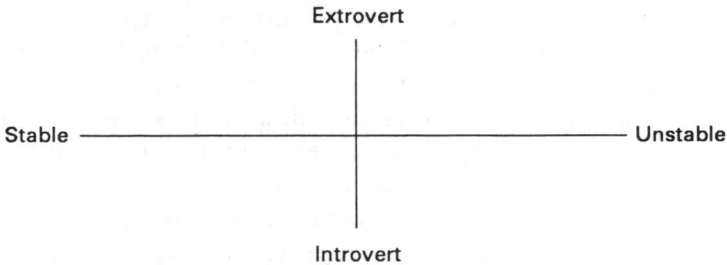

Fig 4.1

ACTIVITY 4.1

Well, what do you think? Are you a stable extravert, an unstable extravert, a stable introvert, an unstable introvert? Do remember the technical definitions given above before you answer; and remember that you are describing the 'I'. Then ask yourself where others would put you, where the 'me' would go. Where do members of your staff go?

How can this help you consider how to manage staff? Like any other way of categorising people – and you may have your own – it simply draws your attention to individual differences, and helps you to consider how different people might like particular aspects of different jobs. If you have the opportunity to allocate tasks of various natures to staff, give some thought to how their personality will fit the role.

Johari's window

There is quite a neat matrix which helps people when they discuss themselves with others, and which is used in counselling, as we will discuss later in this chapter. It is called Johari's Window, and it looks something like Fig. 4.2, 'there are elements of me which are':

	Known to myself	Not known to myself
Known to others	Open	Blind
Not known to others	Hidden	Unknown

Fig 4.2

The idea is to move as much as you can into the open area from the others where it shouldn't be. You can have your own views about that; but you can probably see how useful the diagram is to initiate discussions with those who keep too much in the hidden area or have too much in the blind area.

■ THE SEVEN-POINT PLAN

Organisations and their managers are making selections among people all the time: for recruitment, for promotion, for special tasks or teams, for transfer, for new or different duties, for training and for development programmes. In some cases this is done on judgements with very little system or logic; on the other hand selection is sometimes done on a quite elaborate basis.

When supervisors make selections it is usually for a particular task or set of tasks, or for training. Sometimes they are asked or consulted about staff for transfer, promotion or management development. In this case it is important to have thought about the process of selection if the supervisor is to perform this duty professionally.

One of the best known extended basis for selection decisions is called the *Seven-Point Plan*, designed by the National Institute of Industrial Psychology. This has the merit of being widely accepted in commerce and industry, including banks. Unless you are in the Personnel Department you are unlikely to use the seven-point plan for any selection you might make; but it will sharpen your judgement if you know about it.

It describes seven dimensions along which candidates can be assessed and compared. As you will see, it is particularly developed for recruitment. The seven points are as follows:

- Physical make-up;
- Attainments;
- General intelligence;
- Special aptitudes;
- Interests;
- Disposition;
- Circumstances.

1 *Physical make-up*: what aspects of health, appearance, speech, physiology are needed for the job. The 'hunchback of Notre Dame' might not be too suitable as, say, a police officer, but pretty good for bellringing.

Notice that we are referring both to physical health and to appearance. A candidate's health record may need to be taken into account; and special levels of physical fitness and strength could be important for certain jobs. Appearance is important in some jobs, where people may need to be, not only attractive, but perhaps quiet, or serious, or healthy-looking (such as for serving in a wholefoods store!).

2 *Attainments*, i.e. what they have achieved in the way of education or training. It relates to their schooling and what certificates and prizes they won and what subjects they studied and to what standard. It also relates to posts of responsibility and achievements in educational establishments and in extracurricular activities, such as being a prefect, captain of the school swimming team, or chairman of a local youth charity organisation.

In the case of older people, such training or special work experiences as they have had, and working history, are also part of this plan of characteristics, as are adult responsibilities and achievements, like membership of the local council or school board, chess championships, bank tennis team secretary, and so on.

3 *General intelligence*: while this can be recognised intuitively, it is hard to define and to measure. The term relates to in-born reasoning power, the ability to argue from point to point and to reach conclusions from the combination of facts or principles. It is usually measured by professional tests administered by qualified persons.

Note that it does not refer to the possession of knowledge or of amounts of facts or information. After all, Albert Einstein was very intelligent; but how many high street clearing banks could he name?

4 *Special aptitudes*: some people are born with better artistic talent or musical ability than others, some with certain manual skills or aptitudes. Some may have an abnormally sensitive sense of smell or taste or colour. Some may have special verbal fluency, or a gift for picking up languages. Some are naturally highly numerate.

There are jobs and tasks where these talents are appropriate and there are tests you can apply to demonstrate the extent of such talents, such as the ability of some rather than others to be principal violinist for the Welsh Symphony Orchestra, or as wine-taster for a wine importer, or as striker for Manchester United – or more relevantly, as typist to the Chief Executive, or insurance estimator, or even bank clerk!

5 *Interests* which could be relevant to the job, such as hobbies involving constructional activities, or outdoor activities involving survival or leadership or team techniques like caving or climbing, or the maintenance and upkeep of equipment like care maintenance or motor sports or cycling.

These would have to be long-term genuine interests and not just passing fancies so that they genuinely say something about the person involved. Where jobs can be matched up to interests, of course, there will be a natural enthusiasm to perform them.

6 *Disposition*: this relates to the person's acceptability to others and how friendly and tolerant they are, how they fit in and become generally acceptable to groups; and also how they influence and move those groups, and motivate and persuade people.

It also refers to emotional stability and reliability, and determination to achieve objectives, personal courage and commitment; and how well they are likely to work by themselves with little supervision.

7 *Circumstances*, by which is meant family and home background, how many relatives at home, how many of them are dependent on the candidate, their financial circumstances and the occupation of relatives, and the location/district where they live.

While this is not a characteristic of the person, it can be relevant to mobility, or to the groups they are expected to join, or where they travel to work, or how easy or difficult it might be to send them on training courses (the author can recall a clerk refusing to go on a course because there would be nobody to look after his dog).

ACTIVITY 4.2

(a) Obtain one of your bank's application forms and see whether and how it gets answers in all of the categories of the seven-point plan.
(b) Look at your own job and write down under each category what you might reasonably look for in a candidate to be your successor.

You can see how the Seven-Point Plan is reasonably complete, specifies where tests can be used to see if the candidate has the necessary qualifications, and enables the selector to distinguish objectively and fairly between candidates, which is the aim of selection however it is done.

■ OCCASIONS FOR SELECTION

Look again at that last phrase 'objectively and fairly'. There are few better compliments that can be paid to a supervisor's work, by superiors or by staff, especially when it comes to choosing one or another person to do things. In the ordinary course of business the supervisor will usually make selections between people for specific tasks, or for longer-term job roles, or for training or for (management) development schemes; or they will at least be consulted in some of these matters.

The shorter the term of commitment, the less time needs be taken for selection, so that you would not use the entire seven-point plan to decide who is going to make the tea today (though try it on that as an exercise to help you memorise the points!). This does not imply that selection even for these tasks is not important, or should not be done carefully (the tea could poison the entire branch staff). But the amount of time given to management decisions must be in proportion to the overall importance of the decision.

On the other hand, you may decide to go through a good deal of the seven-point exercise if you were asked which of your staff should be promoted to a supervisory position in another office, at least to make your own thinking more logical and objective, and to be able to defend your decision if anyone asked you to.

In fact the idea of defending your decision is often a good justification for doing things totally systematically: even if you are quite certain that nobody is going to ask you to stand up and give reasons for taking one course of action rather than another, if you get into the habit of going through the process as if they would ask you to do this, you at least assure yourself that you are making decisions for logical, objective and fair – and defensible – reasons.

One of the matters on which you may be consulted is training, and we shall now take a look at this in the context of this chapter's theme; understanding and managing the individual.

■ TRAINING RESPONSIBILITY

Who is responsible for young Lucy's training? That is the kind of question for which an answer springs easily to mind; but it is not in fact an easy question, and there is more than one answer to it.

ACTIVITY 4.3

Before we go any further, write down the answer as *you* see it.

In fact there are at least *five* answers: the organisation, the branch or office manager, the training department, the supervisor, and Lucy herself. You could even add society at large, the government, Lucy's parents, her friends, local authorities, professional associations like the Chartered Institute of Bankers, who also have responsibilities in one way or another for Lucy's training – but apart from the Institute, we will stay within the organisation for the purposes of this discussion.

1 The *organisation* needs trained staff and cannot depend on natural processes or other organisations to provide them. It must not only provide adequate money and other resources, it must demonstrate its commitment to training and development; and in showing that it approves of training, encourage people to develop their relevant skills and talents and knowledge.

Senior people must make statements about the value of training, and attend session on courses, and even entire courses, to demonstrate this commitment, for example; and trained staff should be given work to do which uses the training, and should be those who are promoted.

2 The *office management* derive their responsibility for Lucy's training from the organisation's. They have their objectives and they need trained staff to fulfil them. They must also pursue day-to-day objectives and must balance the investment of time in Lucy's training with getting on with the work.

But it is rarely in large organisations that the impulse for training staff comes from outside the office – you are rarely called on to courses, for example, unless the office recommends and requests training on its judgement of its staff's and its own needs; and so Lucy won't get training unless the branch management says she should.

3 The *training department* is only in one sense responsible for Lucy's training, in that they carry out the training request of the organisation or the office management. They are responsible for doing (some of) the training and doing it well; and they are also responsible for advising those who are doing on-the-job training about contents and methods, which we will discuss later in this chapter.

It is also their role to examine, evaluate and introduce new training methods or materials, and to keep up-to-date with ideas on how to improve working methods and practices as they appear; and to keep materials modern, fresh and up-to-date.

4 The *supervisor*, it will hardly surprise you to hear, has a major responsibility for Lucy's training. Nobody knows better what she needs to know, what skills she has and what she must develop. Nobody knows better which of these Lucy can learn on the job, and which she must learn on courses, or from other training material or devices.

And nobody should know better whether it is Lucy or Gail or Tom who can be spared for a course this week or next, or who was the last person to have formal training. And finally, nobody is better placed to make sure that whatever any of them learn is put into practice at the workplace so that it is not lost or wasted. This can all be done with proper planning, as we shall see in the next few sections.

5 The *candidate*, Lucy herself, has a good deal of responsibility for her own training. Ideally she would wish to be trained to advance herself. This is not always the case, and here supervisors have to press the candidate to realise the value of training, or in the worst case, either simply brook no opposition or select someone else for training!

But it has often been said that you cannot teach adults unless they take responsibility for their own learning; and again it is for the supervisor to make sure that the candidate enters training in this frame of mind, if only because the training will quite obviously be more effective in this case.

6 The *professional association*, and in this volume we might mean the Chartered Institute of Bankers, takes responsibility for industry standards, and provides a measure of what level of study and knowledge Lucy will share with others in her and other similar organisations. It also provides literature and materials to sponsor these standards and this sharing, like its magazine, and books, and examination up-dates and examiners' reports, and the examinations themselves at different levels.

It also must indicate how keen Lucy is on a career in the bank if she is willing to spend spare time – as in reading this book – to prepare herself for certification, or associateship, or higher grades of membership, or her career's professional association; the banks clearly acknowledge this fact in one way or another, by reward, or by making it a condition of promotion or management training.

All these responsibilities interlink, and are dependent on each other: it is rare that you can fulfil one without the others being fulfilled. All the supervisors can do is to ensure that their own part is played to the full.

■ TRAINING AND LEARNING

How, then, shall the supervisor take this learning responsibility and turn it into practical reality? First you must understand some basic points about training and learning; then you must plan systematically for the training of your staff. We shall look now at an elegantly simple concept, called the *training gap*, and then we will look at how adults learn.

The training gap

You will often hear of this concept, mentioned in any textbook on this matter. The idea, as we have said, is very simple: *the training gap is the difference between what I know or am able to do now, and what I need to know or be able to do.*

Supervisors should, ideally, know the extent of this gap for each members of their staff, not to mention their own. They should also keep records of the gaps, what training would fill them, and whether or not/what part of this training has been carried out.

They are also, finally, responsible for testing whether the gap has been filled by whatever training has been carried out, that is, has the training worked, and do I know/can I now do what the training was supposed to achieve? All this can only be done systematically, as we shall see. But now we will take a look at learning.

How adults learn

Adult learning has a great deal to do with problem-solving. We engage more than just the rote-learning parts of our mind. A well-known theory by a man called Kolb indicates that we learn in a number of different modes:

1 by *thinking*, using our mind to calculate, form and review theories and ideas and reasons for things, reading about them, contemplating them;
2 by *doing*, getting involved in trying things out and experimenting for ourselves, being active in the learning process;
3 by *feeling*, engaging our emotions, allowing the impressions to arrive at our emotions, letting how we feel about things influence our learning; and
4 by *watching*, seeing how others do things and observing our own development objectively, noting progress and standing off to watch. In fact these modes occur in a cycle, described in Fig. 4.3.

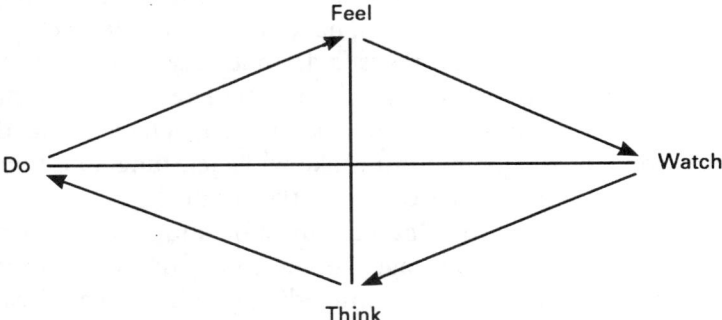

Fig 4.3

You can start where you like: when we get a new experience, let us say we have an idea (think) we then try out its implications (do), let ourselves experience the sensations and emotions (feel), observe the effects (watch), and then modify the idea. Or we watch someone doing something, have a theory and think about it, do it and try it out for ourselves, feel how it affects us, and watch ourselves and the other person to check the thinking etc.

ACTIVITY 4.4

You are walking along the street when all of a sudden you feel a sharp pain in your right ankle. Write down how you would proceed around the above cycle to learn from this little experience starting from the feeling: you experience (*feel*) a sudden pain, then ... what?

Not only do these four key words describe the cycle; they also describe our *preferred learning style*. Some like to learn by thinking logically more than by feeling. Some prefer watching to doing. The trouble is that we will pursue our preferred style and miss out on the others, which, whether we like them or not, do work as well. Whichever is our preference, we should ideally engage in all types of learning, and training should cover all four aspects.

■ ON- OR OFF-THE-JOB TRAINING?

Needless to say, training can take place on or off the job, at the workplace or elsewhere. There are advantages and disadvantages for each location for training, as you would deduce from our discussion of the modes of learning in the previous section.

Off-the-job training is not just out-of-office courses. It can mean reading, or programmed learning texts, or computer-based learning programmes, or off-line terminal practice and the like. An advantage of courses is that they are removed from the workplace, in a protected environment; and the mistakes you can make, to learn, are not costly.

Course trainers are experts in correct methods; and they are themselves trained to instruct. They also have nothing else to do but train. The trainees are in the company of others at the same level of expertise – or inexpertise! – and can share problems and experiences.

One advantage of on-the-job training is that it is for real, and that, while under careful supervision, nevertheless the effects of what you are doing affect the real world, and there is dramatically powerful impact when you learn in real circumstances. It would be a bit like learning to drive in an actual car on the road, instead of in a simulated vehicle. The disadvantage is closely connected: any major mistake while learning, and there is possibly enormous cost – either in the car or in the branch!

This is why such learning must be under close supervision, which gives rise to another disadvantage, i.e. the cost of the trainers' time while they could be doing something more immediately productive. However, the supervisor of your training does know how things are done in practice rather than just in theory, sometimes a problem for the full-time trainer who may not have spent recent time at the workplace.

These are by no means the only advantages and disadvantages, though many more of them are hinted at in these paragraphs.

ACTIVITY 4.5

Draw up a full-page copy of fig. 4.4 and fill in the pluses and minuses for on-the-job and off-the-job training so that you can consider your own staff as well as construct a sensible examination answer.

■ PLANNING AND CONTROLLING TRAINING

Planning training in a systematic manner is not difficult, once you have worked

	On-the-job	Off-the-job
Advantages		
Disadvantages		

Fig. 4.4

out the 'gap' for your staff members. You need to work out what training is needed for each, given the constraint of what is actually available; you can put at the head all the kinds of training available, and you can divide each topic of training into on-the-job and off-the-job sections. A possible scheme for recording this sort of thing is shown in Fig. 4.5.

Name	Training Topic:									
	1		2		3		4		5	
	On	Off	On	Off	On	Off	On	Off	On	Off

Fig. 4.5

You can then tick off, or put planned deadline and actual dates, or make notes, in the boxes, depending on the way you want to operate the plan. This is not the only way to fulfil your responsibility for the conduct of your staff's training, but it indicates the need for being methodical.

■ THE SUPERVISOR AS TRAINER

Apart from guiding the training/learning effort, drawing the attention of staff to available resources, and planning and booking them on to courses, what direct responsibility does the supervisor have for training? This again can be divided into two main areas, responsibility for implementing off-the-job and on-the-job training.

Implementing off-the-job training

It is almost unquestionable that any training that is not implemented soon after its completion will eventually be wasted. People forget knowledge, become rusty in skills and techniques and forget the order of procedures if they get no genuine practice soon after training.

The supervisor has the direct responsibility of putting the candidate on to work which will complete their learning-cycle on return from the course, or after completing the programmed learning or computer-based exercise. Again to do this systematically you must keep records, or have access to your management's records, of what training people have recently received.

Training on the job

This must be done thoughtfully, and the supervisor could do worse than arrange a session with a professional trainer to talk about how it can be done properly. Often it is done by attaching the candidate to an experienced operative, and letting them watch, and try out certain of the tasks, gradually increasing the difficulty of the tasks. This kind of training is, of course, dependent on the careful choice of experienced operative.

The learning cycle should be closely watched, by the supervisor arranging to review lessons learnt at regular, arranged times, so that problems are raised, difficulties can be ironed out, and supplementary activities arranged where necessary.

■ MOTIVATION

However well trained a person is, they will not implement that training or make an effort if they are not motivated to do so. What do we mean by 'motivated'? And how can the supervisor contribute to the motivation of staff? To say that it is part of the supervisor's role is easy enough: to define exactly what the supervisor has to do is less simple; it is indeed fairly complex. We will start the next few sections on this topic by looking at what we mean by it, then we will look at ways in which the effective supervisor can make a practical contribution towards the motivation of staff.

Essentially motivation means two different things, which we will put in the form of two questions:

1 What systems does the organisation have to permit the reward of staff effort?
2 What is it that motivates people to do anything at all, let alone work harder towards organisational goals?

■ THE SYSTEM AND STAFF EXPECTATIONS

Nobody does anything, and certainly nobody comes to work, without expectations. We expect the place to be open, we expect that there will be something for us to do, we expect to have to stay for a specific period, we expect to be in certain relationships with others, we expect others to behave in certain ways, we expect that others have expectations of us.

In this section we are dealing with our expectations concerning a return on our effort, what we expect in terms of reward for our labour; because however much we all love the business of clerical or junior management work, most of us at least do not just do it for love. In fact we do not just do it for money either, as we shall see as this chapter progresses. But for the present we shall look at whether organisations set up adequate systems to reward their staff as the staff wish to be rewarded, and what the supervisor can do to ensure that those systems operate properly.

In an ideal situation — and let's be perfectly clear that there is no such thing as an *ideal* situation — we could start off with *effort*, to which we must be *motivated*. Effort leads to *performance* giving rise to *reward*, which in turn motivates us to greater effort, and so on. Figure 4.6 shows this in diagram form. If only life were as simple as this, however!

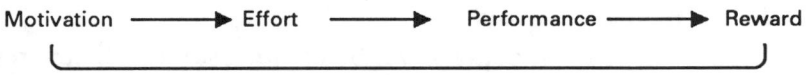

Fig. 4.6

This process never actually works like this, of course, and good supervisors do not concentrate so much on the elements of the diagram but on *what comes between each of the words in the figure*, which we will now go on to consider.

Motivation to effort

Is it possible that motivation might not lead to effort? Is it possible that you might actually want to try something but don't?

Of course it is, when for example the organisation won't let you do something, because you are too junior, or too senior, or in the wrong department.

What can a supervisor do about these situations? Take whether the organisation will let people do what they want to do: you can alter that within your own jurisdiction by letting Karen try something which was traditionally exclusively a male domain and in doing so help to break down organisational barriers.

When people don't do things they would actually like to do because they don't think it is part of their job, this too can be adjusted: by talking to them about their self-image and what should be expected of them. For example, if they want to try work which is 'above' them in grade, they might try it if they knew that by doing so this would help qualify them for that grade.

Effort to performance

Is there anything which can prevent extra *effort* leading to better *performance*? If I try harder, surely I'll perform better?

Well, not if, say, my competition is also trying harder and equalling my efforts; or if my equipment is faulty and breaks down however hard I am trying; or I don't have the resources and run out of expenses money before I can contact all my customers; or the weather changes and fewer holidays are being taken when I am trying to beat Holiday Insurance sales targets, for example.

And however hard I try, it will be of no avail unless my ability or training is sufficient for the tasks, to start with.

Can supervisors do anything about the barriers between effort and performance? Indeed they can in certain circumstances: for example, they can ensure that staff are properly equipped, that equipment is maintained, and then they can keep the resources at the correct level for performance. There is not much they can do about competition, except for monitoring their performance, which they should certainly do; and not much about the weather, except that when targets depend on such external factors, they can help to adjust the targets sensibly in line with what is actually happening in the world outside the organisation.

Performance to reward

Surely if I perform better I will be commensurately better rewarded?

Unfortunately, the direct relationship does not hold in the short term in most organisations, and not even in the longer term in some of them. There are two sets of problems here: first, organisations can simply have no system for rewarding people directly. So for instance if you do hit targets in terms of selling a particular number of specific banking service packages, or you attract a certain number of new customers, are there ways in your bank of giving you a direct related bonus or prize? Possibly so, but more likely not.

Second, even where there are such mechanisms, are you invariably recommended for them by your local management? Are you quite sure that they know about all of these mechanisms? Are they sometimes blind to your achievements?

Again the supervisor can play a part in improving the relationship between performance and reward. There is not much they can do about organisational systems; but they can certainly make sure that any reward that is due to the staff arrives with them. They can only do this if they are vigilant and pay constant attention to the staff's achievements.

Reward to motivation

Finally, will such reward ensure that I am motivated for the next round of tasks?

This depends on two elements of the staff's expectations. First, it depends on whether they actually believe they are going to be rewarded as a result of effort. If we keep on working hard and hitting targets, but get absolutely nothing for it, you cannot persuade us that working even harder will result in special bonuses; nor will we believe you if you exaggerate what we will get for working harder.

Second, it depends on whether what you offer is something they want. It is no good offering a can of the finest fishing-worms in the world as a prize for better performance to most people – unless their all-consuming passion is fishing, in which case, nothing better! You must therefore have some idea of what the staff value as reward.

Once again, and finally, you can affect both of these elements. You can adjust whether they believe they will get reward for effort by being consistent in awarding whatever they can get for genuine performance; and you can also adjust how they value rewards, for instance by showing them what the longer-term values are of whatever may seem less valuable in the short term (i.e. by showing people how in the long term promotion can result from efforts which are apparently fruitless in the short term).

ACTIVITY 4.6

To get all this straight, take a piece of paper and write the words motivation, effort, performance and reward on it, well spaced; and based on the above sections, write in between each of the words what supervisors can actually do to ensure that the process moves smoothly, for their staff, between one stage and the next.

■ INTERNAL MOTIVATION

Why do you come to work at all? The instant response to that is 'For the money', of course. But it has already been hinted that this is only the basic, simple answer, and life is never as simple as that! For example, it would not be difficult to find perfectly normal people who sacrifice extra money in one occupation to do what they like better in another. Stop and think if you know anybody who has done that.

Now all of what has been written above concerning how organisations set themselves up, and how supervisors can contribute to motivating staff must all be set in context: what is it that motivates anyone to do anything?

Whatever I do starts from a drive inside me. For instance, if I eat it is because I am hungry and I have a drive to satisfy that hunger, or even because I fancy a piece of chocolate when I'm not hungry and I am driven to buy and eat some chocolate. In effect, I have needs; and *motivation is the drive to satisfy needs*.

Having made that simple statement, by definition it is now necessary to consider people's needs if you want to understand what motivates them. This is less simple, of course; but we shall now proceed to take a look at the needs of the people you are likely to come across. There are eccentrics, and people who are difficult to classify; but the majority of people working for your bank will have the drives and needs we will outline in the next section.

■ NEEDS

The needs that people have can be classified in order, from the very basic to the fairly subtle and complex. A very famous classification was done by a man called Abraham Maslow; and while you probably will not have to reproduce this classification in detail, it will be fairly fully discussed here, because it does throw light on the motivated behaviour of the staff you may have to manage.

People's needs are arranged in a hierarchy, often drawn as a triangle (*see* Fig. 4.7); we will discuss each level from the bottom up as this section proceeds.

1 *Bodily* (or physiological) *needs* come first. Whatever else you need in life, if you are starving to death or deprived of water, or air, or are in physical mortal pain, you will take steps to satisfy those needs at the risk of anything else.

Fortunately, in our society, we do not normally find ourselves in this position; but that is largely because we earn enough money at work to buy things (like food and clothes and medicines) to satisfy physical needs; or else our society has mechanisms via social welfare to satisfy basic bodily needs.

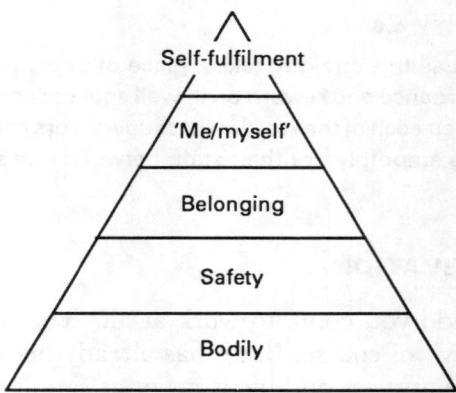

Fig 4.7

2 *Safety* (or security) *needs* come next, and only when bodily needs have been satisfied. If I have eaten, my next concern is to continue to stay alive, both by securing my means of getting the next meal, and by protecting myself from danger.

In the work context, if I have earned enough to feed and clothe myself and my dependants, I shall want to make sure I can continue to do that, and I need to protect myself from threats to that income. I shall want a contract of service, reassurances about redundancy from my bosses or a scheme to handle it if I am made redundant, or life, health or income-protection insurance.

3 *Belonging* (or social/affiliation) *needs* arise after I feel secure: I look around to see who else is similar to me, or will want my company, or like me, or ask me to join their group. This is a need which may or may not be satisfied at work, and I will be anxious that it should, especially if I'm a newcomer.

I would not want to satisfy this need if I'm a hermit, but few hermits join the staff of, say, banks. People like to feel that they belong, that they are not outcasts; and they even like symbols of belonging, e.g. ties or lapel pins or uniforms, or being invited to social, or business-social engagements such as parties or leaving-do's or lunches, or being regarded, not just in the mind but in speech, as 'one of our people'.

4 *Me* (or ego) *needs* are those associated with being recognised as an individual in your own right, rather than just, and having been accepted as, a member of the group. These are needs associated with your contribution to the group, being recognised for special talents or skills or expertise.

These needs can above all be satisfied in responsible work set in group or team activities such as in banks, where people can be given work on which others rely, and being recognised and acknowledged as carrying out that work well: 'We couldn't do without Carol – she's the only one who can make head or tail of those documents' – and Carol will have the need to be seen as a useful individual well-satisfied. As we shall see, it is the existence of this need which can be used by the supervisor, perhaps above all, to motivate staff.

5 *Self-fulfilment* (or self-actualisation) *needs* are the highest order of needs, and are quite individual. What satisfies them is what would really fulfil our

potential, what we would long to do if we did not have to worry about anything else (by which we mean if all our needs were satisfied).

Carol may well be the only person who can make head or tail of the documents, but does Carol think that this is what she was born for? Would Carol be handling the documents still if she won the pools? What in fact would she be doing? Whatever that is in Carol's case, and it will be different in the case of each individual, would be what would satisfy her self-fulfilment needs.

ACTIVITY 4.7
Taking the levels in turn (and we suggest you start from the bottom) what can a supervisor, realistically, do to satisfy the needs of the staff in their office?

Few if any people get to the stage at work where they are satisfying all these needs all the time, and they would probably be in what are known as vocational occupations like medicine, or veterinary, or teaching professions. But all of us like to think that there are occasions on which we will have the opportunity to do something we personally would find really fulfilling every now and then. The point is that while we all have something in common when it comes to what would satisfy our bodily needs, we are all different at this top level.

■ SATISFACTION

ACTIVITY 4.8
Answer each of the following questions.

(a) What single thing at work gave you the most (positive) satisfaction in the last twelve months.
(b) What single thing at work gave you the most (negative) dissatisfaction in the last twelve months?

We have used these questions to illustrate that, having considered needs, we must go on to look at satisfying them and in theory there are two factors to consider: *satisfaction* and *dissatisfaction*. What is the difference?

It is similar to the difference between pleasure and pain. If you are in pain, and I do something to remove that pain, I don't give you pleasure as such — I just remove the pain. In fact you are not likely to be sitting there thinking: 'how nice — nothing hurts me' (unless you are a person normally used to pain as part of your life). On the other hand, I can give you something particularly delicious to eat, even if you are not particularly hungry, and therefore simply give you pleasure, without removing any discomfort (because you were not feeling any). I can even give you pleasure without removing pain so that you feel both independently: you could be lying in your hospital bed, in some discomfort, simultaneously eating and enjoying the excellent grapes I have brought.

Similarly, at work there are factors which, if absent, give you dissatisfaction, but if present leave you not dissatisfied; these we will call dissatisfiers (though the technical term is *hygiene factors*). Then there are factors which if present give you satisfaction but if absent leave you not satisfied (but not dissatisfied!). These we will call satisfiers (the technical term for these is *motivators*).

For example, the physical work conditions you are in are dissatisfiers: you can certainly be reluctant to get out of bed in the morning if your office is a horrible place to work, but you do not look forward to going to work just because the office is pleasant.

On the other hand, what you get in the way of achievement is a satisfier, because you achieve something that gives you positive pleasure; but if you don't, well, much of your routine daily work has to be done without any element of satisfaction, but that does not necessarily actively dissatisfy you.

Other satisfiers are recognition for achievement, the intricacies and interest of the work itself, advancement and promotion, learning, and personal development and growth. Other dissatisfiers are company policy, bureaucracy and red tape, relationships with bosses and workmates.

Salary is interesting, because it can be either or both: part of your salary removes the dissatisfactions associated with not being able to afford to live in reasonable comfort, and is therefore a dissatisfier; and part of it recognises your status and achievement, and is therefore a satisfier.

■ SATISFACTION AND MOTIVATION

How can you use these ideas to be a more effective supervisor, to motivate your staff? The idea of separating dissatisfiers from satisfiers indicates that you must look at both: if there is pain and no pleasure, remove pain and give pleasure, if there is pleasure and pain, remove pain; if no pain, but no pleasure either, give pleasure. It is easy to waste effort and try and give pleasure where I already have pleasure but my problem is that I also have pain; and vice-versa.

Similarly, look at which elements of which of the sets of factors are missing in your staff, and instead of wasting time, effort and resources on the wrong set, ensure that your attempts to solve the problems associated with satisfaction/dissatisfaction are properly directed. It is no good giving more job-satisfaction to those who are perfectly happy with the job but work in extremely uncomfortable surroundings; equally, it is no good trying to persuade the bank to build squash-courts if the problems lie in your staff's lack of job-satisfaction.

We shall discuss the practical application of this thinking when we come to the topic of leadership in the next chapter. Here we have tried to show you that having some sort of structured background to your thinking as supervisor can help you to do the job better and more systematically. We will now go on to look at how people react to the actions of other people; how your interaction with me affects how I react to you.

■ HUMAN INTERACTION

It is quite remarkable how we learn to apologise what others are communicating to us in addition to simply what they are saying in words. We take implications from facial expressions, tone of voice, gestures, body postures, head movements and angles, touch, dress and grooming, even the direction in which their gaze is focused.

Unfortunately we do not have room here to go into the whole subject of the physicals of human behaviour, just into how collections of those non-verbal aspects of behaviour affect our reactions.

There is a model of this action-reaction aspect of behaviour, called *transactional analysis*, or TA – which simply means the analysis of transactions. When I say or do something which is intended to be communicated to you, and you do something in return, that is called a *transaction* (most likely because I expected you to do something in return when I communicated with you.)

What the model says is that I always communicate or transact with you, when I am displaying one of three general aspects of myself, or states I am in at the time, e.g. I am being parent or adult or child. At this point we had better look at these more closely although you will find that in the next chapter we will go into considerable detail.

Ego states

1 The *Parent* is one state I can be in. Parents either look after or nurture you, and say things like 'never mind', and 'I'll look after you', and 'don't worry about that'. They are also critical, and say 'leave that alone', and 'how dare you!', and 'you're not going out dressed like that!'.

2 The *Adult* is the state I am in when I am simply making factual or evaluative phrases, like, 'this book is printed in England', or 'it will take about an hour to read this chapter'. There is usually little in the way of values attached to phrases spoken in the 'adult' state.

3 The *Child* state in the model (they are called *ego-states*, 'ego' being Latin for 'I') is the one I am in when I am being completely uninhibited, having lost my temper or shouting for joy (the 'child natural'); or when I am trying to get my own way by wheedling or by bribing or trading (the 'child manipulative', e.g. I would say things like 'Please get it done by tonight – you can have the morning off tomorrow if you do.').

ACTIVITY 4.9
(a) Think of another 'parent nurturing' phrase and another 'parent critical' phrase.
(b) Think of a few 'adult' phrases.
(c) Think of a 'child natural' and a 'child manipulative' phrase.

These are not just states I am in if I am a parent or an adult or a child in the everyday use of these words. In fact, I am always in one or another of these states. I either address people to look after, criticise or correct them; to deliver factual statements or assessments; or express my emotions or get them to do something.

This model tries to solve the problem of people who spend too much of their time in one state or another: a balanced use of your ego states seems to be healthier. Another use is to help people be more aware of the effect they have on others, this is examined in the next section.

Transactions

We shall not enter the extremely complex – though very interesting – field of transactional analysis until the next chapter. Here we shall just select a point or two of relevance to those in the supervisor-subordinate relationship.

First, how you react to me depends largely on how I act towards you. In terms of the TA model, if I address you, for example, from my parent critical ego-state then I expect you to respond from your child, and indeed I put pressure on you to do so. So if I say, 'How many times have I asked you to put the manual away when you have finished with it?', then I expect, and you will feel pressed to say, something like 'We haven't had it' (child natural), or, 'We're really sorry, it won't happen again' (child manipulative). Or if I come from my child manipulative: 'I'm really in trouble – I've lost the manual. You couldn't help me find it, could you?', then I expect your parent nurturing: 'Don't worry, of course I'll help you' or parent critical: 'How many times do I have to tell you... etc.' and indeed it is your parent which will be stimulated.

However, although the natural response is child to parent, adult to adult, parent to child, with thought it may not in fact be the best one. If someone addresses you from their parent, possibly a cool neutral adult response might work better, as it could if they address you from the distressed child natural, depending on what your objectives are for that interaction.

ACTIVITY 4.10

Increased awareness of human interactions is the first step in developing sharper skills, so try the following.

(a) Think through a few examples of typical conversations at work asking yourself whether the phrases are appropriate to parent, adult or child.
(b) Use this model to look at some of the interactions going on around you the next time you are in the office.

■ ADVICE AND COUNSELLING

It hardly needs to be said about *advice* that unless it is asked for, requested or accepted receptively, it is of no use. That is about all there is to be said about it, too. If you need a textbook to tell you how to give advice, there is little hope for you as supervisor!

On the other hand, *counselling*, would merit, and has on many occasions merited, an entire book in itself! It will have to suffice here to say that the major difference between advice and counselling is that in counselling the objective is to have the subject talk themselves towards their own solution to their problems, not tell them about or urge them towards the counsellor's solutions.

In fact the term 'non-directive' is often applied to modern counselling; and it is a complex interactive skill which is better expressed if the counsellor is trained. Here we can show that it is a systematic activity, and as such there are steps which we can lay out here in basic form, which you can learn for examination purposes, and can consider to improve your supervisory skills.

Thus, the counsellor:

1 *discerns need* in a member of staff for personal or problem-solution counselling;
2 *ensures privacy* for the counselling session, for a reasonable period of time, with no interruptions;
3 *encourages openness* and expression by the staff member about subject of counsel, by assuring of confidentiality;
4 *tries to avoid giving advice* except when specifically requested, and not always even then, unless it will further the interaction;
5 *strongly encourages own solutions* to be developed, courses of action, possible alternatives, by staff member themselves;
6 *supports selected actions*, suggests means of implementation, offers resources, help and support to carry them out;
7 *monitors progress* of solutions, personal development of staff member and emotional progress via solution.

■ INTERVIEWING

Advice is given our counselling offered in the interview situation. You know what an interview is, but we will suggest a definition here for technical purposes:

an interview is a planned interaction at work characterised by objectives.

Irrespective of the purpose of an interview (discipline, grievance, customer, appraisal, briefing, counselling, etc.), it is an interaction between (usually) two people, and all parties have objectives more or less stated which they wish to pursue. There are also certain other characteristics which define it and skills required to conduct it. These are:

- objectives;
- planning;
- investigation;
- role difference;
- formality.

1 Interviewer and interviewee will both have *objectives*, i.e. things they want to achieve by the end of the interview (see Chapter 1). The good interviewer will be able to make a clear statement based on a clear view of them, and will have forecast what the interviewee's are likely to be; and as part of planning will have written them down; and would have developed skills in directing the interview towards them.

Only after this contemplation of objectives would the interviewer plan the content of the interview. Of course, you cannot forecast all that will happen, but you can plan some aspects.

2 *Planning* is necessary, and is the next characteristic of the good interview. The structure should be planned, at least in the form of beginning/opening, middle/body, and end/close; nothing looks more expert than someone who

knows what to say to start the interview, is seen to have a number of planned points to make or questions to ask in the body, and who knows how to end it because they have thought in advance about this tricky aspect of technique.

Planning interviews takes time, as all management does. Certainly there are interviews that you have to do practically without warning but even for these you can often find out what they are going to be about, and ask for a minute or two to collect your thoughts. Thus, plan the *opening* and the *questions* and the *close*. Where you do have warning, it is ridiculously amateurish to go into the interview without a plan at least covering these three elements.

3 *Investigation* or *questioning* is the essence of interviewing, because if there is nothing to be discovered, if all is known, the interview is not an interview, but probably a speech. You have probably been the victim of what the interviewer thought was an interview but was in effect a speech! Investigation requires skills-development, probably via training, and you may find that your organisation offers interviewing training.

One of the central points of that training will be the form of question, i.e. open or closed. Closed questions net you 'yes' or 'no' answers, or offer a single response (like 'how old are you?'). They are far less productive of information than open questions, starting with What or How or Why, or sometimes Where/When/Who. These are much harder to formulate and ask, and much harder to answer; so they must be planned, and sympathy for the responder must be suspended, even if they seem under pressure to answer – because if they give you the richer information open question elicits, you can get nearer the objectives – yours and theirs – for the interview.

4 The *role difference* between interviewer and interviewee also characterises an interview as such. The interviewer should be in charge (though not dominant or aggressive), so that the interview is efficient. Have you ever been in an interview when the interviewer is not in charge? It is frustrating and awkward.

You can establish this authority by having arranged for no interruptions; and also where you sit, your posture, your carefully groomed appearance, your tidy prepared notes, and by your general manner. Open with a clear statement of objectives and the 'ground-rules', i.e. how the interview is to go, how long it is to take, what you expect of the interviewee. Young or inexperienced interviewers find this aspect difficult until they realise how much the interviewee wants them to control the situation for the sake of all.

5 Finally, *formality* is a defining feature of interviews. It is perfectly natural, and expected, and even useful; but it can give rise to tension, which should be carefully managed. Note the word 'managed': quite often tension will need to be reduced, but not invariably, because it could suit the interviewer to maintain its presence, such as in disciplining staff, or even a customer!

It was suggested that formality might be useful. This is because often the formal role you are in is what is really conducting the interview, not 'your yourself'. For example, it is the boss telling the staff off, not the bossy individual shouting at someone, or it is the Personnel Supervisor giving someone notice, not just a usually quite nice person depriving someone else of their living. This affords invaluable protection to the ego of both parties.

It may be deduced from the above that the subject of an interview does not affect what an interviewer has to do to demonstrate competence. It makes little difference whether it is grievance or discipline or selling or counselling.

The subject matter dealt with in different kinds of interviews is covered in various other chapters of this book; here we will rest having described the framework in which the supervisor will set the content, since it is the framework of technique which is basic to developing skills in managing the individual.

■ SUMMARY

In this chapter we have discussed the following aspects of managing the individual:

1. Individual differences, in terms of personality: introvert versus extravert, stable and unstable; and ways of looking at the differences between how you see yourself and how others see you; the 'I' and the 'me';

2. The seven-point plan, a practical way in which organisations classify individuals for recruitment and selection purposes, looking at:

    (a) physical make-up, health, appearance, speech, physiology;
    (b) attainments and what the person has achieved;
    (c) general intelligence and intellectual calibre;
    (d) special aptitudes such as the artistic, verbal or mathematic;
    (e) interests, hobbies and outside activities;
    (f) disposition, character and acceptability to others;
    (g) circumstances, family, wealth, social class, background.

3. Training: who has responsibility. We have looked at several locations for responsibility:

    (a) the organisation;
    (b) the management;
    (c) the training department;
    (d) the supervisor;
    (e) the trainee;
    (f) the professional association.

4. The training gap: the difference between what needs to be learnt and what the learner is currently able to do.

5. The ways in which adults learn: by thinking, working out models and calculating reasons; by doing, trying things out; by feeling, allowing emotions to play; and by watching the attempts and actions of others.

6. The differences between on- and off-the-job training, the advantages and disadvantages of each type of method, and striking a balance. The supervisor's responsibilities in planning and implementing training.

7. Motivation: first, the organisation's systems for motivating the staff, from:

    (a) motivation to effort;

(b) effort to performance;
(c) performance to reward;
(d) reward to motivation;

and the barriers between the elements of each stage.

8 Then, motivation as defined as the drive to satisfy needs, these needs also examined and classified under the headings of:

(a) bodily;
(b) safety;
(c) belonging;
(d) 'me/myself'
(e) fulfilment.

9 Human interaction: how the behaviour of one person in an interactive situation affects and influences the response and behaviour of the other(s), via the model of ego states: parent, adult, child.

10 The difference between, and the different uses of, counselling and advice: counselling is drawing out the subjects to their own conclusions and supporting them, while advice is suggesting and recommending actions to them.

11 Interviewing and its techniques: its objectives, planning the opening, questions and close, handling the role difference of interviewer/interviewee, learning techniques of investigation, and dealing with the formality and rituals.

SELF-ASSESSMENT QUESTIONS

Try to answer these questions to remind you of the content of this chapter:

1 Define personality, in your own terms.

2 What is the difference between the 'I' and the 'Me'?

3 If you were to define someone as an unstable extravert in personality, how would they tend to behave?

4 See if you can name the seven points in the seven-point plan for selection decisions (give yourself good credit for getting five!).

5 How would you generally define intelligence, and what is the distinction between intelligence and knowledge?

6 How is 'disposition' defined as one of the attributes in the seven-point plan?

7 Who is responsible for an employee's training?

8 What responsibility does the training department take in the training of bank staff?

9 What exactly is the training gap?

10 What cycle of activities do adults go through when learning?

11 Give one example of an on-the-job training experience; one example of an off-the-job training experience; one advantage of each, one disadvantage of each.

12 Although others take the direct responsibility for running training courses, what responsibilities do supervisors take for the effectiveness of this kind of training?

13 What barriers are there between effort and performance? How can supervisors approach overcoming them?

14 When is a reward not a reward, and when does it fail to motivate people?

15 How do you define motivation at its simplest?

16 Draw the diagram of the hierarchy of needs: see how accurately you can fill in the names of the levels.

17 What are 'ego' or 'me'; needs? Give one example of how these can be satisfied at work.

18 What is the difference between satisfaction and dissatisfaction?

19 Give at least one example of a parent-critical phrase, and one of a child-manipulative phrase.

20 What elements of any kind of interview can you plan in advance?

5 Managing the group

OBJECTIVES

When you have read this chapter you should understand:
- **The nature of, and reasons for the existence of, groups with organisations;**
- **The difference between formal and informal, and primary and secondary, human groups;**
- **How groups form, and the processes through which they go during their early stages to develop agreed practices;**
- **Group boundaries: their nature and effect, ways of crossing them, and handling the problems they pose;**
- **Group norms and rules, and their methods of maintaining internal discipline and their codes of practice;**
- **Group roles, and the parts which various members take; status and internal group relationships; the supervisor's group role;**
- **Leadership: the differences between leading and managing;**
- **The relationship between personal qualities and leadership effectiveness;**
- **Leading the group: supervisory activities concerned with balancing the needs of task, team and individual;**
- **Leadership and communication, inside and outside the group.**

■ INTRODUCTION

Rarely do supervisors supervise work with no people involved. They usually supervise groups of people, and groups have characteristics which simple assemblies of individuals do not have. In fact, the existence of groups and membership thereof satisfy basic needs which characterise human beings (*see* Chapter 4); and group dynamics, as this topic is known technically, is a very important influence on staff behaviour. We need to know whether we are in or out, what our status is and what is the status of others and what relationships apply. The supervisor needs at least awareness of all this, both in theory and in practice, and in particular needs to be aware of one special group role, i.e. that of the leader and what it implies.

We will begin by looking at the differences, and the relationships between, *formal and informal groups*. The organisation sets up certain formal groups as it sees fit to perform special or continuing tasks, and it determines the rules and objectives, membership and relationships, and responsibilities. Quite separately from this, the people in organisations assemble themselves into groups for their own purposes, social or friendship for example, or even informally to determine the way the work will be done. To indicate what we mean, we could say that one name for such groups would be 'cliques' – but only those outside them would use it! Informal groups also have rules, objectives, memberships and responsibilities, but enforced only by group pressures.

Groups do not spring instantly into existence, even when set up informally. They go through *formation and developmental stages*, until they reach the point where they have routine and harmonious ways of operating, when they can be described as a team. Anyone involved in managing a group needs to know approximately what stage a group has reached so as to forecast and control development towards team status, because untutored attempts to interfere with or change the order of events can lead to damage and delay in development.

It is also interesting and important to understand the existence, nature and location of *group boundaries*. These have a considerable effect, since how you identify yourself as a person, and how you are treated by the group, depends on whether you are inside or outside it. Boundaries are quite firm; but there are ways of crossing. There are certain routes which are normally acceptable, as we shall see, and there are rituals to allow the new member to enter – and this can be important to the supervisor responsible for introducing new staff.

Groups have *rules*, which are more or less explicit, and *norms*, highly prescribed forms of behaviour – 'We *don't* do that around here, Tracy' – both of which help to determine just what people will or will not do. Normally these do not damage the organisation, since people at work usually have an interest in furthering its aims. But they are powerful, and when they are set in resistance to the organisation, it is far from obvious that the organisation will win against the norms of the group.

Everybody likes to feel that they play a special part in life, however modest, and in particular we like to feel we contribute to the formal and informal work of groups we belong to. These will assign us certain *group roles*, from leader down to ordinary worker, from communicator to clown, all of which are carefully if not explicitly defined. The occupation of these roles has a major influence on our self-identification and on our specific behaviour. It also influences how important we feel. There is often a status attached to roles, high, medium or low, which could depend on time served, or personality, age or experience.

Perhaps the most significant elements of group roles for the supervisor is that of leadership. We shall examine in this chapter whether there is any use in categorising leadership qualities. After all, the problem is that you are born with these or you aren't, but even those who are not Napoleon are thrust into leadership positions. We shall then look at the task of leadership, its relationship with managers, and what leaders have to do rather than what they have to be, and how supervisors can bring whatever they have in the way of characteristics to that task.

■ GROUPS: A DEFINITION

Why would we want to define what a group is? Surely it is obvious what the word means. You will find though that there are some difficulties which could arise if we do not agree on a definition, because we could dispute how closely people have to work together, or how frequently, or in what relationship, before what they work in becomes a group rather than a collection of separate individuals. Later in the chapter we will be relating group to team (thus set of individuals becomes group and becomes team); and clearly exactly which of these relationships there is between the members of your staff is important to you as supervisor.

A psychologist called Schein defined groups in a way that many experts agree on, and you may find it interesting. Essentially, to be a group people have to have a good deal of contact with each other; they must know each other at least at a minimal level; and they are not a group unless they also believe themselves to be a group. Schein's definition is a summary of these specifications.

A group is a number of people who interact with one another, are psychologically aware of one another, and perceive themselves to be a group.

How big is a group? Within the above definition, of course, there is no answer to that except to substitute the first word 'A' with the word 'Whatever'. But another answer could lie in the twin ideas of the primary and the secondary group.

1 A *primary group* is a small number, often quoted as 6–12, who constantly work together and genuinely regard themselves as a group, with an official name such as 'the Machine-Room Section' of a branch, and possibly also a nickname, like 'The 'A' Team' or the 'South View Mafia'.

2 A *secondary group* is one whose members meet occasionally, such as a small number of supervisors who have monthly meetings, but do not normally interact constantly as part of the working week, or an Office Representative Committee, engaging in occasional irregular meetings.

There are also, of course, family and social groups, and they are complex and interesting in their behaviour; but we shall be referring exclusively to work groups, which are distinguished by having work tasks and objectives set for them by the organisation in which they operate.

■ WHY DO GROUPS FORM?

In the earlier part of this century it was discovered that work was not just a function of the body as a piece of soft machinery, nor was it something people did because they needed the fuel of money for that machinery.

This was as a result of some famous experiments called the Hawthorne experiments, after the factory in which they took place. There were two main groups of experiments: one in which the behaviour of two groups or cliques of men in one factory workshop were observed, and another where a number of different changes were made in the working terms and conditions of a group of women working together in a small room.

A number of specific findings arose out of each set of experiments. As to the men, it was found that they set norms of work which differed from the company's requirement; but they were just as strict with their own members who fell below the levels they felt were fair, as those who exceeded the accepted work levels — and they had ways of punishing anyone who was stepping out of line.

As to the women, it was discovered that work rates improved as a result of every individual change that was made to their work conditions, whether favourable or unfavourable, which was rather a surprising result at first, but explained later. They also reacted well to being regarded as special, as the experimental group, and to the fact that they were consulted for their opinions by the researchers.

In fact it became clear to managers and researchers and social psychologists that work is a *group activity*. When people join a group and see themselves as members of it, or feel that they have become a group by being distinguished and made to feel special, they behave differently from the way they do as individuals; and groups have different characteristics from simply collections of individuals. They set up their own rules of work behaviour, their own standards, their own roles and relationships.

ACTIVITY 5.1

Think of groups of which you are a member at work and socially. Consider for each of these groups which of your needs they satisfy.

■ SOCIAL/AFFILIATION NEEDS

You will also recall from Chapter 4 that people's social needs, or what we referred to as belonging needs, rank as extremely important. Indeed they come immediately after the need to survive and establish safety and security. As soon as worries about being able to continue to clothe and feed yourself and your dependants are satisfied, your need to find others with common interests who would accept you as one of them, and who would see you as a part of their group, becomes paramount.

It is therefore hardly surprising that as soon as you get a number of people working together over a length of time, or in specific areas, or on particular tasks, groups form, with clearly defined and observable boundaries dividing the members from non-members.

Sometimes they form because the organisation wants them to, and sometimes regardless of the organisation's intentions, and sometimes even in defiance of the organisation, as we shall see in the next section.

■ FORMAL AND INFORMAL GROUPS

A useful distinction can be made between groups which the company sets up for its purposes, and groups which form because of people's needs to assemble together. These are quite appropriately referred to as formal groups and informal groups, and there are some distinctions which we will now examine.

Formal groups are set up or recognised by the organisation, such as the staff at a sub-branch, the above mentioned machine-room people, or a regional section in the personnel department. They exist to perform specific individual or long-running tasks for the organisation.

They have people who occupy certain official roles (for example Senior Cashier, Foreign Clerk, Cashier, Enquiries Clerk) and they may have a Head or Leader (e.g. Supervisor) appointed into that post by the organisation. The structure, relationships, tasks and hierarchy are all officially laid down, and in many cases in writing. Despite the importance of informal groupings, which we will look at next, the formal group is often the only one recognised by the organisation.

Informal groups form by themselves within the organisation, and could be groups of friends or people with similar interests. They can quite easily cut completely across the boundaries of the formal groupings. An informal group may consist of all those who always go to the 'Griffin' for a drink on Fridays, or those who entered the bank in the same week, or the gang in the securities section.

As to this last example, the informal group membership can also coincide with a formal group; but it depends on the context whether they feel a member of one rather than the other. Even in this case, the formal leader may be a different person from the informal leader.

ACTIVITY 5.2

Can you recognise this distinction, and observe informal and formal groupings in your office? Stop for a moment to think about this. Name one formal group and its members and name an informal group and its members.

You need hardly be told how powerful the informal group is, as an influence on how people behave. In fact it is very often more powerful than the formal, and when the management ask its members to do something, especially something out of the ordinary, they look – not necessarily openly – at the informal leadership to check the subtle nod of acceptance before allowing themselves to do it.

What 'can be done about' the informal groupings by those in charge? Very little, in fact, because the point is that management have literally no jurisdiction over the informal group (by definition). However it is extremely important for management to be aware of the existence, membership, norms, sanctions, decision processes, communication and leadership of the informal as well as the formal group, simply because there are circumstances where the informal is as strong or stronger as an influence on behaviour as those of the formal group, and to engineer their acceptance of the management's will is vital.

Much of what follows applies both to the formal as well as to the informal group, and we shall therefore not make the distinction unless it becomes necessary.

GROUP BOUNDARIES

The group boundary is obviously the line drawn around the group defining who is in and who is outside it. If there are problems, or conflict, in a group, this often concerns movement across the boundaries: groups have rules for admittance and for expulsion. For example, nobody minds people entering from the bottom, in most cases, e.g. the ancient banking rule ('The junior makes the tea') ensures a welcome from the last holder of the junior position, at least!

Another normally accepted entry is via attachment to a group member ('Look after Suzie, Anna: she's new and very shy'). For this to succeed, of course, Anna must be a well-regarded member of the group. This is particularly important if you want Suzie accepted by the informal as well as the formal grouping, which is why first you need to be aware of the informal grouping, and second you must choose your 'Anna' with care. Another route in is via the top, of course (and this applies only to the formal group: we cannot reject the new supervisor, except informally). Yet another route is if the newcomer either possesses a significant expertise which the group needs, or is in some other way admired for a specific desirable quality.

Boundaries are very clear and fairly tough. We have defined them as means of indicating quite clearly who is out and who is in. People can be members of separate or overlapping groups, but they are usually sure of their status. It is certainly helpful when you as supervisor can reassure anyone who is not so sure, by reason of a recent conflict, or because they are a newcomer, or because of a doubtful recent status change, about their 'in' or 'out' position at the moment: it is helpful simply because of the need to belong, which this reassurance can bring.

ACTIVITY 5.3
(a) Now stop and think through some examples from your own experience of the effect of the group in and out boundaries, and write them down.
(b) Think also of an admittance rule operated by a group you know of.

GROUP FORMATION AND DEVELOPMENT

Let us now look at how groups get together (formation) and what stages they may go through to become effective groups, from starting as sets of individuals newly formed for a co-operative task (development).

Formation

Formal groups are formed by the organisation to pursue tasks. Informal groups come together because they see or feel a common interest.

Of course this common interest may be, though it is not always, at odds with the organisation; and informal groups may have their origins outside the organisation, such as the group formed of neighbours from a particular commuter area, or of an age group, e.g. the Old Guard, or even of the disruptives, e.g. the 'Wreckers', the 'Awkward Gang'.

Once again, the organisation cannot legislate to ensure that informal and formal groups coincide; but they can have regard to arranging formal groups which would cause difficulties and conflicts, such as, for example, forming two formal groups which are supposed to compete containing people who are close friends; or conversely two which are to co-operate across a couple of informal groups whose members cannot stand each other.

Development

Groups, once formed, go through developmental moves which get them from the point where they are just individuals collected together to where they operate smoothly.

There is a really neat and simple description of the stages of development of a group by Tuckman as follows:

- form;
- storm;
- norm;
- perform.

When group members come together they start by finding out about each other, what they can do and how they behave, and they set out initial ways of co-operating with each other. This then naturally leads them into a stage of conflict, and difficulties and rivalries arise and are expressed, concerning roles and duties and responsibilities and privileges.

When these are worked out, the group members develop new rules and ways of working together, and finally they are in a position to produce really effective work and progress towards their objectives. This can be achieved as follows:

1 *Form*: the coming-together, testing out by each of each others' attitudes and abilities and characters, working out initial roles and relationships, assigning duties and sharing out privileges and perks, setting up hierarchies of status and leadership.

2 *Storm*: when conflict arises, calling for adjustments to be made to the first agreements, often concerning leadership or control: 'We cannot work like this, he just doesn't have my confidence, if she keeps on the way she's going we'll all fail, I can do that better than both of them put together'.

3 *Norm*: through this conflict to the point where rules and norms of procedure are newly decided upon, and relationships have developed, and they can see genuine ways of working together, and progressing as a co-operative fully-fledged group.

4 *Perform*: the group arrives at the stage where roles and relationships and procedures and privileges are sorted out and are stable; and the group can concentrate effort on aims and tasks, and can begin to make real inroads into what it has to do, by working properly together.

The stages of storm and norm are sometimes reversed, and sometimes the storm is a minor one: it is quite possible for groups to become effective before conflict arises. But where it occurs, the storm phase is perfectly natural. If this has not already rung bells with you, now consider examples of group development in your own experience and see whether you can trace the stages as you recall the story of the group, either a long-term group or special project or task group you may have been involved in.

Further, when you next form a group, or allocate a task to an existing group, be calm about the storm if it happens. As you will deduce from the discussion so far, the storm is a natural part of the group process and beneficial in clearing the air if it is sensitively and honestly handled.

ACTIVITY 5.4

Take an example of when you were in a task group set up for a purpose. Make some observations about exactly what happened in your group at each of the four stages identified above.

■ GROUP NORMS

Norms are broadly speaking the rules of proper behaviour, or ways of working, or principles of procedure with which the group agrees to operate. Norms can set production levels, as we discussed when relating the results of the Hawthorne experiments. As an example of this, note how you determined exactly what time to pack up and go home in your first few days at work: it will have a lot less to do with the 5 o'clock you were told about at the start of the day, than what you secretly observe about what everyone else is doing at the end of the day! This could be before or after 5 o'clock; but it is by the agreement of all.

Norms can also concern what language or slang words or nicknames are acceptable. Think how easily people can prove that they are outside the group by using the wrong nickname, one 'we' don't use; and think how irritating or embarrassing it is when someone who is not a member of the group uses group nicknames, or first names, when that indicates familiarity which we haven't invited. Conversely, you can recognise members of in-groups by their language, by what they call Head Office, for example: 'Word has reached us from Lothbury ...', or 'Lombard Street has sent out this circular ...', or 'Cincinatti insists that was ...'.

Informal group norms can relate to major or minor matters, e.g. what relationship we will have with the supervisor, how easily we will react to changes in work routine, whether we do overtime, and how much; right down to who sits at which desk, or who gets the next new chair, or who makes the tea.

Very importantly, group norms can determine whom we shall like or dislike or talk to or ignore. Norms concerning relationships both within the group and outside must be discovered and acknowledged: trying to get us to work with someone the group has decided not to co-operate with, is extremely difficult; as difficult as it might be to change the group's mind on the matter.

When entering a new group, members need to 'find their way about'; this actually means learn the group norms, then acceptance as a full member will be possible.

ACTIVITY 5.5

(a) State examples of clear norms from groups with which you are familiar.
(b) Think through the possible consequences of breaking those norms/rules.

■ ENFORCING THE RULES

Groups have rules and norms and they also have means of enforcing them. In many cases, rules don't need to be enforced, because group members are inclined to conform to them, as it is a valuable sign of their membership, and a way towards acceptance, to be a properly-behaved group member.

However, sometimes rules have to be impressed on people, and sometimes actively imposed. Unless groups have methods of bringing the wayward back into line, and punishing those who deviate, the rules would be meaningless. Groups do have such methods! In other words there is pressure to conform, and there are sanctions for not conforming.

Conformity

Since the membership of an informal group is in any case probably voluntary, people have often joined mainly because they want to do things the group way; thus, their inclination to conform, and their saying so, is a necessary qualification for membership. We need to be members of groups, and the price we willingly pay is to accept the group rules. We don't join the Golf Club and then plant radishes on the 18th green (and if we had signalled such an intention, we would not have been admitted!).

Even when it is not our inclination, groups have ways of pressurising us to conform. They can even do this against our belief in the facts as we see them – they can change our minds.

Some experiments by Solomon Asch showed that when asked to agree or disagree with opinions expressed by the rest of their group, individuals would significantly often agree, against the evidence of their own eyes. For example, when the rest of their group claimed (falsely, for the experiment) to see an illustrated line as shorter than two others, the experimental individual group member also claimed to see it shorter, which it was not. While this might have been because they actually doubted their own observation, it is more likely to have been the need to be liked and accepted that caused the agreement to be expressed.

This conformity is strengthened if the group consists of experts in its field if there is mutual respect and if each wishes to be like the others in many ways.

Think about it: if other members of a group, membership of which you highly value, all tell you of a fact you doubt, and press you to agree, how stoutly and for how long do you resist them? They have ways of making you agree, or at the very least *say* you agree. These ways are called sanctions.

Sanctions

Despite the natural tendency of people to want to conform, groups need to have ways of disciplining those who step out of line, and bring wayward members back within the rules. Otherwise the rules are meaningless. These sanctions come in a variety of powerfulness, depending on the nature and the stage of the rule-breaking, and they tend to be progressive, going through such stages as:

1 *Tacit disapproval:* making sure you know we don't like what you are doing by a look or a gesture or head movement, or showing disapproval by a meaningful word or phrase ('Really, Tracy please!').
2 *Explicit disapproval,* where the rules are emphasised literally: 'Why are you still doing that even when we've told you not to', or 'Tracy, surely you realise that we just don't do that sort of thing here'.
3 *Removal of privileges,* which could include quite severe and hurtful sanctions such as limiting shared information, (Don't tell Tracy Entwistle') or going out to lunch without her, for example.
4 *Suspension* (sending to Coventry) whereby the group will have nothing to do with Tracy, will only talk to her when forced to by the nature of the work, will ignore her existence pending her resolution to reform.
5 *Expulsion:* 'OK, that's it, Tracy, you're out. If you're working here, we are not; as far as we are concerned, you're finished.' This is, of course, coming from the informal group. If it coincides with the formal group, it is not difficult for the informal group to arrange expulsion from the formal one too.
6 Finally, there is even *career damage* in the most extreme case: 'We don't know whether you're thinking about Miss Entwistle for that new job but if so, there's something you may need to know about her ...'.

ACTIVITY 5.6

Think about these and from your experience write an account of groups applying such sanctions.

Notice particularly what we said earlier on this chapter; how important and powerful group membership, group boundaries and group norms are as influences on us, and how important it is for supervisors to understand these processes.

■ GROUP COMMUNICATION

No human enterprise succeeds for long without communication, but it cannot be assumed that all channels are always open, even within a small group. There are times when messages fail to arrive, or are misunderstood, or which hit barriers.

There is, in fact, little that can be said about group communication that has not been covered in the previous chapter. There has been plenty of research done on effective communication patterns, but frankly they are somewhat artificial and academic, and don't relate particularly well to bank branch or office situations, where the channels are at least physically normally open.

The following are, however, important points, and even if there were no research evidence to demonstrate them (which there is) you would be able to accept them on the basis of common sense:

1 The more effective the communication, the more effective the group; communication is the life blood, and we cannot operate well unless we have well-tried means of exchanging information;

2 Communication is a large part of the responsibility of the leader; and unless that responsibility is accepted, the work of the group suffers, as we shall see in ensuing sections; and conversely;

3 Where someone is seen to be the focus of central communication, in the absence of other indications, this person is often seen by members to be the leader of the group, so important is communication to them.

These points take us to the next and major topic in the management of groups, namely, leadership, which we shall now address.

■ LEADERSHIP

This is such an important issue that there are several approaches we could make in discussing it. It also gives rise to a lot of concern among supervisors, in particular the newly-appointed, the young or the less-than-extravert. After all, have we not through our lives discussed leadership qualities, seen on film and read about in novels and at school about great leaders, seen them on television?

How can we emulate these leaders? If we were born with such qualities, would we be in supervisory positions in a bank, or running the country? Even where we are thrust into leadership positions despite our qualities or lack of them, how will the staff react? Does our situation as leader make any difference, or just what our personality and ability is like?

How do we demonstrate leadership, show that we are leaders, make sure people follow us when we set off, indicate that we are exercising such ability that we have. In other words, what do leaders do in their role as leader as opposed to any other role they may occupy?

To answer these questions we shall now proceed first to see whether there is any mileage in looking at the qualities you should have been born with to be a good leader (called trait theory); we will go on to see what effect you simply being there as leader has on the staff (situational leadership) and finally we shall discuss what leaders actually do (action-centred leadership).

■ LEADERSHIP QUALITIES

If we asked to write down a short list of the qualities you need to be a good leader, you would probably find you that wrote such words as:

- initiative;
- drive and energy;
- outgoing personality;
- character;
- vision;
- self-preservation;
- intelligence;
- technical excellence;
- integrity and honesty;
- communication skills;
- decisiveness;
- empathy/listening skills;
- ruthlessness and expedience;
- influence/persuasiveness;

and possibly other, similar qualities.

Now put a mark against all of those qualities which you possess in full measure. You probably won't have a mark against all of them, and you may even have no mark against most of them. But how can this be? You are in a leadership job as supervisor, and you lack those qualities? Look again at the list and consider how you will acquire those where you have no mark. Go on a decisiveness course? As of next week, have character? Start gaining integrity and honesty? Become ruthless? Things are going to get worse in this section before they get better!

To improve as a leader it may be better to think of leadership as something that you *do* rather than a leader being something that you *are*. In-born qualities do not determine whether or not you can be a good leader.

There are great born leaders as there are great born artists; we are talking about the competent leader at supervisor level as we might be talking about the competent draughtsman.

■ SITUATIONAL LEADERSHIP

The idea of the theory summed up in the phrase 'situational leadership' is that *the best leader is the one best suited to a particular situation* with the knowledge of expertise to handle that but not all situations. The Celts and the Sioux Indians, for example, used to select war chiefs for the sole purpose of leading the tribe in battle, and the same leader might not continue as leader in peace-time, because he might not have the expertise or skill or character for peace-time leadership. This happens also in modern politics, when after wars the great war-leader is replaced as Prime Minister to lead the peace.

In management, this would mean leadership passing from one team member to another as the task altered; this might appear in pure logic to be sensible, but it is hardly practical in the standard banking branch or office. It is more applicable to the sort of flexibly structured trouble-shooting team you might find (or rather expect to find) dealing with special projects or major organisational changes, such as mergers. It is, however, noticeable that if the circumstances of a branch changes, the bank may change the manager to cope with the new situation.

Another sense in which the phrase situational leadership is used, and which might be useful for you to consider, is that *if you put someone in a leadership situation they are very often more successful than you, or they, thought they were going to be*. This is partly because, if someone is officially appointed leader, the staff provisionally behave as if that person is the leader. This gives the person confidence to behave like a leader, which reinforces the staff inclination to defer to the leader, which in turn ... and so on. Soon the provisional acceptance turns into real acceptance, and the tentative appointed leader becomes the genuine leader.

■ LEADERSHIP AND MANAGEMENT STYLE

At this point we shall remind you of management style, discussed in Chapter 2. Leaders can choose to involve their staff in a number of different ways in decisions they must make, from autocratically passing down such decisions, to benevolently giving orders with the benefit of the staff in mind, through inviting suggestions and ideas, then making the decisions themselves, to allowing total group participation. Adopting the right style is a major step towards effective leadership. Indeed it is the first step, but there is more to leadership style, other than just how you relate with your staff, or how you effect decisions.

■ ACTION-CENTRED LEADERSHIP

Recently, a consultant author called John Adair suggested that good leadership has more to do with the actions leaders take than the characteristics of personality that they bring to the job. He says you must start from these basic assumptions:

1 what a leader leads is a group;
2 a group has sets of group needs;
3 a good leader does things to satisfy those needs.

So you must know what the sets of group needs are, and take actions to satisfy them, i.e. action-centred leadership. In fact, says Adair, groups have three sets of needs, and the leader understands these and takes observable actions which will satisfy those needs. The better the needs are satisfied, the better the leader. The three sets of needs are:

1 *Task needs:* a group has a need to get its tasks done, well, and indeed competitively well;

2 *Team needs:* a group has the need to maintain cohesion, spirit, team work and morale;
3 *Individual needs:* each member of the group has individual needs which membership of the group helps to satisfy.

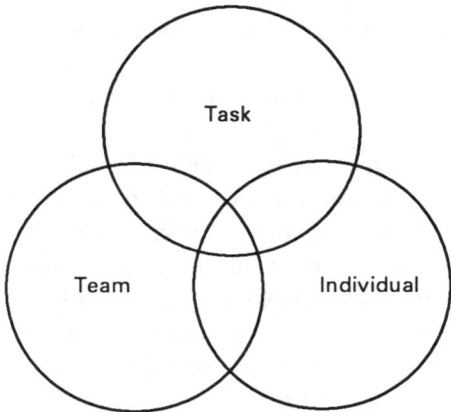

Fig 5.1

We can now illustrate Adair's model, which is always drawn as in Fig. 5.1, in overlapping circles.

Let us now look more closely at these group needs, and what supervisors can do to satisfy them, thus developing and exercising their leadership skills. Note now, for we will say it again later, that we are talking about actions, not characteristics; observable actions, not mental philosophies.

Task needs

What would happen if you formed a task group, then said to them, 'OK, you're a task group but there's no task for you'? Surely they would either try to find something to do, or they would break up as a group, because a group has task needs. Furthermore, if you gave them a task and said, 'You have a choice: you can do the task well or badly', what do you suppose the response would be for any normal group of people? Who would choose to do it badly, all other things being equal? Finally, if you say, 'How well would you like to do it with relation to other groups', don't you suppose the answer would be 'Better'?

So what is expected of the group leader? To whatever extent you have been a leader you will know that your group relies on you to check that they do well. This is very important (and something of a surprise when you first come across it, because you were probably led to expect resistance to your leadership). In other words, they expect you to *do things* to ensure that the tasks get done.

What can you do? Here is a list of observable actions a leader can take to satisfy task needs. You should try to add a few items:

1 Grasp your own brief and understand its details;
2 Get all the necessary information from your superiors and other sources;
3 Define and write down objectives and targets;

4 Clearly divide up tasks, define them, allocate them according to skills, training, inclinations;
5 Make a plan of action and be seen to stick to it;
6 Obtain, and at least be seen to fight for, all necessary resources to enable staff to perform well;
7 Invite and listen to suggestions from qualified or experienced staff and others;
8 Set up systems and periods of control and operate them scrupulously, and maintain task timing;
9 Be, and be seen to be, vigilant for changes;
10 Monitor internal and external influences and communication which may affect the progress of the task; and communicate them.

As you will see, none of these require any personal characteristics except having personally identified yourself as leader. These tasks can be done by introverts or extraverts, the humorous or the solemn, the faster or the slower thinker, the aristocrat or the working person, provided that they have simply determined to do them.

Team needs

Taking the same group, ask them if they would like to be a low morale group, with irritation and back-biting, nobody trusting anyone else, no sense of achievement and no discipline, with very little information about what is going on. Or do you suppose they would wish to be a high morale group, in which everyone trusted and respected each other, with agreed rules of procedure and sound relationships, a group which felt good about its achievements, and set and maintained high personal standards? The answer is obvious: a group has team needs.

Once again, what can the leader do to satisfy team needs? The members look to you to contribute centrally to how they feel about themselves as a group, and once again, here you will find a list of possible observable actions. Note them and add to them:

1 Tell the group about its tasks and the reasons for them;
2 Display to all, the group's objectives and targets;
3 Obtain group agreement to those overall tasks and targets;
4 Agree high standards of personal presentation (including punctuality, dress and grooming) and set a personal example;
5 Summarise progress, not just at the end of tasks;
6 Constructively criticise the group's performance; praise its achievements emphatically;
7 Maintain harmony: face up to and resolve conflict deliberately and courageously;
8 Apply discipline fairly and firmly – and privately;
9 Defend, and be seen to defend, the group against outside attack;
10 Be constantly available, wedge your door open, tour the group workplace at intervals.

Once again, these are things that the supervisor can do to satisfy team needs, regardless of one's character and personality. You would need high personal standards and a measure of courage, but not beyond the bounds of anyone likely to be in a senior clerical position in a commercial organisation. Study and list those actions, and add a few of your own to them.

Individual needs

You do not stop being yourself just because you have joined a group; you do not hang up your individual identity when you arrive at work and join the section. You retain your personality, your hopes, ambitions, abilities; and your individual needs. Being a member of the group satisfies one of those sets of needs, as we have seen above, namely, the belonging needs; but you have other needs too.

As you may recall from the last chapter, concerning the individual, human needs arrange themselves into a hierarchy; and we can satisfy our needs at work, from our needs for food and warmth, through safety, belonging needs, our need to be distinguished as an individual, right through to the need to fulfil our potential. And we look to our bosses and supervisors to do things to help us to satisfy our individual needs at work. Some of those things might come under the following headings, and you should once again be prepared to add to them:

1. Check on the special skills and knowledge of individuals in the group;
2. Discover the personal likes and dislikes of each of various aspects of the group's work;
3. Give each person tasks, but also special-area responsibilities, both within and outside direct tasks;
4. Explain the significance of each task to the job-holder;
5. Consult each person, listen to and acknowledge ideas, and make special efforts to get new ideas implemented;
6. Keep each person in touch with their personal progress and achievements;
7. Be available for the counselling function, for listening to problems, to sort out work and personal difficulties;
8. Make sure each person feels safe, work out areas of insecurity and reassure as far as possible concerning job-security;
9. Defend individuals from attack of any sort from outside the group, including from organisational superiors;
10. Acknowledge special achievements and make them known to significant other people;
11. Make sure that where there are organisational rewards available and deserved, that they are awarded;
12. Apply discipline firmly, fairly, privately; correct incorrect activities or work practices;
13. Indicate the togetherness of the group and its morale to each individual, enhancing their feelings of belonging.

Notice that a good many of these concern what we referred to in Chapter 2 as the 'me/myself' needs, i.e. the needs to feel special and distinguished as an individual. This is the most powerful of practical work needs, or at least certainly the one into which the supervisor can most easily tap. One of the simplest ways of doing this is to day, 'Thank you, Jamie – you did a specially good job this week'.

Provided that it is done sincerely, and not a matter of rota or routine ('Hello, here come the Friday thank-yous'), this can and should be done more than it is. No phrase seems to get more easily stuck in the throat than 'thank you', and the attitude that they know you appreciate without telling them, is simply inadequate.

It is in fact as inadequate as the attitude that you don't have to tell your life-partners that you love them because they know it without your telling them: try getting away with that!

■ THE OVERLAPS

If you have been reading the above lists carefully, it may have occurred to you that items in one list could just as easily be included in one of the others, and indeed that there were some items so similar that really they did occur in two lists. If you were also adding one or two items of your own, you might also have asked yourself if they should be in another category.

If you go back to Fig. 5.1 you can see why. There are overlaps, first of all to account for the fact that one or another section can satisfy more than one group need. Second, these overlaps indicate how important it is for leaders, or in our case supervisors, to do things to satisfy all three sets of needs.

Take for example the overlap between task needs and team needs. If the team or morale needs are not being satisfied, then, as the diagram will indicate, a segment is taken out of how the task needs will be satisfied. Conversely, if task needs are going unfulfilled, then morale needs also suffer and will need attention.

The overlap between team needs and individual needs indicates that if team/morale needs are unsatisfied, then my individual feelings will suffer; and also if I am feeling frustrated, then I will negatively affect group morale, to a certain extent.

Finally, there is the other overlap, between individual and task needs. If my individual needs are not being satisfied, this is likely to give rise to a lowering of my contribution to the task needs; and if the task is not being fulfilled, I shall feel that my own personal needs are being frustrated.

ACTIVITY 5.7

To demonstrate the significance of the overlaps, give an example of a management action which will satisfy:

(a) Both task and team needs:
(b) Both team and individual needs.
(c) Both individual and task needs.

Where is the leader, the supervisor? How do they fit in to the three-circle picture? The answer is across the whole of the diagram, in the business of paying attention to all of the group's needs.

GROUP NEEDS AND LEADERSHIP

This is worth repeating, then: anyone who wishes to improve the leadership element of their supervisory tasks needs to pay less attention to the traits or characteristics of their personality, than to the actions they take as leader/supervisor to satisfy the needs of their groups. It is to this set of actions that they bring whatever elements of strength of character that they have, regardless of exactly what those elements are.

GROUPS AND TEAMS

When does a group become a team? You can answer that yourself instinctively and you will probably be right. Teams have just the right number of people; the relationship between them is characterised by trust; their abilities dovetail and they are conscious of this interlink and know each other's skills and abilities; where there is temporary absence or difficulty, members cover for each other; less communication is necessary because members know things without being told. The team's needs tend to be satisfied, task, morale and individual, and each member has a strong sense of responsibility for their own and the team's collective work.

Is there any way of affecting the development from group to team? To start with you will certainly need a good measure of luck; an employer who will not move key-members out and make other changes which frustrate your efforts; and probably no customers at all so that things run smoothly! Then you can bend all your efforts to satisfy the group needs.

Finally, you can look at certain special functions which groups need one (or more) of their members to fulfil to keep the group process going. Team working is a process: it takes place over time and needs regular maintenance, and special roles to tend to the various parts of the process. A recent set of suggestions as to the various characters that a group needs to advance the team process is suggested by a man called Belbin, and a digest of these suggestions will now follow.

MANAGEMENT TEAM ROLES

A well-constructed team would contain, according to Belbin, someone who would be fulfilling the following roles. Each role does call for a person with a set of particular characteristics, and would it not be nice if you could choose your team with the luxury of selecting their personalities too! Normally, of course, you can't.

However, do not see this and read it as theoretical: it bears a genuine relationship to your own group situation. You may not have all the roles, and their specifications may not be being fulfilled. Where there are gaps, you may have problems. Where the wrong person is taking the wrong role you may also have problems. As you check it out, relate it to the actual people — or the actual gaps — in your own group/team.

1 The *chairperson* would be a disciplined thinker who would organise and coordinate the team, maintaining a balance of effort. This person would be the fulcrum of the group, the cool central person around whom it would revolve.
2 The *shaper* is the outgoing, creative character who provides the dynamism and the drive of the group. This one would provide the motivation and the energy, and some of the leadership in the more enterprising tasks.
3 The *plant* is often a more withdrawn person, the plant is intellectual and thoughtful, and provides a lot of the ideas for the progress of the group's work, by contemplating problems, quietly and privately. Could need drawing into the limelight when it would serve the group's purposes as they would certainly not put themselves there.
4 The *monitor-evaluator* evaluates ideas logically and takes arguments apart to check on their validity, criticises creative approaches and checks on the accuracy and effectiveness of suggestions and solutions.
5 The *resource-investigator* is the monitor of all outside information, and sets up information and social networks to obtain a stream of such information, and many contracts; is relaxed, friendly, outgoing, public-relations and advertising oriented.
6 The *company worker* is that vital person sometimes ignored by those who look for important group roles, the efficient team member who gets on with the job, keeps the records, makes sure that the paperwork is done and recorded and that no details are omitted, keeps the timetables and the charts up-to-date — and likes that role!
7 The *team-worker* tries to maintain the group as a team, works quietly and calmly and unobtrusively in the team to ensure that there is harmony, resolving conflict and making sure of smooth relationships. This person is vigilant for ruffled feelings or for friction, and is the one to whom people will bring personal problems.
8 The *finisher* drives, persuades and nags the group to get jobs done on time, meet deadlines and complies with controls. Sometimes an anxious person, this one serves the purpose of giving the group a sense of urgency when it needs it.

An effective team must have all these roles filled by one person or another, and the same person can take one or more of the functions. Look at them again, however, and note that if any one role is not taken the team can have problems associated with that.

ACTIVITY 5.8
Check out a team of which you are a member.

(a) Are all the roles covered? Go through each one and name the person who covers it.
(b) Which if the roles do you prefer to occupy? Are you given a chance to do this in your group?
(c) Are there any problems caused either by a lack of someone to fill one of the roles or by a role being filled by the wrong person.

■ MBWA (MANAGEMENT BY WALKING ABOUT)

The famous American-multinational computer company, Hewlett-Packard, was founded on the basis of some very forward-thinking philosophies for their staff. One of these summarised much of what we have said in this chapter about managing the group. It is called MBWA which stands for *Management By Walking About.*

No supervisor or manager at any other level can truly manage well by sitting at the desk. To begin with, we have emphasised vigilance, the requirement to keep an eye on what is happening and being ready for problems and exceptions. Managers cannot see things through doors or hear of difficulties through walls; they must appear on the spot.

It has also been pointed out that management is voluntary and active, and the supervisor must be seen to be a person involved in the work of management, both by superiors and by staff, and this is not possible if the supervisor spends all the time sitting down. Even if the move through the office is seen as a routine tour, it is better than being closeted, and the staff know that the supervisor will appear at certain times.

The manager/supervisor who is seen to be at the workplace of the staff rather that at their own workplace all the time, will be available for the 'Oh-by-the-way' comment or question. It would not be appropriate for the asker to leave the workplace, go to the supervisor's office or desk, make contact, ask and return; but it would be very valuable to say 'Oh-by-the-way' if the supervisor were to appear in the vicinity of the staff-member's workplace occasionally.

The most successful American, Japanese – and even British – companies are characterised by managers who are in close contact with their workforce at all levels, are frequently to be found on the shop floor (daily and routinely, rather than on the odd occasion) and see themselves as different from – not better than – their staff only in terms of the jobs that they do, not their importance.

ACTIVITY 5.9

Reflect here by making a note or two:

(a) About a time when a so-called approachable manager wasn't.
(b) About a time when a manager took action to approach you to help you rather than being merely 'approachable'.

■ SUMMARY

In this chapter we have discussed the following aspects of managing the group:

1. The definition of a group, the best known of which is: a number of people who interact with each other, are psychologically aware of each other, and perceive themselves to be a group.

2. Primary groups, which are those which meet constantly; and secondary groups, occasionally.

3. The formation of groups, as a result of a natural inclination to satisfy human needs, and because work is to a great extent a group activity.

4. Formal groups, set up by the organisation to fulfil its purpose, with objectives, rules, structure, tasks imposed from outside; and informal groups, formed by the members for their own purposes, with all these elements created and maintained from within; and the supervisor's responsibility is discerning the differences between each.

5. Group boundaries: the invisible but very detectable line around the group, showing who is in and who out; and the problems of crossing boundaries.

6. Formation and development has shown us a simple and effective analytical pattern, a way of understanding group behaviour, namely:

    (a) form: when groups come together, find out about each other, test their own members out, get to know each other;
    (b) storm: when they discover differences, conflicts, awkwardnesses and rivalries, sometimes arriving near to breakdown;
    (c) norm: where they come under task-pressure to get things done and they know that they must, and they do, find ways to progress;
    (d) perform: the group, having developed ways to work together, now starts to produce results and begins to develop team characteristics.

7. Group norms, internal rules of behaviour which the group firmly imposes on its members, and which they must obey to stay in; and conformity, methods of enforcing the natural inclination to conform; by sanctions, a series of increasingly severe pressure methods:

    (a) tacit or silent disapproval;
    (b) explicit or spoken disapproval;
    (c) removal of privileges;
    (d) suspension, sending to Coventry;
    (e) expulsion, at least from informal groups;
    (f) career damage.

8. Leadership qualities, and how these are acquired by those who must lead small work groups.

9. Situational leadership: either 'the best leader is the one suited best to the task in hand', or, 'put someone in a leadership situation and they will behave like a leader'.

10. Action-centred leadership, where we elaborate on the activities of the leader, whose essential function is to satisfy group needs:

(a) task needs, to get the jobs done effectively;
(b) team needs, to have high morale and cohesion;
(c) individual needs, of each group member.

11 Groups and teams, and the various roles desirable in a management team: Chairperson, Shaper, Plant, Monitor-Evaluator, Resource-Investigator, Company Worker, Team Worker and Finisher.

12 MBWA: 'Management By Walking About', the need for the supervisor to be available to the team, by being at their workplace.

■ SELF-ASSESSMENT QUESTIONS

Try to answer these questions to remind you of the content of this chapter:

1 How would you define the term 'group'?

2 What is a primary group? What is a secondary group? What is the difference? Give an example of each.

3 What is the precise difference between a formal and an informal group?

4 What are group boundaries, and what difficulties can they cause for supervisory staff?

5 What are the stages through which a group may go before it gets into ways of effective working?

6 What are group norms? Give one or two examples of norms from groups of which you are a member.

7 Give an example of jargon or a nickname which would only be understood in your group, or your branch, or your bank.

8 What kinds of sanctions can a group apply to get Julie to conform to its rules? What is the worst thing it can do to Julie?

9 What are the problems associated with discussing leadership in terms of personal characteristics or traits?

10 What is situational leadership?

11 Why do people tend to become possibly better leaders than expected just because they are thrust into leadership situations?

12 What is action-centred leadership?

13 Give three examples of how a leader can satisfy task needs.

14 Give three examples of how a leader can satisfy team needs.

15 Give three examples of how a leader can satisfy individual needs.

16 Draw the three-circle diagram. Then make one statement, in writing, about each of the three overlap areas.

17 What makes a group into a team?

18 Name at least three of the managerial team roles suggested by Belbin.
19 What does MBWA stand for?
20 How can a supervisor adopt the MBWA philosophy, and why would it be valuable to do so?

6 MANAGING YOURSELF

OBJECTIVES

When you have read this chapter you should understand:
- The importance of time management to the good supervisor;
- How efficient supervisors go about getting themselves organised initially;
- How to set up and use personal planning equipment;
- The importance of managing personal as well as business life, so as to be more effective in the latter (and the former!);
- Self-knowledge, and the ability to understand and use strengths and weaknesses in your own personality;
- The supervisor's deployment of training for self-improvement;
- How assertiveness can help to effect the supervisor's plans and intentions;
- Techniques of assertiveness, and how these can be developed in the supervisor and in staff;
- Taking responsibility for problems which are your own, and sensibly unburdening problems which are not;
- Designing a personal supervisor's self-development action plan.

■ INTRODUCTION

So, now we have discussed managing the group, and the individual member of staff; but what about managing yourself, the supervisor? This is possibly one of the most difficult tasks you have, because it is actually easier for most people to see clearly and to deploy the strengths, weaknesses, skills, abilities, qualities and faults of others, than to be objective about themselves. But how you manage yourself is a vital aspect of how your staff and your management react to you as a business-person and as a supervisor, never mind as a private individual.

In this chapter we shall first of all look at how supervisors can engage in *time management*: on the rather cynical assumption that a good number are less than well organised at the beginning we will look at moves to sort out initial problems. These may be straightforward matters, such as getting your desk tidy, clearing the decks for action, and composing lists of things to do, and getting those sorted into priorities.

We shall then go on to look at physical *planning devices*: making the best use of your walls, your desk, your pockets or handbag for visual planning methods, open diarying of significant events now and in the future; we shall take a more detailed look at the various ways in which you can keep and use your conventional diary; and we shall go on to look at taking notes as you proceed through the day. As we do so, we shall consider in what form and using what media we can make effective notes to help complete the day's tasks and the longer term projects.

Sensible supervisors do not discount the importance of *planning private life*, both intrinsically and in the way it affects the way they work. If you are to manage yourself properly, you must have your private life in reasonable order (and chance would be a fine thing!). Some of the efficiencies you adopt at work can be transferred to home life so as, in fact, to detach it from work problems. It would not be sensible to ignore the interface between work and home if we really want to discuss self-management realistically: we shall therefore open it up for debate in this chapter.

The better you know your staff or your colleagues or your manager, the better able you are to manage them. This principle must also apply to yourself. We shall explore *self knowledge*, ways of looking at yourself, by yourself and/or in the company of others. We will take another look at the transactional analysis model referred to in the chapter on Managing the Individual, and at the personality categories: but this time we will turn our focus on the supervisors themselves, and how they can reach a closer understanding of how they see themselves, and at how others see them; and we will look at ways of analysing these things outside the ambit of reading a textbook or preparing for professional examinations.

How often do even good managers, especially at the supervisory level, have good ideas, or know the right course of action, feel they let themselves and others down just because they don't like to say something but perhaps they think it may embarrass or hurt themselves, or that the idea is too unconventional. In many cases this results from a lack of *assertiveness*, a way of behaving which has gained a good deal of currency in recent years. There are clear assertiveness techniques which can be learnt and developed, so as to make your plans and intentions more personally effective, without causing anyone else any harm in their expression.

When supervisors take on responsibility, unfortunately they are *taking responsibility for problems*: it is taking responsibility for the problems of everyone else which can get in the way of managing effectively. In this chapter, and indeed correlated closely with being assertive, we shall look at ways of separating what is the supervisor's problem and what is someone else's, and how first to locate the problem where it can and should be solved, and then how to help the solver sort it out, without the supervisor carrying the excessive burden: indeed we shall introduce you to Saint Supervisor the Martyr, before hopefully disposing of that character for good!

Finally, we shall look at how all of these things can be collated into a personal supervisor's self-development plan. This will, as you will discover, extend the philosophy inherent in everything you will find in this volume, which is that if you take time to plan and systematise the way you operate, that investment of time will pay off, both for the way you feel about yourself, and for the effectiveness of your operation as a member of a management team.

■ TIME MANAGEMENT

Time management is largely an act of will, and to decide that you will handle the affairs of your day, your week, your month, your year, is to be almost there in doing it. Remember the idiocy of the phrase 'I haven't got time to plan', which really only means I haven't decided to take the time to plan.

Time management, by the way, doesn't simply mean time to plan: it also means time to think. Managers have to think about all the aspects of their job: operations, finance, personnel, marketing, information flow, the allocation of resources – indeed, all the things that this book is about. They are actually paid to do this, and therefore actually paid to take time to do this. Everyone can manage time: all it takes is systematic thought about certain activities which will avoid wasting it.

At this point, you may like to take a pause and list some of the ways managers at all levels, including supervisors, waste time. Your list could include:

- looking for things they can't find, because they are personally disorganised;
- wasting time making up for things they have forgotten to do, because they can't keep it all in their heads;
- doing things that others should be doing, because they think it's quicker if they do them themselves;
- doing things that others could be doing: failure to delegate;
- missing opportunities to save time by handling the wrong issue at the wrong time;
- filling in quarter hours before timed events by idling.

ACTIVITY 6.1

Make up your own list, and add other ways that people waste time, from what you have observed of them – and yourself!

Remember that these things do not just waste the supervisor's time, but almost invariably waste the time of others too. So what can be done by sensible supervisors? They can get organised, set up planning devices, sort out their personal lives, and force a ten-minute planning period into every day. We'll look at these in turn.

Getting organised

How many times have you heard – how many times have you said – 'I must get organised'? Well, you are absolutely right, you must. But rarely is one 'in order' when one decides to get organised, so the first thing good supervisors do when they make this decision is to tidy their office space.

Most importantly, if you have a desk or working surface, this should be sorted out. There are several things you could consider about getting tidy:

1 The One-Pile principle: most desks are cluttered with several piles of work under some vague and temporary principle of categorisation. Get it all into one pile, and you will feel better, then take time to sort and dispose of every item you can.

2 The No Pendings principle: There's really no such thing as 'pending'. A good way of getting a pending pile off your desk is to determine to take at least one action, however small, on each item in your pile, write this action on it or on a little adhesive note attached to it, then file it or dispose of it.

Please note that there actually are things which may be in your pending file which you can throw away. Do take care, of course, and do check: but don't keep what you know you will never need again.

3 Tidying Time: if you can't keep your desk tidy constantly (and few normal people can), diary a weekly tidying time, say, 2.00 pm on Thursdays, or whatever fits in well with your office routine. You'll find that that tidying time also gives you time to think through what you are sorting out, especially if you are using the No Pendings principle.

Please note that tidying up doesn't apply just to desks, but also to where you carry informational material about your person: pockets/ briefcase/handbag. Regular timetabled sortings of these does no harm, indeed help to avoid wasting a significant amount of time.

ACTIVITY 6.2

Tidy your desk!

The TTD list

It stands for 'Things To Do'; and it can be asserted with some confidence that *all* organised people have one and carry it about with them at all times. Disorganised people have them too: they are on bits of cigarette packet, old envelopes, on a six month old note from Charlotte, on the back of Alison's old shopping list, or on a fluff-covered ice-cream wrapper, secreted about various parts of their desk, their kitchen and their clothing.

The TTD list is easy to operate. First you compose a list of everything you have to do, divided, if you like, into personal and work, into short, medium and long term. But however you divide it, it should still be one list, and bound into your diary, notebook or personal planner (of which more later, and if you don't possess these devices, write down the acquisition thereof as one of the TTD items ...). These items, by the way, include everything from buying a pound of carrots to writing to an important customer.

Next, prioritise, that is rank order the things you have to do. Using any device you like, put a mark – say, an asterisk – beside every item which is *important*; and another mark – say a circle – beside whatever is urgent. What is the difference between *important* and *urgent*? Simply a matter of time: important means what it says, but urgent matters which may in fact be relatively unimportant sometimes have to be done first (e.g. if you know you have an important late meeting with the Managing Director of a client company, it is quite urgent to ensure that the car-park will be open when you want to leave late that evening).

Another way good supervisors will classify their list is to divide it into *must* do, *should* do and *would like to* do, and then they will do them – in that order. And while they are about it, they will seek to plan to delegate certain items on their list. Delegation has been dealt with at length elsewhere in this volume (in Chapter 3, mainly) so there is no need for repetition. But the first steps to sensible delegation is the listing of the supervisor's own tasks.

ACTIVITY 6.3

Create a *single list* of everything you have to do and then apply the above techniques to prioritise the items which appear on it.

Equipment

For supervisors to equip themselves to be more time-efficient can be fun, and they can wander into the treasure trove of the stationer's shop with great enjoyment – and not too much expense, if done sensibly (not to mention use of the Petty Cash or Stationery Budget, if done honestly, and according to company procedures).

To begin with, making your plans visible is very important. Many people put off getting organised, then planning, because they are afraid of what will be revealed as 'swept under the carpet'; the horrible realisation of what they have not done and should have done. But it must be confronted: and a *wall-chart* or *year-planner* puts all that must be done, short, medium and long term, in front of you and your colleagues.

The *diary* is vital. Most line managers are issued with one by the company, and banks are reasonably sensible about giving them to those who need them. However, the company diary may not suit everyone's personal style, and a large variety of shapes and sizes, with everything from one line to two pages to the day, are inexpensively available from the stationer's. Whatever is chosen, it should be such that it can be kept to hand. Indeed inspectors have been known to assert that the best managers never let their diary leave their person, even if they are taking a short trip from one side of the office to the other.

A familiar device to branch bankers among others, the office *file-card diary systems* also work well, if those delegated to work them are efficient: on the due date, a file-card is delivered from the system to the desk of the involved individual, for action to be taken that day, and the card is collected or returned when the action is taken.

A *notebook* is also the feature of the personal effects of the good supervisor. Nobody can remember everything, and a notebook is useful when talking to customers, taking briefings from management, absorbing information from mail or circulars, or studying and remembering incidents and information for later use. It is also in the notebook that the Things To Do list can appear, although it could also be incorporated into the diary, if the day-space is large enough to accommodate it.

An *address-book*, or just a telephone list, is important to most supervisors, with internal, external, business and private addresses and telephone numbers all located in one place. Somewhere where business and personal *expenses* can be recorded is useful, and for *personal details* such as Passport, Inland Revenue, National Insurance and Medical Certificate numbers, not to mention bank account numbers and next of kin and the like. Emphasis can be placed on items by using your own personal system of *visual aids* such as fluorescent or coloured small sticker shapes, or a highlighter pen, or coloured symbols.

All of the above can be combined into one handy object, the *personal planner*. Filofax is perhaps the best known of these systems and the one which has given its name to the generic object: but whatever the make of the system, it is no more than a loose-leaf folder containing all of the above items and more, to be organised and reorganised according to the will of the possessor. Never mind the image: they work for those who possess them – just ask one! And they can be purchased at a wide range of prices from the luxurious down to the extremely affordable.

ACTIVITY 6.4

The next time you pass an office stationery shop, go in and browse and see what items of inexpensive equipment you may find useful. Now why not buy such items and see if they improve your work performance.

Using the equipment

It is very easy to kid yourself that if you simply possess the equipment your problems are over. For example, when studying, have you noticed that once you purchase a good textbook you feel you 'have' the information, even if it is not in your head, so that you think that you don't need to worry about revision? Which is wrong, of course: you must use the textbook for study – and you must use your planning devices rather than depending on them to remind you automatically of diaried and planned events.

The ten-minute planning period

It is therefore vital to consult your diary systems ad hoc when necessary: but even more effective additionally to set aside ten minutes, preferably at the beginning of the day, to check out all your planning devices: wall chart, diary, notebook, TTD list. Become known as eccentric, if you like: put off with some ferocity calls on your time during this ten minutes ("Don't talk to Pamela in her ten-minute-planning-time – she'll bite your head off").

Coping with the incoming bombardment

Let nobody believe that you can sort everything out at once: as soon as you have, the incoming mail arrives. How does the good supervisor handle this? Without explanation, it is now suggested you work your way through the flow chart in fig. 6.1.

ACTIVITY 6.5

Copy out fig. 6.1 and put it on your wall and apply it to tomorrow's incoming mail.

Private and personal

People do not cease to be themselves just because they have come to work. The whole person has a family, a home or a personal life; and it is really difficult

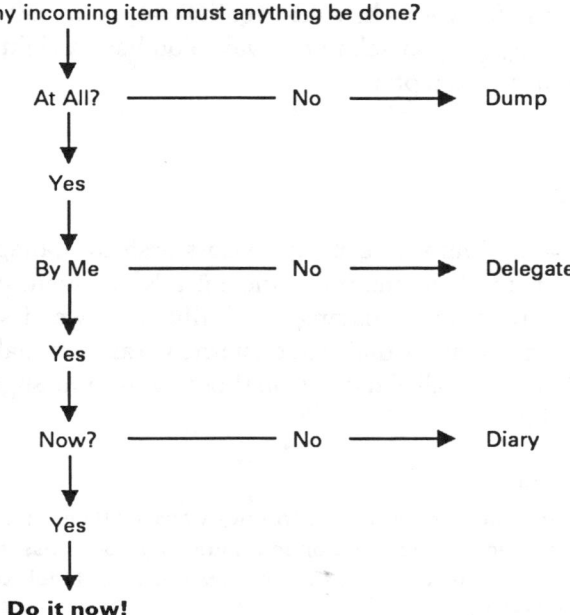

Fig. 6.1

to leave absolutely all of that behind when you come to work. In other words, if you are disorganised in your personal life you cannot be as effective as you would like in your work life. There are one or two ways in which the good supervisor can gain more control over their personal lives, or can advise their staff to do so:

1 Get organised at home. Tidy up, list what needs to be done.
2 Use home diarying devices. A wall-planner at home is as useful as one at work, particularly if the household consists of more than one person. Encourage all to make entries on it, including children; and consult it, in conference if necessary.
3 Maintain control of social life. It can be overdone, and staggering from one excessive event to another removes part of the enjoyment of the next one as well as some of the partygoer's effectiveness at work.
4 While on the subject, however personal, the effective manager maintains control of health and of weight, and can advise staff on these matters too where necessary. A balanced intake of oxygen, food and drink means a more efficient brain and body. It is best to engage in routines, such as of daily or weekly exercise.
5 Speaking of routines, it is sensible to set aside certain periods for certain tasks: for example washing on Saturday morning, shopping Saturday afternoon, ironing on Sunday evening. Ask the real experts when it comes to domestic routines: the professional housewife or househusband.

And, by the way, whatever your status in the household, commandeer a regular time for yourself: your evening out, your half-day at the weekend, in which to recreate yourself in my way. You have a right to this time, as we shall see later in this chapter.

■ SELF KNOWLEDGE

It is above all important, if supervisors wish to manage themselves, for them to know themselves (the most ancient advice given, by the Delphic Oracle). In the chapter on managing the individual, we described two models for discerning personality differences, namely transactional analysis, and Eysenck's model; here we shall elaborate on those, with some suggested exercises for self-examination.

ACTIVITY 6.6

Suppose you have been called to your boss's office. The boss says something. In response to each of the three opening lines by your boss listed below, write down a brief, honest, realistic description of how you would feel, and what you might say to start your response:

1 The Boss says:
'How dare you come in here: how many times have I told you I am not to be disturbed today?'
How would you feel?   What would you say?

2 The Boss says:
'Oh, thank goodness you've come. I'm in a terrible mess, and only you can sort me out.'
How would you feel?   What would you say?

3 The Boss says:
'Well, now, let's talk about your career. I've got some positive ideas, and I'd like to be the one to help you.'
How would you feel?   What would you say?

4 The Boss says:
'Hey, its our senior manager's birthday tomorrow: let's arrange a really embarrassing Kissogram or something!'
How would you feel?   What would you say?

We shall get back to these examples after discussing the *ego states* which are represented both by these sayings and by your probable responses, later in this chapter. As you will recall, the *parent ego state* is where you feel, act, speak and behave in a caring or nurturing, or a dominating or critical manner. The *adult ego state* is where you speak and behave in a logical, neutral, unemotional or evaluative way. The *child ego state* is where you act emotionally and uninhibitedly, or in a calculating or manipulative manner.

ACTIVITY 6.7

Try these little tests to get to know how you personally behave, speak, feel, when you are in one or another of your ego states.

Getting to know your *parent ego state*

1 Write down three things your parents didn't like.
2 Write down three things your parents did that you liked.
3 Do you do any of the above six things yourself, with/to whom?
4 Write down, verbatim, two important 'Parent' messages you still hear in your head, or can easily recall.

Do these messages still influence your behaviour? When/where? With whom?

Getting to know your *adult ego state*

1 Think of three decisions you recently made, either at work or at home. To what extent were they made on a purely logical basis? To what extent did 'Parent' traditions or 'Child' feelings influence?
2 Give examples of ways you use your 'Adult' in social gatherings.
3 In what situations would you like your 'Adult' to operate, but it's difficult, and you sometimes fail? And which of 'Parent' or 'Child' often operate in these situations?

Getting to know your *child ego state*

1 Write three things you do now to express your 'Child Natural', when you simply express your feelings without inhibition.
2 Write three things you do now to express your 'Child Manipulative', where you try and influence someone emotionally.
3 Think of an occasion or occasions when you use 'Child' words or behaviour, and jot them down. Were they/are they 'Child Natural' or 'Child Manipulative'?

How similar are these behaviours to the ones you used in your actual childhood? Or how different?

And so what?

Now look back at the exercise in which your boss made statements, and you reacted. Each of the boss's statements came clearly from an ego state, and it is worth betting that your feelings and your response came automatically from a complementary one. Without looking at the next paragraph, go back and identify which ego states we mean.

The first statement is clearly from 'Parent Critical'. Did you react with shock, anger, guilt, or by attempting to pacify? That is your 'Child' state. 'Parent' naturally stimulates 'Child'.

The second statement comes from the boss's 'Child'. Did you feel protective, flattered, ready to help out – or even irritated that the boss should be so weak-kneed? This is your 'Parent', nurturing or critical.

The third statement originates in the boss's 'Parent Nurturing' state, and should have stimulated in you feelings of being looked after, or of gratitude (or suspicion?): your 'Child' state.

Finally, the last statement comes from the boss's 'Child' natural. You might have felt conspiratorial (it is clearly aimed at your own 'Child state') or you may have felt contemptuous, or have been inclined to advise against the proposed course of action: your 'Parent' state.

Still, so what? Well, awareness itself is beneficial, but you are not in fact forced to react as the model suggests you might.

Crossing the transaction

If the reactor takes time to think, the reaction can come from whatever ego state seems more advantageous, and that might be not the one stimulated. This is called crossing the transaction. Whatever the initiator may intend, if the reaction comes from somewhere else, the reactor has a little advantage. So a logical and calm, 'Adult' reaction to the boss's 'Parent' irritation, and a similar one to his silly 'Child' suggestion, can take the boss into a complementary 'Adult' ego state, especially if done with patient persistence.

Conversely, when you are stimulated to a logical response, sometimes, on consideration, a freely emotional 'Child' reaction may be more effective, or a caring 'Parent' one. It is the pause for thought, and the deliberate choice, which indicates a supervisor who can manage the self. Do find other textbooks and writings on the subject of transactional analysis. It is interesting, and you can develop skills beyond the scope of this book.

Stable or unstable, introvert or extravert?

As you will recall, a person can be described as anything from extravert to introvert, meaning that they check to know what is their real identity either by relating with others and seeing themselves reflected there, or seeking within themselves to find their true selves as they see it. They may also be stable, or unstable, meaning in this context changeable in mood, or changing only slowly or rarely.

ACTIVITY 6.8

Try the following abbreviated test to show yourself where you are located on the diagram. But before you do, how would you describe yourself in colloquial terms: a stable extravert? An unstable introvert? An unstable extravert? A stable introvert? Neither one extreme or the other?

Now answer the following questions with either 'yes' or 'no'.

1 Do you sometimes feel cheerful and sometimes depressed, without any real reason?
2 Do you frequently lose concentration on the subject when taking part in a conversation?
3 Are you inclined to be moody and difficult?
4 Do you sometimes bubble with energy, but are other times very lethargic and slow?
5 Does your mind often wander, and you find difficulty in trying to concentrate?
6 Do you experience ups and downs of mood, with or without good reason?
7 Do you prefer to do things than to plan?
8 Do you usually take the initiative in making new fiends and starting conversations?
9 Are you happy and stimulated when you have to act quickly?
10 Would you describe yourself as lively?

11 Are you usually confident and sure in action?
12 Would you be very unhappy if you could not meet new people from time to time?

You get a point on the extravert/introvert axis for every 'Yes' in the first six questions; and a point on the stable/unstable axis for every 'Yes' in the last six questions. Mark your position on the following diagram, and you will find yourself in a quadrant. No point on the diagram, by the way, is abnormal: so now mark yourself on it, and see how you have described yourself with the reflective time it took to answer the questions:

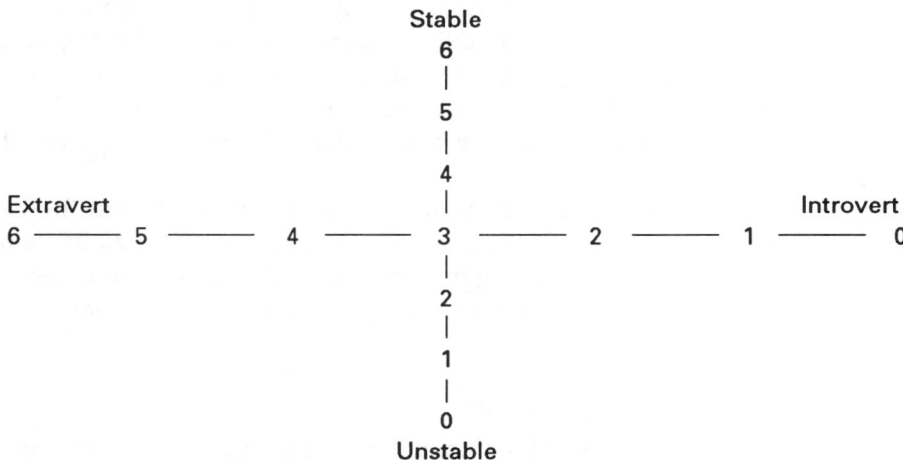

And again, so what? Well, in itself, a little more self-knowledge is useful. But it is even more interesting to get someone else to answer the questions on your behalf, and then contrast what they say about you with what you have said about yourself: because self-knowledge also includes knowing what others think about who or what or how you are.

Self-analysis tests

These are just examples of self-analysis tests, and you may have been interested in the results. But they are only restatements of your own statements about yourself, as are most such tests. There are many others. Good supervisors, knowing that their self is their managerial stock-in-trade, will seek out further such tests to develop their awareness of themselves. A good source of these are courses, either in-company management development or supervisory courses, or professional courses such as those run by local colleges for the Chartered Institute of Bankers: most tutors are ingenious enough to discover and apply these in the context of this part of the syllabus.

■ ASSERTIVENESS

The study of assertiveness started in the late 1960s/early 1970s, with the movement towards the liberation of women, whose power and permission to express themselves were at the time severely limited by custom and practice. Much has been written and spoken about assertiveness, and a good deal of this is about building up people's rights to defend themselves.

It can be said now to have come to mean the management of the expression of what there is in you. This is much more difficult, of course, than it seems. It takes some skill to strike a balance between saying the things you feel or believe in a way which is aggressive, and saying them so mildly that nobody takes any notice – or indeed not saying them at all, and feeling bad about it.

Good managers are able to express themselves firmly, even when saying unpopular things, without causing damage in their relationships. This does not mean to say that when you are being assertive you are always popular: but you do feel that you have said or done the right thing, not inhibited by fear of others' reactions.

We shall discuss this management of your expression by looking first at a wider definition of assertion versus aggression. We shall introduce a character called the 'Dominant Aggressor'. We shall establish some rights that you have; then we shall examine certain specific techniques which can be learnt and used.

Assertion or aggression?

There is a clear difference, and you actually know what it is. To prove this, try this activity.

ACTIVITY 6.9
Draw a line down the centre of a piece of paper and write the words 'aggressive' and 'assertive' at the head of each half. Then write below words associated with assertion, and words associated with aggression.

You will find that under aggression you have such words as violent, shout, hard, fight, hit, attack; under assertion, calm, clear, strong, insistent, confident, logical, cool.

Assertion can be defined in many ways. We have suggested the management of expression; you could also say expressing your views and feelings strongly but in a way which does not impinge on the rights of others. Indeed, rights are important: you have some, and we shall discuss them now.

A 'bill of rights'

Anne Dickson in *A Woman in your Own Right: Assertiveness and You*: London, Quartet, 1982, suggested a full list of personal rights. Here you will find a shorter, and incomplete, list of some of the rights you have as a person in our society. Think of an example or an anecdote when you exercised each right, or had it curtailed.

1 I have the right to be treated with respect as an intelligent person with my own capabilities.
2 I have the right to express my feelings.

3 I have the right to take time, to complete my tasks, and for my own recreation.
4 I have the right to hold my own values.
5 I have the right to say 'yes' and 'no' without anybody else saying them for me.
6 I have the right to make mistakes.
7 I have the right to say I don't understand.
8 I have the right to ask for what I want.
9 I have the right not to apologise for the actions of others, where it is not my fault.

The 'Dominant Aggressor'

Few readers will disagree that they have these rights. So why do we have to list them? Simply because they are all too frequently denied. This is often done by a person who feels, because of personality or position or status, that they can be dominantly aggressive: the petty official, the bullying boss, the supercilious shop assistant, the heavy parent, the ebullient life-and-soul of the party, the over-confident flirt.

It is counter to the 'Dominant Aggressor' that the above rights are to be asserted.

Asserting

To assert means:

- to examine and acknowledge something you feel;
- to establish immediate objectives;
- to determine that action needs to be taken;
- to decide on what that action should be;
- to take that action calmly and deliberately;
- to avoid denying rights to others by taking that action.

Taking action, of course, almost invariably means saying something. The first thing that the assertive person will do, then, is to *acknowledge and trust their body*. When you feel bad and are denying yourself saying something about it, or someone else is denying you, you feel bad physically: a sinking feeling in the stomach, feeling hot or flushed about the neck, sweaty palms. Similarly you feel physically elated when you feel good and want to say so.

Next, the assertive person will *fix a clear objective*. If you are taking something back to the boutique with the snooty sales assistant, you decide: 'I intend (not hope) to get my money back' (or a replacement, or a credit note – whichever you decide).

Finally, whatever is said must be *without apology* for something which is not the asserter's fault, though it is sometimes true that what is asked for might give the object of the assertion some discomfort or call for effort on their part – which is not the asserter's problem, as we will see.

We now turn to some learnable, named techniques of assertion.

Assertiveness techniques
The broken record

It is not easy to express yourself in the face of aggression: but if you have decided to do so, you can repeat your assertion until it is heard: broken records are eventually heard and dealt with!

(a) Identify a clear, simple goal or set of goals, e.g. 'I don't want to go out for a drink: I want to stay in and watch TV.'
(b) Assertively deflect counter-arguments. Use phrases such as 'I don't think you heard me'; 'The point at issue is...'; 'Let me say this again', and 'We can deal with that later. At the moment, I want you to be clear that...'
(c) Repeat your assertion – 'No thanks, I am not coming to the pub, I'm staying in tonight' – calmly and *as often as is necessary*, with appropriate non-verbal signals: as we said, broken records are eventually dealt with!

Initiating conversation

Non-assertive people find it hard to start conversations, even when they want to, and even though they gratefully respond to the initiatives of others. The reluctance to begin can be overcome, however:

(a) Start with and use Open Ended Questions: 'How do you think people will react to Profit-Related Pay?'
(b) Identify 'free' information and use it:
Them: 'Well, I didn't think much of it.'
You: 'Oh, you've experienced it then. When was that, and why didn't it work for you?'
(c) Self-disclosure: offer some free information yourself, and see if it's picked up: 'I'm not confident I'd be able to make much extra in a scheme like that...'

Saying no

This is not easy to do: even when we think we are politely refusing something, we omit actually to use the word. We sometimes think we have said 'no', but in fact we haven't. Common reasons for avoiding saying 'no' are:

- avoiding feeling guilty;
- avoiding making the other person feel guilty;
- softening the blow (pussyfooting);
- submitting to power;
- anxiously wanting to cooperate;
- preserving one's image or stereotype.

Some of these might be quite reasonable but saying 'no' is still an uncomfortable thing to do. How can you cope with this?

(a) remember you are rejecting the request, not the asker;
(b) trust your body: a sinking feeling, or one of pleasurable anticipation?
(c) give yourself time (*see* the following section);
(d) practice saying 'no' without apology or excuses: in front of a mirror and let your body-language match your words.

Asking for time

How many times has someone demanded an instant response, or given you too little time to do something, or pressured you for immediate decisions? The lending banker will tell you that whenever a customer asks for an instant response to a lending decision, the customer may by all means have that instant answer: it is 'no'. But if the customer will wait while the proposition is considered, of course it may well be 'yes'.

When pressured to respond immediately, you might use the following assertiveness technique:

(a) Listen carefully to what is being asked of you.
(b) Clarify by asking questions. Take your own measured time to make sure you are clear about what is being asked.
(c) Think about it, and verbally acknowledge that you really understand what the request entails.
(d) Say 'I can't do that now – I need time to sort that out.'
(e) Be sure, however, to specify how much time, and in what way you will convey your decision or complete the tasks.

Win or lose?

Do note that after having been assertive in the face of the dominant aggressor, or even in an ordinary interaction situation, you may still not win. You may sometimes quite effectively assert yourself, and still lose the situation, or have to give in for reasons other than your own reticence: and that is the point. If you lose, but can say to yourself, 'There is no more that I could have done', you cannot accuse yourself of being ineffective, and you avoid all the bad feelings of self-recrimination associated with having been dominated.

■ NOT MY PROBLEM – YOUR PROBLEM

In the introduction to this chapter we spoke of introducing the reader to Saint Supervisor the Martyr. This is a person, possibly known to you, who takes on the burdens of everybody's problems, and thereby not only fails to solve any of them, but adds to them by complaining about the burden! This particular saint would receive everybody's blessing if they adopted the phrase used as subheading to this section: 'That's not my problem: that is your problem'.

At first glance this seems rather off-hand, or cruel. But the good supervisor, and especially the assertive one, will know that your own problems are your own, and others' problems are theirs. More specifically, let us divide the phrase into its two parts.

'That's not my problem' is quite a reasonable philosophy. Over-enthusiastic or overburdened supervisors have often multiplied their difficulties by taking on the burdens, tasks and problems of others, when they need not have done so. Other people's problems can often be solved without actually accepting them as your own. It does no harm, calmly and coolly and deliberately to consider whether a problem being presented to you is your problem. If not, you may assert that it is not: but this does not preclude your right to help to solve it, indeed it may even help you to solve it.

'That is your problem' is also not only reasonable, it is usually the best way to gain a solution. Supervisors must make sure that their staff, their colleagues and even their managers take responsibility for their own problems, which in most cases can be solved only by the problem-holder – and indeed often more easily as soon as the ownership of the problem is established.

While the philosophy of these phrases is sensible for the supervisor, the expression of them has to be done with some care: they too often mean only the abdication of responsibility by someone who does not care about the problems of others. The good supervisor does care; and is establishing the ownership or otherwise only to locate the responsibility for the solution of the problem.

Supervisor self-development

Managing yourself does not simply take place in the present: it is constant, and it needs to be extended into the future, and techniques of forecasting and planning can be applied to supervisors' own objectives for themselves.

Objectives

Sensible supervisors will have set certain medium and longer term personal objectives in terms of work, having planned for the future. As part of good appraisal systems, such planning is often done in conjunction with the supervisor's boss.

Unless they are denying their humanity, however, such supervisors ought also to be incorporating their personal life-plans; their objectives in terms of what they want to achieve in their non-work lives, in terms of their hobbies, or artistic or literary ambitions, or sport, or family, or personal possessions, or homes.

This is not only because they must harmonise with work-plans, but because a clearer view of the future means more realistic planning in the present.

The development gaps

Similarly with the training gap of the subordinates, supervisors have development gaps, the difference between the objectives suggested above, and the present position. These gaps have first of all to be discerned and calculated. Then they have to be filled, by training, by personal development and by new experiences calculated to move the supervisor in the right, planned direction.

Supervisors can do this for their personal lives by themselves in consultation and participation with their life-partners or parents or other significant people in their lives.

They can also take responsibility for doing it at work, to a certain extent. It is not always sensible to put the training needs of staff above those of the supervisor: sometimes it is actually advantageous for all if the supervisor takes priority. This needs to be thought through carefully, justified and then implemented.

Naturally quite a lot of training and development needs have to be catered for by the supervisor's superiors or by personnel departments. But again, the supervisor can take responsibility for drawing the need for development to the attention of these people, within the structures and procedures of the organisation, of course.

Professional training

The best defence against the accusation, or excuse for not advancing your career, that 'You are not professionally trained' is to gain the necessary training and qualifications. To sign on and study for a certificate or a diploma or even a degree (say in the Open University) is seen as advantageous by most employers; and not only do you qualify, you may even learn something useful on the way!

The progress towards higher qualification is almost endless, and provided that you achieve a measure of success, it is usually neither unpleasant or onerous to continue up the education ladder.

Life-enhancing training

As an additional activity, remember that there are also hobbies and pastimes in which you can get training, or attend courses, or buy manuals for improvement. But what has this to do with the role of the supervisor?

Well, first the better you are at whatever you do in your private life, the more integrated a person you become as a supervisor at work; and secondly, there are often useful and interesting parallels to be drawn from private to professional activities, like teamwork, for example, or concentration, or the joys of achievement.

The self-development action plan

A self-development action plan would have all the same features of any other action plan, as suggested in a previous chapter. It would have a number of different topics to cover, such as domestic and professional, training, development and different responsibilities. It would also be divided into short, medium and longer terms; and it would state what needs to be done, how it would be done, involving whom, and by when. As an exercise, it might be useful if you were to pause at the end of this chapter and design one, sketching out a sensible series of headings.

There is no specific or best form for such a plan. But good supervisors will at least create it, and will possibly discuss it with trusted other people. In this plan, supervisors can indulge themselves, by concentrating for a change on themselves rather than the others who are under their care.

After all, if you are organised, and feel in yourself that your working (and your personal) life is under control, you are bound to be more effective in your job as supervisor. This includes achieving the objectives of your organisation, being sympathetic and helpful in dealing with the problems of others, and achieving fulfilment for yourself.

ACTIVITY 6.10

We're not going to suggest that you do anything as elaborate as a full-scale self-development action plan but you may like to consider clearing the ground for one by answering the following questions.

Look now at your future career. Being realistic, if you stay in banking, where would you see yourself:

(a) in 12 months' time?
(b) in five years' time?
(c) in ten years' time?
(d) at the peak of your career?

■ SUMMARY

In this chapter we have discussed the following aspects of managing yourself:

1 The importance of time management to good supervisors, which is central to their work and effectiveness; and how time management is an act of will, breaking into the planning-cycle dilemma;

2 How efficient supervisors go about getting themselves organised: tidying working space, the TTD list, prioritising into urgent and important, or must, should, would like to do.

3 Delegation as a time-management device (and *see* Chapter 3).

4 The importance of personal planning equipment, such as wall charts, diary, notebooks, personal planners and other stationery.

5 The importance of managing personal as well as business life, for the benefit of both:

(a) planning for weekly domestic routines;
(b) keeping home planners and diaries;
(c) maintaining control of private, or social life;
(d) health and fitness.

6 Self-knowledge, and the ability to understand and use strengths and weaknesses in your own personality:

(a) Strong feelings as 'Parent', as 'Adult', as 'Child', and discerning where the supervisor personally spends time;
(b) Deliberately crossing the transaction: being in control of interactions with others by being detached and aware;
(c) Stable and relatively unchanging, or unstable and volatile in moods? Extravert, and seeking views of self via others, or introvert, checking self only with self? And so what?

7 Getting educated; being more effective by having a broader view of the business and banking world about you; doing this systematically:

(a) having sorted everyone else's training out, how the supervisor can and should deploy the organisation's training philosophy, budget and facilities for self-improvement;

(b) how the supervisor can use educational, press and other public media to develop personal and business awareness.

8 How assertiveness can help to effect the supervisor's plans and intentions; not feeling guilty when saying 'no', and then understanding the difference between assertion and aggression.

9 How to handle the 'Dominant Aggressor'; and understanding the rights a person has: your own, and everyone else's, 'bill of rights'.

10 Techniques of assertiveness, and how these can be developed in the supervisor and in staff; how to adjust your manner: calm, firm, and non-impinging; and how to set your immediate objectives. Then how to develop techniques, such as:

(a) the 'broken record'
(b) saying 'no'
(c) asking for time
(d) initiating conversation

11 Winning or losing assertive interactions, but feeling at least comfortable with the outcome; and how this affects longer term effectiveness in dealing with self and others.

12 How good supervisors take responsibility for their own problems and not those of others: avoiding playing at being a martyr to everybody's difficulties; but being effective at helping others to take possession of their own problems, then helping to solve them – at arm's length.

13 How to work out and operate a personal supervisor's self-development action plan, and to keep the relevant parts of it in the consciousness of managers.

SELF-ASSESSMENT QUESTIONS

Try to answer these questions to remind you of the contents of this chapter:

1 What could be the main reasons why supervisors do not organise their time effectively?

2 What would be the first step in sensibly getting organised?

3 What is the difference between 'urgent' and 'important'?

4 What is the no-pending principle? How do you comply with it?

5 What items of stationery are useful in managing yourself?

6 What does TTD stand for?

7 How should the good supervisor organise to give time to keep the TTD list up to date?

8 What is an *ego state*?

9 Suggest a phrase which characterises the 'Parent Critical'.

10 How do you cross a transaction?

11 What is the technical meaning given in this chapter for 'Unstable?'

12 And what is an extravert?

13 State briefly the difference between aggression and assertion.

14 Describe three of the things you feel you have a right to, in interacting with other people.

15 What is a Dominant Aggressor?

16 What do you do first, with your emotions and bodily feelings, when you are being confronted with dominant aggression?

17 Describe how and when you might ask for more time for a decision.

18 What is meant in this chapter by the 'broken record'?

19 Why is 'Not my problem' a rational philosophy for a good supervisor?

20 Why is it important for the supervisor to have a reasonably planned and ordered home life?

7 The rules and the law

OBJECTIVES

When you have read this chapter you will be familiar with a variety of rules, set externally or internally, for behaviour concerning:
- Health and safety, the law and the supervisor's responsibilities for staff safety;
- The protection from outside agencies of the organisation's property and that of its customers currently in its custody;
- Rules concerning absence caused by illness or disability; confirmation by self and by medical practitioners;
- The terms and conditions of employment in banks, the basis for the contract of service;
- The contract of service: what it contains, what the employers' and the staff members' responsibilities are as laid down therein;
- The declaration of secrecy and staff responsibility for the security of confidential information;
- Employment protection, the law and the organisation's agreement with the staff;
- Equal opportunity legislation, and organisational policies towards sex and racial discrimination;
- The conduct of staff bank accounts and finance;
- The supervisor, the staff and relationships with internal audit.

■ INTRODUCTION

There are many environments in which work takes place, e.g. social, political, organisational, cultural and technological. There is also an environment characterised by rules, whether set by the organisation or by the society in which it operates. Supervisors are at least negatively responsible for the rules: if they are broken, the supervisor carries the can. For this reason, they are well advised to note that ignorance of the law, or the rules, is rarely accepted as an excuse, and more positively, that correct operation within the rules is respected. In this chapter we will not divide between the rules and the law: all must be understood by those with managerial responsibility.

We will begin with *health and safety;* and we shall not simply be rehearsing the law but genuinely examine the supervisor's responsibility for the physical well-being of the staff. Of course you will be responsible for the organisation's instructions to comply with the law, as well as to protect your staff against the organisation when its recommended practices break the law. But the staff will also look to you for practices which will characterise their work as healthy and safe within your own jurisdiction at the workplace.

There are also important administrative rules concerning the recording of accidents and of absences due to illness, both to comply with the law and for insurance purposes, for the correct application of which the supervisor is responsible, and which could cause loss to organisation or to staff if supervisors are ignorant or negligent of their duties.

In some organisations, rules for the protection of outside people and their property – such as customers – are also vested to a significant extent in the staff, and especially in the supervisor; banks are a perfect example of this. Those in charge down to the first level of management are responsible for the security of premises, and must follow well-developed and clearly-expressed procedural rules for the storing and handling of valuable property either belonging to the organisation or entrusted to its care. Ignorance of these rules or their misinterpretation or mishandling can be literally perilous.

How much of one's total person is committed to the organisation depends on many things. Formally it is determined by the *contract of service* and other related documentation. This sets out positive prescriptions for the bargain between the staff member and the employer, and negative rules which outline what happens if the bargain is breached, on either side. As background when supervisors represent the organisation vis-à-vis their staff, they should be aware of these prescriptions, and those of related documents, such as any declaration of secrecy into which people enter when they join.

Just societies look to improve relationships between people and work-organisations, to minimise problems of the oppression of the weak by the powerful in either direction, such as by *employment protection laws,* so that the organisation cannot summarily deprive people of their means of earning, nor can staff associations of one sort or another heedlessly damage the organisation's operations. Supervisors, to operate within the law, should understand it.

Similarly, *equal opportunity rules* are to give people a better chance of success, not hindered by prejudice about sex, age, race or beliefs. The law cannot change attitudes, but it can make unjust extremes unacceptable, or ineffective, by sanctions. A characteristic very often applied to the best managers is fairness; and the laws on equal opportunity, if understand and operated in their spirit as well as their letter, help in this aspect of supervisory skill.

Finally, wherever staff have responsibility for money which does not belong to them, their supervisors are made responsible by the organisation to see that the conduct of staff with relation to *handling money* is correct. This is done by more or less strict and elaborate rules, with a greater or lesser involvement in the conduct of the staff's personal finances, in banks, for example, to an extent which would horrify non-bankers!

■ THE NEED FOR HEALTH AND SAFETY

People spend their adult life at work, most of the daylight hours of most of the weeks of the years between leaving school and retiring, around two-thirds of the way to the grave. This would be a fairly depressing thought if it were not for the fact that many can satisfy a good number of their human needs by doing this.

If you were to check out the discussion of these needs conducted in Chapter 3, you would be reminded of the fact that the need for safety arises immediately after the need for physical survival, and is a very basic one.

Connecting these two points, it follows that safety and health at work are very important as part of daily life, and in our age a good deal of attention is paid to it. It was not always so: you need not know much about feudal times to know that working people were regarded as a disposable and replaceable resource, and all the landowner or mine-owner wanted to know if one of his workers was maimed or disabled or died, was, how soon a replacement could arrive.

This was echoed through the Victorian era, although reformers were having to be steadily at pains to put Acts through parliament, to force employers to take a more humanitarian view of worker safety. The growing union movement was backing this in government and on the shop-floor.

Now it seems so natural as to take it for granted that employers actually want to keep their staff healthy and safe. But it still takes an Act of Parliament to ensure that it is done adequately, and if you mention Health and Safety as a phrase most will assume that you are referring to the Health and Safety at Work Act 1974.

We will go on to look at the main provisions of that act as they refer to clerical/office based staff, and where the supervisor's responsibility, formal and incidental, lies. We will then go on to look at the proper responsibilities of the supervisor outside the act; and then move on to the special problems faced by those whose offices are the repository of items and sums of money of great value, such as bank branches, by looking at some of the practices that may be recommended by your inspectors.

■ HEALTH AND SAFETY AT WORK ACT 1974

The Act was introduced to cope with a very considerable piecemeal collection of legislation, one of the features of which was that all responsibility lay with the employer as an organisation, and very little with the management or staff. The commission which examined the matter suggested that things would be more positive if the staff were to be involved in the preservation of their own safety.

The Act is long and complex; and all that needs to concern us here is Part 1, referring directly to the health and safety of staff at work (and also of the public; the handling of dangerous substances; and the emission of noxious substances into the atmosphere).

It lays down sets of duties, among them those imposed on the employer, on the suppliers of tools and other such materials, and on the employees.

The employers' duties

Premises

The general responsibility of the employer for health and safety is specified. First, the premises and the plant shall be designed and built for health and safety, with proper access to safe areas outside where necessary, and with proper availability of fresh air and warmth, for example, and provision for protection against harmful gases or dust or dirt.

Questions of this sort do not normally arise in bank offices, except in exceptional circumstances of building and refurbishment, and you may like to check out your procedures for what happens in these cases. Check also what the rules are for the evacuation of the premises and keeping exits clear for this eventuality.

Equipment

Working equipment shall also be designed and set up so as to minimise the possibility of unhealthiness and danger. This sort of requirement has implications more obvious in the case of, say, the movable mechanical blade that cuts material in the manufacture of shirts, or in automatic lathe machines. Employees must not be charged for any necessary safety equipment or clothing.

Nevertheless it applies also to office premises. For instance, when did you last see a document spike which is straight and vertical, inviting you to impale your hand as well as the document? Strictly illegal! If they still exist, document spikes are now curved over like a question mark.

Materials

Materials to be handled must be safe, or there must be strict safety procedures for handling, storing, and transporting it. In fact this rarely applies to materials handled in the clerical context, like cash, because there are few associated health hazards in the sense of transmittable disease or noxious substances (although have you ever counted the takings from a wholesale meat-market dealer?).

However, many of the precautions taken to protect the customers' money from theft, especially of the type with violence associated, also help the bank comply with the Health and Safety Act; such as strict rules as to where in the branch you may or may not count money, and how much may be held in one or another counter till.

Training and information

Training and information sufficient to equip the staff with the skills and knowledge they need to stay safe, and keep others safe, must be provided by the employer. This comes in the form of posters, circulars, and training courses; and it is associated with the appointment of staff as safety representatives and on to committees, which we shall cover later on in this chapter under Health and Safety Committees.

ACTIVITY 7.1

Under each of the following headings write down an example of exactly what is done in your office to comply with the Health and Safety at Work Act 1974.

- Premises
- Equipment
- Materials
- Training and information

The suppliers' duties

Anyone who supplies material and equipment must also make sure that it is designed to be, and manufactured to be, safe and free of hazard; and instructions, and where necessary training, must be provided in a way that is clear enough to minimise the dangers of working with it. They must also take the responsibility of examining and testing the equipment as often as necessary for safety purposes.

The staff's responsibilities

They must *take care* of themselves, within reason, and not deliberately do anything which would be hazardous to health or safety, either of the employee's own or that of colleagues.

You are therefore in breach of the Act if you play the fool in a dangerous manner likely to cause damage to yourself or others. In fact the relevant section reads 'It shall be the duty of every employee while at work... to take reasonable care for the health and safety of himself and of other persons who may be affected by his acts or omissions at work'. This means that you are, strictly, in breach of it if you knowingly turn up with an infectious disease like 'flu!

Employees must *comply with rules* laid down by the employer, co-operate in schemes and carry out duties imposed by employers to preserve health or safety.

Thus, where there are rules concerning bank branch or office security so as to protect the staff from attack, you cannot, under the law, decide not to obey those rules, even where it is only your safety that is affected and you don't care. You have a duty under the Act so to comply, and co-operate with the employer.

Interfering with safety equipment, or particularly any such equipment provided so as to comply with the Act, is against the rules of the Act, and misuse of such equipment, either recklessly or intentionally, is a breach of the Act. So please do not drink the distilled water provided to counter ammonia attacks, or play the fool with the fire-extinguishers at the office party!

ACTIVITY 7.2

Recall an example where the rules concerning health and safety were breached by a staff member failing to accept responsibility for themselves and others.

(a) What action did the management take?
(b) What action do you think they should have taken? (This may be the same or different.)

■ HEALTH AND SAFETY COMMITTEES

As a result of government regulations subsequent to the Act, health and safety officers can be appointed at the request of trade unions representing the staff, and these can be formed into committees if more than one of them requests it.

Where there are such representatives, they have a number of duties and functions, e.g. to consult, and be consulted by, the employer, to help make the arrangements necessary to comply with the Act, or generally to promote health and safety. They must also investigate complaints, potential problems or hazards, and the cause of accidents; they must make representations to the employer in general cases of problems and represent specific staff in particular cases. They must also represent their section staff on safety committees.

Health and safety representatives must be given time off, with pay, and in working hours, and such facilities and training as they need to carry out their duties in a reasonable manner. The regulations covering this will be agreed by employers and staff representatives, such as unions. With certain reservations, they must also be given company information.

Your organisation may well have set up mechanisms for the appointment, briefing and training of such safety officers. So get hold of whatever documentation you can concerning their rights, duties and accreditation. If it is not freely available in the office, try contacting your union or staff association. Look at it with care and check out its main provisions. In examinations you are not likely to be asked about the detailed technicalities of health and safety, but this documentation should give you a good idea of what your employer believes about the matter.

■ POLICY STATEMENTS

See if you can get hold of a policy statement made by your organisation concerning its commitment to the health and safety of the staff. Look at it carefully, and note in your mind to what extent it is in fact operated in your office. Look out for shortfalls, not in any spirit of antagonism, but see if fresh attention should be paid to it by your employer, or more pointedly, by yourself as supervisor.

■ HEALTH, SAFETY AND THE SUPERVISOR

Supervisors, as part of local management, clearly have responsibilities under the Act. They also have general responsibility if only in the sense that, should anyone in their charge suffer an unavoidable accident or harm or damage, they will inevitably shoulder part of the blame. The best of them will accept that blame as part of the supervisor function.

It therefore behoves supervisors as part of their managerial function to make efforts to preserve safety and health, and take steps, and be vigilant, to prevent accidents. It is not a bad idea to diary for a regular, say monthly, safety check. You could examine your premises, your office, the electrical fittings, equipment, furniture and fittings and so on; and pay attention to corner-cutting practices the staff may have drifted into. Do this, if at all, with the co-operation of, or delegated to, your safety officer, if you have one.

The Royal Society for the Prevention of Accidents (RoSPA) provides leaflets and other material giving checklists of areas for attention to safety and health, and your personnel department, training department and union will also have such material. Indeed you may find that such a checklist forms part of your bank procedures and that you are, or your management is, actually required to carry out a periodic check of safety matters. Find out about this; and as an exercise, build up a portfolio of such material by contacting these agencies and asking for it. (When did you last check that every employee has 40 square feet of floor space?)

Supervisors have special responsibilities in bank branches, where breaches of company safety rules can lead to serious consequences such as injury or even death. It is a pity to mention this so brutally, but it is also easy to fail to face it and to tuck it into the back of the mind under the general heading of 'It won't happen here'.

ACTIVITY 7.3

Create a portfolio of published items, such as leaflets or booklets, on the matter of health and safety at work. Discuss your portfolio with your local health and safety officer. (Good sources of information are RoSPA, your local library, or Citizens' Advice Bureau, and your Local Authority Information Centre.)

■ BRANCH SECURITY IN BANKS

It will not be possible to describe all the steps to be taken in branches to maintain the security of the bank's and the customers' property, and the staff's safety. First of all, it could form a nice set of instructions for the odd criminal reading this book; and secondly there are too many to cover in the available space. As a check on the detail of these instructions, listen carefully to the inspectors the next time they visit; or preferably, imagine they will visit tomorrow – and they might! – and check out at least your own area.

There is one principle that is certain, i.e. *that there is not a single bank regulation for branch security that you can afford to relax,* however irrelevant it may seem to be to your particular circumstances. This is simply because if anything should happen as a result of relaxation, you will quite rightly be blamed, and probably penalised for it; and if harm should come to your staff, you will have to live with it for the rest of your life.

What if the rules are in fact inappropriate because of the geography or design or special circumstances in your case? If there is a good argument that a change would improve rather than weaken safety you can formulate that argument in writing. Then you must simply take steps so that your management obtains approval in writing from Inspection or from the top domestic banking authorities for an appropriate modification or change.

There is one other certain principle: it is wrong to believe that a disaster will not happen in your branch but the next one down the road. You should always behave as if it will happen to you, and as supervisor your staff will, or should be made to, appreciate your concern even if it involves nagging them. You must be able to put your hand on your heard and say, 'In my supervised section we were always as careful as we should have been. There was absolutely nothing more we could have done, nothing we should have done that we ignored, no rule broken'. If you are not able to say that, you will have to carry the burden.

The traditional areas in which care should be taken to comply meticulously with agreed rules are:

1 morning admittance of staff to branch;
2 public admittance outside office hours;
3 cash and valuables transport and delivery;
4 entry to the safe or strongroom;
5 cash control and movement during working hours;
6 small and sub-branch staffing and security routines;
7 hostage alarms and bomb threats.

Supervisors must be familiar with the up-to-date, fully detailed procedures in these matters. Once again, the least you can do is diary, at short intervals, branch security checks. You should be able to obtain from inspectors, or examine in your procedures manual, the various items which should be attended to. Do an exercise when you are next in the office as part of these studies and resolve to make a practice of it. If this is not your overall responsibility, establish what part of it is yours, by consultation with your management, and make sure that your own operation, at least, is immaculate.

■ DRILLS

How boring fire and bomb-threat drills are. Yet it is your responsibility to check that they are not only done properly, but in the right spirit, and that everyone fully understands the serious reasons for all the moves involved. Have you ever considered holding a raid drill? How well do your staff know the procedure, how smoothly could they operate to ensure their safety and limit loss (in that order)? How confident are you in this ability? Don't you think a raid drill, or at least a 'walk-through' of what they should do in case of a raid, would be beneficial?

ACTIVITY 7.4

(a) Write down the steps through which everyone in your office should go when a fire-alarm sounds: personnel, routes, routines, location.
(b) Write down the steps which everyone in your office should follow if there were to be a raid drill.

■ SICKNESS PROCEDURES

No less a body than the EEC has involved itself with standard regulations concerning your rights when absent from work due to sickness. However, at the workplace level all a supervisor needs to know is the procedure for recording the absence of staff. It may not be your direct responsibility, but it is something on which your staff would expect you to be informed.

Check on your office procedure. It is likely to state that anyone who is absent for reasons of sickness must:

1 notify the office early on the first day;
2 give certain information about the illness, such as date of commencement, nature of illness and likely duration;
3 record (self-certify) the illness absence on return;
4 provide a medical certificate if the illness lasts more than seven days and send it to the office.

There are special provisions if the illness turns out to be highly infectious or dangerous. Management must inform central personnel departments in this case, and check on contact with other members of staff, for example if the disease is German measles and the sick person has been in contact with a pregnant staff member or if the disease turns out to be the Black Death and it would be useful to close the branch (and paint crosses on the doors!).

Take note of the situation concerning the payment of salaries during illness. While the bank will probably reserve the right to do as it pleases, there are arrangements which will normally apply and they will be related to length of service, and the payments will be reduced by the amounts of state sickness benefit payable.

■ CONDITIONS OF EMPLOYMENT

Either with or incorporated in your contract of service you will find a statement of the main terms and conditions of employment.

By law, if a member of staff works more than 16 hours per week they must be issued with a contract of service within 13 weeks of starting employment. The contract will have a number of detailed specifications, and before you go on find yours, read it and think about what you have contracted to do.

Many people sign such a document at the beginning of their career, and also agree to the conditions of employment, and never think about it again until it causes them trouble. Do you know, for instance, to what extent the bank can insist that you move house? Is overtime compulsory? Exactly what is your period of notice? Under what terms may you earn extra cash from an outside employer?

The Statement of the Terms and Conditions of Employment will answer those questions. A typical document of this sort in banking might include the following pieces of information. Your own may have additional, or varied, or different clauses.

1 *General statements* about the document. You may (or may not) be amused by one which states that 'Where the male gender is used, this applies equally to the female gender', immediately followed by 'The bank is an equal opportunities employer'.

2 *The mobility clause,* which is in all bank contracts, and which says you must work *wherever* the bank wants you to, and in whatever subsidiary company in its group.

3 *Salary structure* general statements, statements about London allowances and about holding and conducting bank accounts.

4 *Hours of work* are generally specified, and policy on overtime. It will probably state that reasonable amounts of overtime must be done on the request of management to complete essential work, at rates specified elsewhere.

5 *Illness procedures* will be outlined.

6 *Grievance and discipline procedures* will be referred to, and the location of detailed information will be given, as well as a brief statement about the right to appeal.

7 *Outside employment,* if referred to, will probably be prohibited except with the permission of the bank, in writing.

8 *Periods of notice* will be referred to and may be specified.

9 *Further documentation* which it would be useful for you to read will be specified, such as the bank's procedures manuals.

ACTIVITY 7.5

See if you can find your own contract of employment and conditions of service and compare the clauses in them with those suggested on the above list.

■ THE DECLARATION OF SECRECY

Nothing could be more straightforward than this document. You have simply signed it to say that you will not disclose anything which you may have learnt about customer accounts or about other banks' business which would harm the bank. It is not under oath, but you declare as firmly as if it were, that you will be bound by it. It is also interesting to note that its provisions extend for life, and beyond when or if you leave the bank's service.

The legal consequences of breach of this declaration are fairly serious (for both you and the bank); but the honourable intention when signing it is equally serious. Unfortunately the document can be treated lightly or taken for granted; but the good supervisor will draw its importance to the attention of the new staff member, because it is the foundation of your profession (in fact, without it, it is doubtful that banking could be called a profession).

Customers are entitled to take confidentiality and secrecy concerning their accounts completely for granted, and indeed they have many legal rights to this secrecy. The subject forms a good part of your study of banking outside this field. But give thought to the fact that the whole fabric of banking as it is conducted would have to be overhauled if a bank clerk could quite legitimately gossip about customers' financial affairs down at the pub.

Supervisors should be at pains to keep this matter before their staff as a central matter of ethics and proper behaviour. Those interested in certification by the Chartered Institute of Bankers should note the motto is *Probus et Fidelis* – honourable and faithful).

There is only one class of people in the world, every detail of whose banking affairs are freely available to their colleagues, friends, subordinates, bosses, other staff members and employers: and that is the employees of a bank!

■ EMPLOYMENT PROTECTION

Employment protection is enshrined in the law basically in the Employment Protection (Consolidation) Act 1978 which covers fair and unfair dismissal and redundancy, and in the Employment Act 1980, which modified that, and in a Code of Practice for dismissal agreed by the government and designed by the Arbitration and Conciliation Advisory Service (ACAS) in the late 1970s.

You do not need, as supervisor, to know of the details of the law, or to be able to name the Acts of Parliament but it is useful to memorise them for examination purposes. We shall be dealing in detail in the next chapter with your bank's procedures for redundancy and dismissal; but here we will go through the outlines of what our society, via the laws, lays down as desirable in employer and employee behaviour ('acting in a reasonable manner' is the frequently used term) when it comes to deciding to terminate employment.

Let us begin by examining the ACAS Code of Practice on Disciplinary Practice and Procedures, and its main provisions; you will almost certainly find that your bank will comply absolutely with these, as we shall discover later.

The Code of Practice

Essentially, the Code provides that:

1 dismissal shall be preceded by a series of progressive disciplinary steps;
2 actions concerning dismissal must be taken promptly, so that delay does not lead to extra unfairness or to distress;
3 there must be a series of warnings;
4 employees should be allowed to defend themselves and have the opportunity of stating their case;
5 time should be given for the staff member to improve performance;
6 there should be the right to, and a system of, appealing against a dismissal notice;
7 particular dismissal matters should be in writing; and
8 there should be written rules concerning grounds for dismissal, and the step-by-step consequences of breaking the rules.

So, no stage in a disciplinary procedure, even to dismissal, should come as a surprise because it is all deliberate and open; there should always be time to reform behaviour or correct working practices or improve skills; and there should always be a chance to defend yourself against dismissal, or have someone else defend you.

ACTIVITY 7.6

For the purposes of the examination, it would be sensible to memorise the eight essential elements in the Code of Practice.

Fair and unfair dismissal

An employer can no longer, in our society, fire someone instantly without good reason, and that the employer does not like someone, or cannot stand their attitude, or does not like their politics or union orientation are no longer regarded as good reasons. In other words, we have decided that employers do not have dictatorial rights over whom they may fire.

However, the law does suggest that there are some sensible, acceptable grounds for summary dismissal (immediate, without notice) and it is not difficult to think of examples of where it would be perfectly reasonable for banks to fire people on the spot (theft, misconduct relating to customer accounts, breaches of security procedures, and the like).

Conversely, there are also certain grounds on which employers cannot dismiss people at all, such as for joining a union, or refusing to join one, or for pregnancy.

Normally there have to be procedures of discipline or redundancy before dismissal, which must be reasonable. Dismissal includes 'constructive dismissal', which is essentially driving someone to the point where they cannot stand the employment any more; this sort of resignation is regarded by the law as exactly the same as normal dismissal.

Fair dismissal is basically on grounds which seem reasonable to the employer provided that the steps of the procedure have been gone through and those steps are according to the Code of Practice. Because each is an individual case, we cannot examine all the grounds for fair dismissal, but they can fall into areas of *incompetence,* of *conduct,* of *redundancy,* and of continuing employment *contravening some other legal duty.*

The question of fair or unfair dismissal only comes up if there is resistance; and the Act provides for the dismissed person to appeal to an industrial tribunal. It is for this tribunal to decide on the facts of the case, and it is up to the tribunal to judge the dismissal fair and that the employer behaved reasonably in leading up to the dismissal. It is therefore accurate to say that what constitutes fair dismissal in every particular case is what the industrial tribunal says is fair.

Redundancy

Yes, it does happen in banks. When it does, it must be according to the procedure, which we will examine later. The Employment Protection (Consolidation) Act 1978 determines that people can be made redundant if the company goes out of business, or changes its place of business, or if its business no longer needs the particular contribution of certain employees. There must be a special redundancy payment, based on the age, length of service and pay of the redundant person, and the government will repay the employer some of this payment, from the Government Redundancy Fund.

Those to be made redundant may not be selected by race or colour or membership of a trade union; and if they are members of a recognised union it must be consulted about the matter. If more than 10 employees are to be made redundant within 30 days, the government must be informed.

Should it ever happen where you work, note that as supervisor your duty to yourself and your employer is to ensure it that the strict rules of procedure are carried out. In particular you will check on the methods used for the selection of staff for redundancy, which must be strictly correct, and that every step is meticulously taken. You can only live with yourself when it comes to depriving people of their living if you are sure that it was not done haphazardly and as a result of unfair or incorrect or even illegal procedure.

ACTIVITY 7.7
Find your own bank's statements on redundancy, in procedures manuals or contract of employment or conditions of service? What are the main provisions?

■ EQUAL OPPORTUNITY

If you go by official statements, the banks have quite good records for equal opportunity. Equal pay for men and women was introduced in the late 1960s by some banks, ahead of the Equal Pay Act 1970, and in all by 1972. Nowhere will you find any official statement of a discriminatory nature on race or religion; in fact you will not have to look far in staff manuals before you find the statement 'The Bank is an Equal Opportunity Employer'. In fact over 60 per cent of clearing bank employees are women, and about half the men are in junior clerical/secretarial jobs.

Now observe that 99 per cent of managers in banking are men; 85 per cent of appointed officers are men; and 90 per cent of the women are in clerical/secretarial jobs. This is not only unbalanced; it is even odder by national standards, where at this time in British industry and commerce, around a quarter of all managers are women.

ACTIVITY 7.8
Before you go on complete the following activity.

(a) Count and record how many men, how many women, how many people of ethnic minority communities, work at your job location and work out what percentage each figure is of the total workforce there, even if the figures are small.
(b) Where there are inequalities, jot down some possible good reasons (nature of the work, location of branch, peculiarities of office history, odd recent events).
(c) Relate these figures to the managerial status of the staff: how many men, women, ethnic minority people are at different status levels?
(d) Ring and ask your personnel department (in the spirit of study) how many women managers, and officials, there are in domestic (branch) banking in your bank, and in the whole bank. Carefully record exactly what they say in response, whatever that response may be. First of all you may find it interesting; second, this verbatim or word-for-word response scores you examination points in answer to questions in this field.

(e) Now ask them how many people of Afro-Caribbean or Asian racial origin work for the bank, and how many of them are officials or managers. Again, record in writing the word-for-word response.

The law

There is no biological or psychological evidence that shows that men or women, Caucasian or Afro-Caribbean, Asian people are any different in levels of intelligence, skill or ability to learn.

The three relevant Acts of Parliament acknowledge these facts. They are the Race Relations Act 1968 (amended in 1976), the Equal Pay Act 1970, and the Sex Discrimination Act 1975. In summary, these Acts make it unlawful to discriminate on grounds of sex or race at any stage of the career, or in recruitment, terms of service, training, advancement and dismissal. There are certain jobs in certain occupations where either male or female, or persons of a particular ethnic origin, may be specified because of the nature of the work, where there is a particular physical or social qualification required (such as, for instance, a counselling job among Moslem men where only men would be acceptable, and possibly only Moslem men).

Banks have meticulously complied with the successive Acts in their regulations as to discrimination, though this occasionally meant tightening up on male privilege rather than having females share the privilege.

For example, before 1975, staff loans were much more easily obtained by males than females, and by younger males than females, and by married males than married females. After 1975, they become more difficult for males simultaneously with becoming at least available to married females.

The facts

Some of the actual facts of the present situation have already been alluded to; and if you have performed the exercise on counting males/females/minorities as suggested above, you will have some more facts at your fingertips and in your files.

You will have discovered that the law is one thing and reality is another; it would be unreasonable to expect a change in the law to change people's attitudes. But is anything changing in banking?

Check on your own bank. As to sex-equality, some banks are permitting women who leave to have babies not just the statutory birth-and-after period to return to work, but up to five years to return at a guaranteed commensurate grade, with refresher courses in those five years to keep up-to-date. Some have special career advisers, and working parties, and workshops, to look at what is actually happening in terms of on-the-ground equality and discrimination, and are making official moves to eradicate quotas where these exist, formally or informally.

Check also – and record the answer in writing, either for your personal interest or for examination purposes – what similar measures are being taken, concerning having the banking proportion of ethnic minorities match the population at large. Also, get your union to send you whatever research material they have on this matter, as well as on sex-equality.

Having checked out that your bank's policy is making inroads into past inequalities, you may wish to contrast the policy with the practice as you observe it. Banks are undoubtedly ahead of the law in their policies that they state and the facilities that they make available for this purpose. However, where there are still problems they are rooted in the attitudes of those who put the policies into practice. (You will always get good marks in the examination for cool, objective observations of the contrast between policy and practice.)

Equality and the supervisor

Let us be frank: this is a sensitive and difficult area. However, as supervisor, in particular in a bank, you have no choice but to be totally non-discriminating, as hopefully you would anyway be inclined to be.

To begin with, you should check your own behaviour, and ensure that at all stages you select and judge and reward people for their performance and ability, rather than for their sex or race or colour, without bias in any direction.

Remember in this context that in any job-evaluated grading system people are paid for what they do, not for what they will do in the future. So that 'she may get pregnant and leave' is not only illegal, but also illogical, grounds for failing to recommend for promotion.

Second, the best of supervisors defend their staff from discrimination by outside agencies, including their own management. The least that is required of you by your organisation is to be vigilant that all regulations and procedures are adhered to; the least your staff expect is that you speak out against injustices, or breaches of law or regulations calculated to have a bad effect on them.

The good supervisor, speaking out, may fail; but the good supervisor will not fail to speak out.

■ THE STAFF AND MONEY

The last set of topics we will deal with in this chapter relate to a dangerous substance that anyone in a clerical situation, and in particular banking people, tend to take for granted, namely, money.

In some ways it is a good thing that they do take it for granted, and that it does not constantly occur to them how much of their own financial problems one cash-dispenser load, or the contents of one till, would solve!

Since anything that 'goes wrong' with cash in the supervisor's section has at least something to do with the supervisor's responsibility, we shall now examine this aspect of bank/office work. Starting with general principles of cash-handling, we will then look at the conduct of staff bank accounts and finally the relationships between staff, supervisor and the inspection and internal audit departments and staff.

Cash

It is not appropriate to set out here all the rules that your organisation is likely to impose concerning the handling, storing and moving of cash. It is, however, entirely appropriate to suggest that whatever those rules are, there is neither flexibility nor choice in obeying them to the letter, and additionally, as supervisor, you must ensure that they are obeyed in every detail, on every occasion, and by every member of your group.

If there is the slightest gap between what they should do and what they actually do, and anything goes wrong, then you shall be apportioned some of the blame, and with every justification.

Cash handling rules come in a variety of areas:

- Storage
- Delivery
- Movement
- Counting.

1 *Storage:* there are rules about getting cash out ready for use during the day, about putting it away and especially about how many people and at what level should be involved. Remember that these rules are principally for the protection of those people, against later accusation.

There are also rules about how much cash should be held at tills; and on busy days time must be set aside to remove cash to storage areas, however inconvenient it is (as it will be, almost by definition, on busy days!). It is a supervisory responsibility both to keep an eye on the levels of cash and to arrange for people to be allocated to its removal to storage.

2 *Delivery:* the staff involved, and all other staff, and the supervisor, must all know the rules concerning delivery; and must co-operate in every sensible way with the security people who deliver. A supervisory eye should be kept on the transfer from delivery to storage point, too.

3 *Movement:* cash is often moved within the office, and there are rules for this too. Cash is at its most vulnerable as it moves; you cannot be or be seen to be lax in the rules of its movement, nor take it for granted by drifting into careless practices.

4 *Counting:* refresh yourself on the rules about where and when and how cash should be counted, how the sums should be recorded and who checks the figures. Any locally-decided variations of the rules incur possible trouble, either from intruders or from inspectors.

For instance, there may be a rule about not counting cash on the counter. In the case of your counter, you might not be able to see any way in which the cash could be stolen even if it were counted there. On the other hand, if you count it away from the counter there wouldn't be any way of its being stolen from the counter.

ACTIVITY 7.9

If yours is an office which deals with cash, such as a domestic banking branch, write down one of the rules which apply to each of the above cash-handling stages.

Staff accounts

It is possible that the supervisors in your organisation have no responsibility for their staff's bank accounts or the conduct of their finances. But these things affect people's work, and the supervisor is responsible for that.

Their own money has the same effect on bankers as it does on anyone else: it brings pleasure and pain, security and worry, about the surplus and the shortfall. The difference is that branch bankers have cash in their hands all the time. Staff members who, like other human beings, have the occasional money problems, are in danger of at least foolish acts and at worst criminal ones.

It is for this reason that the rules about the conduct of accounts are far stricter for bank staff than for their customers, and this is why so many people have the right to investigate your financial affairs. For managers and inspectors to be able to, or indeed to have the duty to, ask you why your Auntie Carla has deposited £100 in your current account would be outrageous if you were a customer; and to have to ask your boss if you can borrow £50 beyond belief for your friends outside banking; but to you it is perfectly natural. They must be assured that you are nowhere near the point where the day's cash would be too much of a temptation for you.

Where such examination is freely and physically available, supervisors can and should keep a discreet eye on the more extreme of money movement or shortfalls in their staff accounts. Depending on the relationship with the staff, they can either then offer counselling, or recommend that management engage in such counselling, with the staff in question.

In any case, it does no harm to have it known that you are available for the discussion of these problems, and that you can help with your personal knowledge of the bank's loans and schemes for staff.

■ INSPECTORS AND AUDITORS

We shall examine in turn routine inspections and special investigations.

General inspections/audits

The inspection function — as any inspector will tell you — is to a large extent a training function. What inspectors exist for is to improve performance, and it is largely to their regret that they have to do this negatively, that is, by correcting faults. In this function they should complement the supervisor's responsibility very precisely.

For this reason, at least, inspectors and auditors should be welcomed as they arrive, and carefully and considerately accommodated during their visit. Note that inexperienced or younger members of your staff may be quite apprehensive of the inspectors. Therefore, it is the supervisor's duty to explain their presence and to indicate the positive purposes thereof, rather than perpetuate the traditional myths of the suspicious secret police, or the rampaging destroyers of tidiness and order.

The most sensible behaviour, once the inspectors/auditors have arranged their office 'base', and set off, with your co-operation, is to get on with your job. But it does no harm to take an interest in what they are looking for, and what they are finding, as they go along. In fact, they will normally tell you, or your management, if there are items you can advantageously alter on the spot (although certain of their fathers in inspection would have cheerfully saved it for the bombshell report to your seniors: this should no longer happen).

If your management is doing its job properly, you will be involved in reading at least the directly relevant parts of the eventual inspection or internal audit reports. In the ideal world the report will be one sheet long congratulating your perfection. In the almost ideal world it will be a little longer but will contain no unpleasant surprises. What it will undoubtedly include is areas for improvement in your work, and recommendations as to methods of improvement, delivered in good faith.

Take an interest in the actual report, as good supervisors must, and make sure that you do get a sight of the next one. Now, as an exercise, ask to examine the relevant parts of the last one on your branch or office. Unless you were involved yourself, try and trace the steps taken to comply with the report's recommendations, and the changes that have taken place as a result.

ACTIVITY 7.10

Contact your inspection or internal audit department and discuss with them their checklists for good office practice.

(a) Ask them where the more common faults lie;
(b) confirm with them the location in manuals of such checklists for good practice; and then
(c) with this guidance, locate and examine the checklists.

Special inspections

Rather more dramatic by their very nature are the special inspections or non-routine investigations which have to take place because of incidents or sudden changes in circumstance. Once again the supervisor has a part to play in the effective and smooth operation of such visits, which are not relished either by the investigators or the investigated.

Your bank will have procedural guidelines to cover such eventualities. You should take this opportunity to get hold of, examine, and absorb the main points of the procedure. It will probably emphasise that the inspectors or auditor's principal task is to eliminate people from suspicion as a result of the enquiry; and to do this, unfortunately, they will have to investigate closely and thoroughly.

During the interview, inspectors may come to believe that a staff member may be personally involved, and they will notify the person of the belief, and continue the interview on a formal basis. At this point the staff member may on request be accompanied by another, possibly a union office representative, or selected colleague. This accompanying person should have been ready, and standing by, and it would be the supervisor's responsibility to make sure that all staff members knew of this rule in advance, and that contingency cover for their work is planned, to avoid delay in continuing the process if it has to happen.

You may also find that staff will be permitted to make written statements not under the eye of the inspectors/auditors. They will probably be entitled to guidance from the inspectors, from their accompanying representative or colleague, and possibly from their supervisor if they want it, as to what matters should be included.

Most importantly, you should understand and make sure you convey to your staff that the best interests of the bank are the same as the best interests of the staff, in the long run. While being vigilant that your staff are receiving fair and just treatment from the inspectors, everybody under your guidance must be very positively encouraged to co-operate in special investigations just as much as in general inspections and audits.

■ SUMMARY

In this chapter we discussed the following aspects of law and rules of supervision in banks:

1. Health and safety in general, and people's needs and rights concerning these elements of the working environment.

2. The Health and Safety at Work Act 1974:

   (a) The employer's duties, concerning premises, equipment, materials, training and information;
   (b) The supplier's duties;
   (c) The staff's responsibilities, to take care of themselves, to comply with rules, and to behave responsibly.

3. Health and safety representatives, committees, and policy statements.

4. The supervisor's formal and informal responsibilities for health and safety, and some methods of checking staff practices.

5. Branch security in banks: the supervisor's (and all staff's) responsibility to keep to the rules, or apply in writing for local variation; and the various areas in which the rules apply; for instance admittance to the branch; cash transport and delivery; entry to the safe/strongroom; cash control and movement; small branch staffing; and hostage and bomb threats.

6. Fire, bomb and raid drills.

7. What to do when you or your staff fall sick and have to be absent from the workplace.

8. The conditions of employment, often as incorporated in the Contract of Service, which in most banks will contain agreements and specifications concerning: mobility, salary, hours, holidays, illness, grievance, discipline, outside employment, notice and further documentation.

9 The Declaration of Secrecy, and the banker's obligation of honour in the matter of customer's confidentiality.

10 Employment protection: the various laws, and the ACAS Code of Practice;

11 Fair and unfair dismissal: summary dismissal, then the various grounds on which dismissal will be considered unfair, and then fair; and the role of the industrial tribunal.

12 Redundancy, as a special case of dismissal, with its own procedures.

13 Equal opportunity, relating to race/colour or sex: the law and the facts; and the supervisor's responsibilities, both under the law and in terms of a civilised society, for handling the ramifications of prejudice.

14 The supervisor, the staff, and the handling of cash:

(a) storage;
(b) delivery;
(c) movement;
(d) counting.

15 The conduct of staff accounts: the supervisor, the staff and their money affairs.

16 General inspections and audits; special investigations; the supervisor's responsibility, and effective attitudes towards, and co-operation with, the inspection and internal audit staff.

■ SELF-ASSESSMENT QUESTIONS

Try to answer these questions to remind you of the content of this chapter:

1 What are the employer's duties under the Health and Safety at Work Act?

2 What special duties do suppliers to companies have under the same Act?

3 What responsibilities do staff have to comply with the Health and Safety at Work Act?

4 What are the principal points made in your organisation's statement of policy concerning health and safety at work?

5 Think about your office situation. Is there any one practice which a purist would describe as dangerous, or unsafe, or unhealthy? What can you do about it?

6 In what areas should you be concerned with security if you work in a branch? And in what areas if in a non-branch office?

7 What do employees of your organisation have to do, according to its rules, if they are absent because of sickness?

8 Exactly what does the mobility clause in your contract say?

9 How long is the declaration of secrecy that bank staff sign binding upon them?

10 What is the motto of the Chartered Institute of Bankers? What does it mean? What is its significance for the business community in which banking operates?

11 What actions must an organisation take before dismissing an employee?

12 What is summary dismissal? On what occasions is it fair? On what grounds does your bank state that it will dismiss staff summarily?

13 How do you define fair dismissal?

14 On what grounds may an organisation simply not dismiss staff?

15 What proportion of bank staff of managerial rank are female? And what proportion of your bank's managerial staff are women?

16 What formal arrangements are there in your organisation for women who become pregnant and wish to return to work?

17 What arrangements, and what rules, are there for overnight cash storage in your office?

18 What is the principal objective of the inspection or the internal audit department?

19 Give one example of an action recommended in your office's last inspection or audit report, and recount what was done about it.

20 What rights does a staff member have if subject to a special inspection investigation?

8 Procedures

OBJECTIVES

When you have read this chapter you will be able to investigate your own organisation's procedures concerning:
- Staff representation with relation to trade union membership, and the role of the office representative;
- The relationship between the supervisor and the office representative;
- Other systems of consultation and participation;
- The formal appraisal system and its relationship with ongoing staff assessment;
- The handling of staff grievances, both informally and formally, via normal management practices and procedures;
- Discipline and the relationship between on-the-job management control and the formal system;
- The organisation's arrangements for training, and the formal role of levels of management in implementing that training;
- Procedures and rewards for entering, and for success in, professional qualification examinations;
- Mobility and the needs of the organisation and the individual: procedures and allowances;
- Other procedures: leave of absence, including pregnancy, late work, overtime, dirt allowances, meals, expenses and so on.

■ INTRODUCTION

In their capacity as first line of management, supervisors are responsible for many procedures concerning the relationship between the organisation and its employees. Staff will look to the supervisor for information on representation, formally or informally, by the union, the staff association or others. The supervisor should also be up-to-date about schemes of participative or consultative decision-making. Then there are the formal arrangements for appraisal, discipline, grievance, training, mobility, redundancy, sickness and the like. Nobody can be the complete expert in all of these; but the staff will look for information to their immediate superior, who should at least know where to lay their hands on a route-map, as it were.

The law allows for formal *staff representation*, and the sensible organisation makes special arrangements for it. Banks, for instance, have at least permitted, more normally encouraged, membership of staff associations or trade unions recognised by both sides. Supervisors should be clear on company policy as well as the arrangements for membership and payment for it. They must also be familiar with the rights and duties of the *office representatives* and how they relate with full-time union officials and the supervisors.

Then there are also informal schemes in which staff are invited to participate to one degree or another in organisational decision-making, such as in *consultation and participation* programmes, where organisations propose changes in policies or practices and call for comment on a regular basis, taking staff comment into account; or in *quality circles,* where operational staff are given responsibility for developing ways of improving customer service.

Performance appraisal schemes involve the supervisor: even when not being the appraiser, the supervisor should at least be consulted, and be familiar with the paperwork, the interpretation of the categories on it, and the procedures. Really good supervisors are sufficiently familiar with this topic to make comparisons with systems outside their own organisation, and by this and other means use the system for the improvement of staff performance rather than just complying because it is the rule to do so.

The supervisor is involved in *grievance* and *discipline procedures* at least in a consultative capacity, but usually directly. Acting in ignorance of these procedures is risky and could be damaging to all parties. Indeed there are those who would say that this is the point at which the supervisor's organisational responsibilities truly begin.

Supervisors have a formal responsibility in terms of the organisation's provision of *training* and how it is obtained. Resources are rarely unlimited, and there are rules and procedures for when staff are entitled to training, depending on experience, grade or status, location, order in precedence and so on. There are also rules for the monitoring of the effectiveness of training. Since supervisors have first responsibility for discerning training needs and recommending how they will be fulfilled, they must be familiar with these rules.

Few organisations in what are referred to as professions do not encourage their members to enter for, study towards and pass examinations in their profession, via such bodies as the Chartered Institute of Bankers. There are regulations as to who is eligible, for leave, loans, rewards and expenses.

There are occasions on which any large organisations require their staff to move to another location where their work will be more valuable. We naturally take for granted that they would make arrangements for the staff at least to suffer no loss when this happens, that they are compensated for the disruption. The requirement of *mobility* is not confined to senior staff, and supervisors should be familiar with the main provisions of their company's schemes.

Finally, there are other company procedures concerning such topics as leave of absence, pregnancy leave, dirt allowances, late work and overtime, etc. It is clearly in the supervisor's responsibility, as well as interest, to know about these.

■ STAFF REPRESENTATION

It is not within the scope of this book to detail the whole of the industrial relations structure of the UK, nor even of the banks; but in the spirit of all the foregoing, rather to call your attention to a list of topics, about which you should know the details concerning your own office.

There are a few things that all the banks have in common as employers, i.e. they are happy to have their staff represented by bodies set up for the purpose, such as trade unions or staff associations; and in the normal course of business, they have always been happy to negotiate with those bodies. They have set up their own joint bodies for negotiation; they work within the letter and spirit of the law; and they behave in the usual spirit of constructive conflict that usually characterises British industrial relations.

Various bodies represent banking staff: the Banking, Insurance and Finance Union (BIFU), which also has members who are not in banks, and is affiliated to the Trades Union Congress; the Clearing Banks Union (CBU), which has only bankers as members, is not affiliated to the TUC, and is really a loose confederation of the staff associations of various banks; the Association of Scientific, Technical and Managerial Staff (ASTMS), largely only in one clearing bank; and other bank staff associations which are not or are only tenuously connected with the CBU.

Until the late 1980s, most collective bargaining was done nationally between joint bodies representing bankers in general on one side and the employers on the other (although there was some wrangling between BIFU and CBU and separate talks often had to take place).

Since then national negotiation has broken up, and domestic, i.e. bank for bank, negotiation is the norm. Each individual bank negotiates with whichever body it considers to represent its staff; and while conditions of employment and wages do not differ very much among banks, nevertheless the agreements reached are in the nature of individual agreements.

Staff look to training and personnel departments to give them formal information on where they stand and what happens in such negotiations; and whether or not to join a union or staff association should be their free choice in the light of the fullest information they can get.

A majority of bank staff are members of, and are protected and represented by, staff corporate bodies and pay a subscription. Any decision not to join must therefore be in the light of the fact that staff benefit from the efforts of the officials of these bodies whether or not they join.

ACTIVITY 8.1

As supervisor, you should know exactly what the staff representation situation is in your bank. So ...

(a) Which union or association has most members in your bank?
(b) Are there any other unions or associations with members in your bank?
(c) Which of these unions or associations are recognised by your bank?
(d) What is the annual subscription?
(e) In what ways and over what period can it be paid?
(f) How can you get more, and official, information direct from the union or association?

■ OFFICE REPRESENTATIVES

There are two kinds of people who can represent staff in negotiation with the management of an organisation, in the context of local or low-level discussions or of domestic matters: first, full-time paid employees of the union, often known as *union officials;* and second, full-time employees of the organisation who are given time and allowances by the employer to serve that purpose and provide an on-the-spot service for the staff, usually known as shop stewards. Work out for yourself why they are not called that in banking but, where they exist, are called *office representatives.*

Certainly in banks where BIFU is recognised, there is a well-established structure of office representatives, elected to 'constituencies', which usually are a group of sections in large offices, or a medium-sized office, or a group of small offices. There will be an agreement as to office representation, and you should obtain it and read it carefully. In particular, as supervisor, you should find out what the bank and the union or staff association have agreed should be the office representative's official rights, duties and functions.

Office representatives are the staff's first recourse after they have failed to solve a problem themselves, and subsequently with management. The office representative will then take it up on their behalf, either directly with management or first with the union official and then with management. In grievance, disciplinary or special inspection procedures, where the staff may be accompanied or represented, it will often be by the office representative.

The office representative also has a responsibility for vigilance concerning the terms and conditions of employment and the carrying out of agreed procedures; and to represent their constituency on office representatives committees.

The supervisor and the office representative

From the above you can see that the supervisor and the office representative could have overlap in their functions, if from different points of view; and they could have official contact at one point or another.

If all is trouble-free in the office, then you may never need to know how an office representative works, because the staff will not need recourse to being represented; and the office representative who is well-trained and properly orientated, will certainly not want to be 'activated'. However, a good supervisor will take some actions in advance of trouble.

For example, see if you already know or can discover the identity of the office representative for your office. Arrange an official meeting simply to establish contact and talk about office representation and relationships with supervisors. If both find it of possible value, you could diary for, say, monthly chats about the office and the staff.

A brief conversation ought to establish a good relationship including the exchange of information on attitudes and personal policies for the welfare of staff, so that any future problems of an official nature can at least be dealt with on a reasonable basis, and not between complete strangers. Should there be any need for an official relationship at all, you should be aiming for one of the type that exists between colleagues, and not between rivals or antagonists. You could privately record the arrangement, content, tone and conclusions of this meeting, for your own interest and as an anecdote for use in a possible examination answer.

The benefits of staff representation

ACTIVITY 8.2

As a final activity on the subject of staff representation, think through the benefits and drawbacks to both employers and staff of properly organised staff representation by filling in an expanded version of the chart below.

	Benefits	Drawbacks
To employers		
To staff		

If you have not cheated and looked at the following list, congratulate yourself if your list looks something like this.

Benefits to employer

- Unions/staff associations speak for the majority.
- Ability to talk to/negotiate with a single or small number of bodies.
- Wide membership includes larger moderate element.
- Unions/staff associations co-operate in discipline.
- Proper procedures enable stable wage-planning.
- Staff enjoy sense of justice.
- Influential channel of communication to staff.

Benefits to staff

- More powerful body to right injustices.
- More powerful body to negotiate wages/conditions.
- Union/staff association provide staff with time to negotiate.
- Representation in grievance and discipline matters.
- Forum for free expression of views on employment.

Drawbacks to employer

- Possibility of higher-cost wage settlements.
- Staff organised to withhold labour (strike, work to rule).
- Possible confrontational attitudes.
- Necessity to set up negotiation mechanisms for staff.
- Restrictions on freedom of staff deployment.
- Loss of management 'power'.

Drawbacks to staff:
- Cost of subscription.
- Benefits available in any case, without membership.
- 'Image' (especially in banking).
- Worries about effects on career.
- Problems of isolation in low-membership areas.

■ STAFF CONSULTATION AND PARTICIPATION SCHEMES

Quite separately from official union or staff association negotiations, the bank and its staff may wish to have a forum in which matters of mutual interest can be discussed, and whereby staff views can be conveyed to management, and management ideas put to staff, with no threatening or binding elements. You may recall discussion in Chapter 2 of consultative styles of management, where decisions are taken in the light of, but not bound by, staff opinion. Most British banks adopt that as a style policy (or make statements to that effect).

At least one clearing bank has instituted a system of quarterly consultative meetings, where topics suggested by management, together with any topics staff may wish to raise, are discussed by office-based groups at a meeting, and the minuted resolutions and recommendations are sifted and collated by a body representing all divisions and departments. A digest is then sent to the executive, indicating such actions taken to fulfil the resolutions.

ACTIVITY 8.3

Find out any details of any such scheme in your bank, and check whether or not they still operate, and if so when (and if not, why?).

■ QUALITY CIRCLES

Quality circles, or quality control circles, have been operated with varying measures of success in British industry and commerce. They originated in Japan, where high quality at a low price has been the genuine aim of industry for many years.

Essentially a quality circle consists of a small group of people, say, 6–10, who meet to discuss, analyse and implement ways of improving the product or service they are involved with. The group may have a leader or chairperson, and there will be a facilitator or trainer to check on their group harmony, and techniques, and liaison with outside people.

Their objectives are simple: to improve the product or service on which they work, by study, analysis, discussion and the pooling of their creativity, skills and technical knowledge.

They are given a range of problems to attack, from which they select the one(s) on which they want to work. They go through a problem-solving process from the setting of objectives, through the gathering and analysis of data, via the consideration of alternative solutions, and to selection. They then recommend their solution to management.

Whether under this name or another, quality circles have been tried in banks. They are being discussed here because, not only do they have the main aim of improving quality, but they also have the additional objective of involving the staff, with theoretically motivational results, in the bank's decision-making (as part of a consultative style); and where it has been introduced, it has been as part of a major bank scheme, with procedures attached.

As supervisor, you could quite easily not be a member of a quality circle operating in your area, because normally management is the recipient of, and not a contributor, to the ideas. The point is to let them get on with it. As management, you would probably have the following duties:

1 to implement as well as you can, and in the spirit of the scheme, such procedures and guidelines as have been laid down by the bank; and however you may personally feel, to indicate your positive support for the scheme and its intentions to the staff;
2 to facilitate the time, space, personnel and resources that the circle may need to get on with the creative/analytical task;
3 to listen to the eventual ideas positively and interestedly.

Remember that creative ideas are by definition unusual, new, even revolutionary!
4 to make such efforts as are in your power to pass the recommendations on to where they will be heard, and to do, and be seen to do, all in your power to get them implemented.

Note that some of them can be totally within your power: the quality circle is encouraged to develop local solutions to problems; and if you are receptive to ideas, and there is one you can put into effect within your own jurisdiction, do it.

There are two major ways in which quality circle schemes can be allowed to peter out and eventually fail, and unfortunately they are easy to do: one is to fail to reward the creative efforts in any way – the simple idealistic satisfaction of seeing the fruits of our creativity implemented, and that our company is a better place as a result of it, is really not enough to keep us at it.

The second is even easier: failing to implement any of our suggestions in the first round you don't get many in the second round, and we don't even come to the third meeting.

The idea of quality circles is obviously sensible and valuable, and if there is success or failure, this is very largely due to top management commitment and behaviour. Well-designed and well-run schemes must fulfil the twin objectives of productivity and motivation.

If your organisation has such a system, your supervisors' duty, however well or badly the company's scheme is designed, is to be the local expert on its mechanics even if you are not a member of the quality circle, and unfailingly to fulfil the functions allocated to you, with the aim of improving productivity.

ACTIVITY 8.4

If your bank has ever engaged in a customer care programme or the like, quality circles would probably have formed part of the scheme.

(a) Describe 'your' quality circle: what was it called, and in general what was its purpose?
(b) How was it structured? Was there a chairperson? Did it have a formal relationship with local management/the organisation?
(c) What were its specific objectives?
(d) It will have achieved successes. What were they, and what were the reasons for them?
(e) It will have had failures. What were they, and what were the reasons for them?

■ PERFORMANCE APPRAISAL

We now come to a set of procedures which are central to the career progress of those who would move up through an organisation, and to the whole of the job of those who are in jobs at levels at which they are satisfied, namely, the performance appraisal or assessment system.

Every bank has a different appraisal system and possibly even different names for it, and certainly different sets of forms.

ACTIVITY 8.5

(a) Obtain a complete set of appraisal forms, and preferably also a copy of any instructions and guidelines, and such procedures manual material as you can assemble.
(b) Ideally, study this chapter further in the company of a friend or colleague from a different bank to see how the systems differ. What we will ask you to do is to compare and contrast (a good school phrase which means look at what is similar between what we are about to say and your system, and what is different about it).

This activity is important because your and your friend's documentation will bear out what has been said in the introduction to this book, which is that the best textbook in this subject is bank documentation.

Let us now see if we can highlight some points to increase your understanding of the whole matter of appraisal. We shall look at the objectives of appraisal, and typical content of an appraisal system; then, go on to discuss how appraisals can be carried out well or badly and look at problems, and finally at the supervisor's possible roles.

The objectives of appraisal

There are at least three sets of objectives for appraisal:

- those of the organisation;
- those of the person appraising; and
- those of the person being appraised.

1 The *organisation* has a manpower plan which it needs to keep up-to-date, and

it can get a good deal of information from the incoming appraisals as to everybody's position and status. It needs also to review its stock of talent, and who is now trained to do what and who has developed new skills or characteristics. It must have sufficient information for promotions and moves, i.e. the current state of people's readiness and willingness to move and advance. It needs to be able to diagnose and anticipate problems of staffing at certain levels, or in certain geographical areas, or in certain departments or functions. It may need to adjust provisions made for training, or premises, or service, or welfare, or other resources, based on information received centrally as the appraisals come in.

2 The *appraiser*, as a member of local management, must sound out staff's attitudes and feelings about their work. They need to motivate individual members of staff to their best efforts. They must adjust training provision in the branch or office to maintain the current work standards at their best. They need to solve problems or grievances which might not be raised except at the occasion of an appraisal. They should wish to review their own performance and will be able to gauge this in the expression of the appraised.

3 The *staff being appraised* wish to obtain feedback about their competence to do their current job, and future jobs, as currently judged by their managers. They want to remind the management of their own achievements, just in case they have been forgotten! They may need to suggest, or remind management of, needed or even promised career moves, extra responsibilities, changes in duties. They will need to express their own views on their performance and its qualities, and reasons for possible shortfall. They will have the objective of obtaining guidance on improvements they can make in their performance. They may aim to obtain some reassurance at least, and motivation at best, to continue to want to do a good job, or to improve to a better one for everybody's sake.

Is yours a good or a poor appraisal system?

ACTIVITY 8.6

(a) Does your appraisal system have a set of (stated) objectives?
(b) What is your initial feeling about whether it satisfied the objectives?
(c) How do the objectives compare with the ones you find above?

Note that we are really not talking yet about whether the appraisal system works; this depends on its objectives, its structure and its implementation, as we shall see.

The elements of an appraisal system

What are the bare essentials of a sensible appraisal system? We shall suggest a list of essentials here. Check whether yours has each element, and you may like to look for gaps. It is more likely that yours will have extra elements not noted in this checklist; if so, add a marginal note to this effect, stating what are those extra elements.

Most appraisal systems have:

1 a form on which the manager will make written comments on performance, including some element of 'scoring' certain skills, abilities, characteristics or elements of performance;
2 an interview to discuss what is written on the form, and other matters of performance over the specified period;
3 the right, and a system, for the appraised to comment on what has been said on the report, in writing, on the form itself;
4 a separate right to contact central personnel to appeal or comment on what management have written on the form;
5 a written self-appraisal component, usually a separate form, handed to the appraiser;
6 a compulsory annual periodicity;
7 a voluntary interim appraisal in special circumstances;
8 different formats, and elements appraised, at different levels in the organisation.

Some systems require the filled-in form to be handed to the recipient before the interview, so that they may formulate ideas and comment, say, 24 hours in advance. Some systems are directly related to salary review; some are quite deliberately set at a different time of the year with strict instructions that the thoughts of performance review/improvement, and remuneration, are separated.

Aspects of the appraisal form

Appraisal forms contain several major sections: one on which there is confirmation of a number of *personal details* useful for information, such as age, date of birth, grade, length of service, health record, family circumstances and the like.

Then there is a section concerning *elements of performance*, with a scored section on which number or letter gradings assess a number of qualities employed on the job, sometimes accompanied by an open comment section.

There is a section which concerns *personal* or *career development*, with recommendations as to future moves, promotions, or career changes in the longer run, and added or changed responsibility, and courses or other training, in the shorter term, or other suggested future actions.

Finally there will be a section in which the person appraised can make *written response*, comments on what has been said, usually open in the sense of being simply an unguided space to do this.

ACTIVITY 8.7

Look at your forms, and/or any other you have available, identify the areas suggested above and note any different or additional ones.

Performance areas and qualities assessed

It would not be possible to delineate here all the possible qualities which might appear on your bank's appraisal forms. They ought, however, to fall generally into two main areas: *personal qualities and characteristics,* which have to do with abilities and behaviour and appearance and manner, and so on; and *performance and achievement,* not how the staff are but what they have done over the last appraised period, or can do, or can now do that they have not been able to do.

ACTIVITY 8.8

(a) See if your qualities fall into these categories.
(b) Are they deliberately so divided?
(c) Or do they so divide, but the categories are mixed into each other?
(d) Investigate the availability of instructions and definitions. (Are you sure that you know what is meant by 'leadership', 'initiative', 'adaptability', 'persuasiveness', 'manner' or even 'appearance'?)

Problems with appraisal

For the supervisor to get a clear picture of the appraisal system, we ought to face the fact that appraisal also has its problems. Some of the criticisms levelled against what has now become a traditional element of commercial life, are as follows:

1 An annual appraisal is too infrequent. Managers forget what you did even months ago, and only really appraise you on the last three. Therefore, a good appraiser ought to keep a confidential diary to record of good performance points over the whole period.
2 Continuous appraisal is the mark of the good manager, so there is not much point if all the annual session does is to confirm what has been said all year round; it can be a waste of time. However, what it does is focus exclusive and direct attention on the person appraised.
3 Appraisals suffer from personal bias. It can hardly be denied that to a certain extent, however small, grades and comments depend on personal relationships. Appraisers should guard against it and be vigilant with themselves, cross-checking with colleagues when biased in favour of or against a person.
4 Graders mark differently. You can suffer from 'hard' markers, or even known 'soft' markers. You can get a lower score for a better performance one year than the last, just because of a change of marker; personnel departments must, and usually do, know who is hard and who is a soft marker.
5 Beware the 'halo-effect': if a candidate is good in one area they will be marked well in others.
6 Appraisers are neither necessarily competent or well-trained. The best organisations include appraisal training on management courses, or offer special appraisal training to those who need it. Find out what your organisation does in this line.

The supervisor and appraisal

Appraisals should obviously be conducted by people who are entirely familiar with the people being appraised. On the other hand, they should be done by someone with the rank commensurate with being able to put whatever is planned and decided into effect. This can cause difficulties, since in most cases the person who knows the appraised staff member and the performance best is a supervisor who is not of sufficient rank to be permitted to do the appraisal.

Regrettably, the power/status argument tends to take precedence, and this is a quite legitimate practice in a hierarchical organisation. However, the best systems allow for, indeed insist on, consultation between the official who conducts the appraisal, and the supervisor closest to the work; thus the best way of carrying out this consultation is for the official to allow the supervisor to draft or pencil in the appraisal form, before the official finalises it in discussion with that supervisor.

If you want to be involved, as you should, and you want to make your contributions to discussions as suggested above to be worthwhile, you should record events during the year, and keep a constant eye on the performance of your staff, as if you were going to do their appraisals yourself.

Good supervisors stoutly defend the right to be involved in their staff's appraisals. Give thought now to your own involvement; discuss any changes you would like to see in that process with your superiors and record the responses.

■ GRIEVANCE AND DISCIPLINE

In any human organisation there will be times when the individual is unhappy about the organisation (will entertain a grievance) and when the organisation is not satisfied with the behaviour of the individual (will need to apply discipline). In banks there are properly laid down procedures to handle both types of situation.

It is important that distinction should be made between formal and informal discipline and grievance procedures. In the great majority of cases, grievances and disciplinary matters can and should be dealt with locally, informally, and in the normal course of business, by a complaint to the supervisor or local management on the one hand, or by a telling-off or other corrective actions directed at the staff member on the other.

Now, what do you know about the formalities of the grievance and disciplinary procedures in your bank? In fact, you can go through the whole of your career without ever having either direct or indirect experience of either of the formal procedures in question. However, it is best for supervisors to have generally familiarised themselves with them, so as to make the process as smooth as possible, in the unfortunate event of the formal procedures arising.

The formal procedures will only ever be invoked after it has become locally impossible to deal with the problem. These procedures exist to ensure fair treatment for both parties in the extreme cases in which they are appropriate. It should be made clear, and in writing, the object of the procedure and then a number of carefully specified steps should be taken.

Ideal grievance and disciplinary procedures

Before we examine the differences between them, and the steps taken within them, we should look at some requirements for such procedures to be really satisfactory. These should be:

(a) written, they will be complex and detailed;
(b) clear and understandable, with clear rules of progress;
(c) logically constructed with one step leading to the next;
(d) progressive, leading to higher levels in the bank;
(e) time-limited, to deal quickly and efficiently with the problem;
(f) allowing for either party to be represented by union or association;
(g) equipped with appeal procedures after decision.

In addition, grievance procedures should be:

(a) easily accessible to anyone with a grievance;
(b) specific in who can deal with what sort of grievance.

Disciplinary procedures should also have additional qualities. They should be:

(a) according to the ACAS Code of Practice discussed on page 145;
(b) fair and seen to be fair to all parties;
(c) clear about what steps come next, in what period of time;
(d) specific in what behaviours are/are not permitted, what penalties attach to what misdemeanour, what disciplinary powers lie where;
(e) permitting the time and the means for the correction of the cause of the discipline.

Try to find out all you can of the grievance and disciplinary procedures in your bank, their nature and general provisions. If they are any good you should be able to do this easily! It would also be of enormous value if you could work with a colleague in another bank, or any other organisation sophisticated enough to have such procedures, and compare notes. Since they will probably follow the ACAS Code of Practice, they should not be highly confidential.

Study them carefully and give thought to their qualities in the light of the above suggestions as to the ideal systems (they will more than probably comply; and you may be well-advised to tell your superiors why you are doing this). As you study them, make brief notes so that you could reproduce the steps to be taken if you had to explain them to anyone else. You might have to explain the essence in an examination answer; you may, sadly, have to explain them to anyone who is having to go through them; or even to your management.

The grounds and the steps

Whatever else you know about, you should be familiar with the grounds on which the disciplinary procedure may be invoked, and the steps it goes through.

The grounds are likely to involve poor performance on the one hand, and misconduct on the other. The latter will be divided into ordinary misconduct, such as insolence or dressing inappropriately or persistent lateness; then financial misconduct, misusing bank accounts or staff loans, at a minor level; then gross misconduct, serious breaches of bank rules, or security, or any criminal conduct related to bank affairs.

The stages through which disciplinary procedures go, after the first local attempt to correct the behaviour involved, will be via verbal warning from management (and the person involved must be told that it is a warning under the procedure, and not just a general telling-off); then if there is no improvement, a written warning, sometimes with an accompanying formal interview, of which there should be written notice, and at which the staff member may be accompanied by a union representative or another colleague. Clear instructions must be given as to how to improve performance. After this, if there is still no improvement, downgrading or dismissal will be among the choices open to the employer.

ACTIVITY 8.9

Check and note:

(a) The grounds on which disciplinary procedures may be applied in your organisation.
(b) The grounds on which a staff member may invoke the grievance procedure.
(c) The steps in each type of procedure in your organisation.

Grievance, discipline and the supervisor

By definition, when these procedures are invoked, things have come to a very serious point; and it is absolutely essential, if you are involved as supervisor, to comply meticulously and completely with every detail of the procedures, keeping a record in writing for the sake of the procedure where it is required, and for your own sake where it is not.

Whatever the range of your loyalties may be, they will include the staff member involved, your section, your employer, your profession and yourself. At this point, all are best served by the correct application of the procedures.

You may not be directly involved at all in the formalities. In this case, if it is one of your staff involved, then remember that compassion is permitted within the grievance or disciplinary steps; and that they may look to you to keep them informed of their formal situation.

For this, if for no other reason, you should be knowledgeable and accurate about your organisation's procedures.

■ TRAINING PROCEDURES

To a large extent we have covered the topic of the supervisor's managerial responsibility for training in Chapter 4. However, we did not at that time look at procedures for obtaining training facilities, handling periods when staff are away on training courses, and the monitoring, evaluation and use of trained skills as a formal activity; and we shall now address those issues.

Remember that we did apportion a good deal of the responsibility for Lucy's training to Lucy's supervisor or immediate superior. Having the right philosophy, in accepting that responsibility is not enough: actually making use of its must also take place.

Obtaining training

Your organisation will have taken its own responsibility for providing training, or at least *making training offers*. What do we mean by this phrase? Of course where you will find such a set of offers will be in documentation held by, or preferably published to, staff by personnel or training departments.

It will be in the form of a manual or booklet or descriptive list of materials and courses and other facilities offered. In some companies, only management have access to this descriptive list (let's call it the 'training guide'); but ideally everyone should be able to consult it; and you as supervisor, should in any case have access to it on request.

Since we are now going to assume that such a document exists and that you have access to it, the following few sections will be more effective if you now obtain your equivalent of the training guide and read these sections in conjunction with it; though you can proceed without it, if necessary.

What should this offer document include? Let us pass through the statements of policy and intention, and go to the part on what training is appropriate to what stage of the career, because in sophisticated organisations, training is progressive, and the higher you are, the more complex it is. There should also be some form of guide as to how to find appropriate courses by topic or banking area.

Now let us look at what are necessary details on each item of training. Whatever form it takes, the following should appear:

1 A sensible *name* or *title* which accurately, though briefly, describes what it is. Most importantly it should not be ambiguous. It can be embarrassing if you ask for an entirely inappropriate course because the title gives you the wrong impression of its content;
2 A statement which determines the *level* or other appropriate qualification for the training, including details of *previous experience* or training necessary (don't ask for Part II before Part I);
3 A set of *training objectives* must be included, i.e. what is it for, what training effect should there be, what should the candidate be able to do/should know about, by the end of the training experience?
4 A good clear *outline of content*, to clarify and orient both the candidate and the supervisor/manager;
5 A description of any *preparation* or pre-training requirements or experiences might be included;
6 *Supervisory requirements*, if any, after the training, might be specified, such as necessary on-the-job post-training experiences, or feedback to candidate or trainers of training effectiveness;
7 *Instructions for access* to, or the obtaining of, the training must appear here

or at a clearly directed place in the training guide. There could also be an indication of how long after requesting the training it is likely to be available, so that you can plan more accurately.

There should also be a consultation facility, whereby anyone responsible for training should be able to talk to the trainers and get some explanation or clarification of any of those points in person or by telephone.

ACTIVITY 8.10

Obtain any documents you can on the training available to your staff. For any individual item of training, check whether it has the features suggested in the list above.

■ PLANNING FOR TRAINING

There are a number of simple physical steps to take which will make training much more effective. They are connected with planning for the training period, getting the trainee tuned in to the training, and the encouragement of pre-training activities. While much of this will apply to any kind of training, we shall centre it on off-the-job courses.

Planning

If you have charted a succession of timed training experiences for your staff, as suggested in Chapter 4, you will have planned for their absence and for cover during that period.

Provided that such experiences are well shared out, and your staff understand the benefit to all of a well-trained staff, they will willingly and mutually make covering efforts. While one of your staff is out, your own supervisory vigilance, and ability to 'pitch in', will also be put to the test.

Orientation

It is not professional for managers to arrange to send people on training courses, and then forget about that fact until the time that the course starts ('Oh you're on a course next week – good luck') though it is only too common.

Time should be set aside to discuss with the candidate the objectives, the 'training gap' (the difference between what you need to be able to do and what you can do now), the content of the course, and what will happen on return. Staff who believe that the course is important, not just to them but to their management, must be better 'turned on' to the training.

Preparation

Sometimes in the training manual or as part of the joining instructions, there is the recommendation to do certain pre-course activities, such as watching the activity to be trained, or trying out part of it, or doing some reading or programmed text work.

Most people invited to do this pre-training work are very keen to do it, but can be faced with one obstacle or another; some would quite like to do it; some cannot be bothered. In each case, encouragement from the supervisor is essential; and in some cases, the work cannot be done unless the supervisor makes it possible, rearranges schedules, obtains necessary permissions or co-operation, obtains resources or material, etc.

Supervisors should find out for each piece of training that their staff undertake whether there are any such preparatory activities, and what they are; and they should see it as part of their job, part of their duty, not just to enable but to ensure and check that it is done. It would not have been suggested if it were not a good idea, and can even be so essential that the training will be very much less effective without it.

In the interests, therefore, of bringing the work of the section to its best possible pitch, you should see to it that candidates are properly prepared, as well as properly orientated, to the training.

■ AFTER TRAINING

Look again at what was said about the learning cycle in Chapter 4 (*see* page 75). People need to learn in adult life by feeling, watching, thinking and doing, and unless they think about the training on return to the office, and try it out, it will simply fade. People talk of 'closing the training loop', and this is done very soon after the training experience.

There are really three simple phases to the proper completion of training on return: debriefing, exercise/monitoring and feedback.

Debriefing

'Ah, you're back: there's your in-tray – get on with it'. Is this an exaggerated summary of the normal attitude? It is a caricature of the poor management reaction to training, and it certainly is not unknown. The effect it has is to kill the training stone dead.

People usually return from training at least motivated to try new and improved work methods, and certainly ready to talk about them. Time should be diaried in advance, and set aside, to discuss all aspects of the training with the candidates on their return, and to plan their introduction to the use of the new skill and knowledge.

Indeed they should know that this form of debriefing is the normal practice for anyone, on the first day back from the training, or after completion of any training activity.

Exercising the skills

Clearly implied by all of the above is the need to try out the new skills. This should have been planned for, and should, under pressure from the supervisor, take place almost immediately. The early performance should be closely under review, and corrections fed back, positively and encouragingly, as the work progresses (this is called *positive reinforcement*, for obvious reasons, and is a very effective learning tool).

Gradually, and carefully, the monitoring should be reduced until the training is fully effective. Please realise that this is not just the act of kindness of a mature supervisor, but a central part of the supervisor's job.

Feedback to training personnel

Nobody can complain about the quality of training unless they have contributed to that quality by letting trainers know about the effectiveness of training. In most cases there are formal feedback methods, such as forms which the candidate, and sometimes the supervisors, must fill in and return. You should at least ensure that this is done by your staff, e.g. by diarying to check its return, say, a week after the course, or at whatever period is specified.

To the good supervisor it is also more effective, when training does not seem to work so well, to contact and discuss this with the training department, than to mutter to themselves and colleagues and staff about it. If this is done in a reasonable manner and spirit, it is welcomed by trainers who want to improve staff performance as much as line management do.

■ PROFESSIONAL QUALIFICATIONS

Modern organisations understand that the training they provide in-house may be insufficient as the staff move upwards in their career, and that there are professional organisations and institutes which can add supplementary education to help staff to take a further interest, and to become qualified, in their work. These institutions set industry-wide standards confirmed by examination systems.

Banks are in the forefront of companies encouraging this professional qualification. You will somewhere find a statement that there is encouragement and support, some of it financial, to obtain professional qualifications. This does not just apply to banking as a subject, but to whatever qualifications are appropriate to the work, such as personnel, or accounting, or marketing and the like. Indeed you may find that the path to training, management development or promotion is smoothed by qualification, or even blocked without it.

Principally banks favour the qualifications offered by the Chartered Institute of Bankers, which operates at three main levels: the Banking Certificate, followed by the Banking Diploma and Associateship of the Chartered Institute, and finally at advanced level, the Financial Studies Diploma. You can find out details of these via easily obtainable documentation from the Institute or your training department.

But you should also be familiar with the procedural process whereby the banks tangibly encourage participation.

ACTIVITY 8.11

Find out what your bank's procedures are for:

(a) study leave and study loans;
(b) expenses for attending examinations;
(c) leave for examinations and refresher courses;
(d) gratuities and rewards for success;
(e) consequences of becoming qualified.

It would be for your own as well as for your staff's sake that you are fully aware of these rules and procedures – and rewards!

■ MOBILITY AND CHANGES OF LOCATION

In at least one bank's terms and conditions of employment, very near the beginning of the document, there appears the following sentence:
'Members of staff must be prepared to serve at any office or subsidiary company of the bank, where bank terms and conditions apply, in the UK including the Channel Islands and the Isle of Man.'
Literally, this means that the bank can send you or your staff anywhere they like, and if you refuse to go, you are in breach of contract. In fact no bank would forcibly move anyone, nor would they invoke this clause except in the most unusual or extreme circumstances; and it is practically unknown for them to do this, because quite obviously the damaging effect of this force would negate any positive effect the move was to have.

Your organisation will have clear rules concerning mobility. We shall not go into them in detail here, because they will be found in your staff manuals, and may differ from organisation to organisation. However, you should examine them and become familiar with their main points, simply because, once again, the first person a staff member is entitled to look to for knowledge and guidance is their immediate superior.

There will be details concerning the following:

1 who can be moved, and at what level;
2 legitimate reasons for moving people;
3 details concerning house sale and purchase:

(a) house purchase loans;
(b) improvement loans;
(c) advertising expenses;
(d) house search visit expenses;
(e) bridging finance;

4 rules concerning taking out equity or proceeds from the house sale;
5 separate rules for non-house-owners, including temporary hotel accommodation and the like; and rent differential;
6 expenses of removal, including:

(a) removals company;
(b) replacements;
(c) travel for candidate;
(d) travel for family;
(e) insurance;

7 additional payments for re-settling/inconvenience;
8 expenses for new/different living conditions;
9 rules and concessions for initial period after move;
10 allowances or concessions for return visits.

ACTIVITY 8.12

(a) Check for the presence of all these in your own company's scheme and add to the list if necessary.
(b) Note the specific rules, details and amounts in your organisation.
(c) Write some notes as if you expected to have to explain this matter to a staff member.

■ OTHER PROCEDURES

If a number of other procedures are collected together under this heading, it is not because they are to be consigned to an unimportant status. Whatever procedure you or a member of your staff is involved in, is vital at the time. For example, we shall not deal here in detail with organisational arrangements for the handling of maternity leave though that is very important to the person in question!

The reason is that many other procedures relate to benefits available to bank staff, which we will deal with in Chapter 8, or to special categories of people, rather than the whole staff body, or that there is too much detail to cover concerning very rarely used procedures. For all of those miscellaneous procedures, the least you need to know is that they exist, and it would be preferable if you had at least read them, and knew of the general principles involved in their operation.

It is quite remarkable, for instance, how many headings you would find under, say, the Maternity Absence entry in your staff or personnel procedures documentation: probably some or all of the following, which you can check in the contents section of the documentation:

1 advice of impending absence;
2 work during pregnancy;
3 child care arrangements;
4 intending to return to work;
5 not intending to return to work;
6 eligibility for leave;
7 notice of return to work;
8 right, and loss of right, to return;

9 illness absence in pregnancy;
10 maternity pay;
11 timetable of pregnancy leave;
12 postponing return date;
13 state benefits;
14 time off for ante-natal care;
15 time off for post-natal care;
16 jobs and amended conditions on return.

There are procedures for overtime, Christmas parties, gifts from customers, retirement – and retirement parties! – leave for jury service, your wills and executorships, attendance at conferences and shows, the company tie and scarf, change of name, club subscriptions, fire precautions and compassionate leave, etc.

You name any conceivable aspect of human activity with any remote connection with your organisation, and there will be a procedure for it! The index to the Royal Bank of Scotland's Staff section of the Procedures Manual is twenty-three pages long!

ACTIVITY 8.13
Look at the index in your own bank's staff procedures manual: for your own amusement make some notes about a procedure for an event which you really did not expect to find in such a manual!

Many of the procedures, happily, refer to the packages of rewards and benefits available to members of staff. These merit, and therefore have allocated, the following and final chapter of this book.

■ SUMMARY

In this chapter we have discussed the following aspects of bank procedures:

1 Staff representation and the unions and staff associations which represent bank staff.

2 The role and function of the office representative, a sort of banking shop steward; and the difference between their role and that of the full-time union official.

3 The supervisor and the office representative, and the interface between their relative roles, and the need for co-operation.

4 Consultation and participation in organisational decision-making, apart from formal negotiation procedures.

5 The nature and function of quality circles, in making suggestions for improving service, and in having those suggestions implemented, and recognised; and the role of the supervisor as first-line management, facilitating the work of the circle and pressing their case.

6 The performance appraisal system: its objectives, for
   (a) the organisation;
   (b) the appraiser/local management;
   (c) the person appraised.

7 The elements of a sound appraisal system:
   (a) the form;
   (b) the interview;
   (c) the right to comment;
   (d) the self appraisal;
   (e) the frequency.

8 The appraisal form; elements assessed and the system of marking and comment; staff notes of guidance.

9 Grievance and discipline procedures: the different but complementary nature of formal and informal processes.

10 Ideal procedures: written, clear, logical, progressive, time-limited, permitting representation, having appeal mechanisms, accessible.

11 The grounds for setting the disciplinary procedure in motion; and the stages through which it goes.

12 The supervisor's role in the implementation of the formal procedures either of discipline or grievance.

13 Training: obtaining training for your staff, and the way training offerings are described in guides or manuals:
   (a) the title;
   (b) the level;
   (c) the objectives;
   (d) the content;
   (e) pre- and post-training requirements;
   (f) instructions for access.

14 Planning for the absence of staff on courses; and the supervisor's responsibility for preparing the candidate for training.

15 The supervisor and the trainee after the training: debriefing, and the early exercise of newly-acquired skills, knowledge and techniques.

16 Mobility and changes of location: the details of bank procedures and benefits to those whom the bank wishes to move.

17 Other bank procedures and the importance of supervisory staff knowing about access to information about them.

■ SELF-ASSESSMENT QUESTIONS

Try to answer these questions to remind you of the content of this chapter:

1 Find a statement by your bank concerning its attitude towards trades union or staff association membership. What does it say?

2   Which bodies does your organisation recognise for negotiation on behalf of the staff?

3   What is the difference between a union official and an office representative or shop steward?

4   What are the principal duties of the office representative?

5   Does your organisation have a system of staff consultation other than via the union or staff association? How does it operate?

6   What is the principal function of a quality circle?

7   What are the objectives of an appraisal system, from the organisation's point of view?

8   What are the objectives of an appraisal system, from the individual's point of view?

9   What are some of the main problems and difficulties associated with a formal appraisal system?

10 What steps does your organisation take to train people specifically to conduct appraisals?

11 What is the difference between the informal and the formal disciplinary procedure?

12 What would be a set of specifications for good grievance or disciplinary procedures?

13 On what grounds may your organisation's disciplinary procedure be started?

14 State as closely as you can the training objectives of at least two training courses offered by your organisation.

15 Exactly how would you have to arrange, according to your bank's procedures, for one of your staff to attend a course? Write down each step.

16 What is the best way of getting staff to have the correct orientation towards a course before they go on it?

17 How can supervisors ensure that the best use is made of training; and that the training department maintains high training standards?

18 What are the three main levels of qualifications offered by the Chartered Institute of Bankers or the equivalent institution regulating your industry?

19 What different terms are offered for *house purchase* for those asked to move on behalf of the bank, from the ordinary house purchase loan (HPL)?

20 What is your organisation's procedure for leave for jury service?

9 Benefits

OBJECTIVES

When you have read this chapter you will be able to explain:
- **The variety of the elements of the reward system in your organisation; the supervisor's responsibilities;**
- **Wages and salaries, grading and job evaluation: how it was developed, and the current state of arrangements;**
- **The relationships between grades, promotion, merit and pay;**
- **Pecuniary benefits: bonuses, profit-sharing schemes, share options and allocations;**
- **Material benefits: car schemes, leasing arrangements, mileage and travel allowances;**
- **Location (large-town, London), and relocation allowances;**
- **Leave and holidays: procedures and entitlement for grade and length of service;**
- **Working conditions at the place of employment, and the supervisor's contribution to them;**
- **Staff house loans and home improvements loans: qualification, conditions and costs;**
- **Other staff loans; and concessions concerning the conduct and cost of staff bank accounts.**

■ INTRODUCTION

While one of the main forces impelling us to go to work is the rewards package, it is remarkable how little we tend to know about the details of its constituents, except where it relates directly to our own case. It reflects extremely well on immediate superiors when staff are aware of their full entitlement to the rewards of their labour, and for this to be the case, supervisors must be clear themselves on the details and be able to explain the benefits to their staff.

To begin with, *wages* and *salaries* are neither random nor individually negotiated, but are part of a system, based for example in banks on a job evaluation and grading system. This is fairly complex, but the principles are simple, and knowledge of them forms a sensible basis for discussion of apparent or felt anomalies raised by staff, as does a knowledge of their history, development and rationale. In particular we shall look at the relationships between promotion from one grade to another and different levels of pay; and we shall examine the difference between promotion from one grade to another, and rises in pay within a grade, as rewards for performance.

Although we tend to quote basic annual salary if we say what we earn, there are other *pecuniary benefits,* or monetary rewards, in our package. There are bonuses based on individual or group or company performance, or which are formalised as specific percentages of salary; there are profit-sharing schemes which can be taken either as cash or as company shares; there are share option schemes where shares may be purchased at any time at advantageous rates; and shares are even allocated, in some companies, freely as a reward. The sensible supervisor knows about and can explain these – and especially the rules of entitlement – to staff.

One of the most popular non-salary benefits in modern commercial organisations is the *company car*. Distinction will be made concerning the award of the car as a reward for status; the award or subsidy of a car as a job-necessity; and subsidised car-loan or leasing schemes permitting the staff to obtain their own car at advantageous rates. Once again, it is to the supervisors' advantage to be familiar with the rules.

In the previous chapter we discussed the location at which people worked, and procedures for alleviating the problems of displacement. There are staff benefits associated with *location* and *relocation*. There are certain locations in which special allowances are applied because of the cost of living there; there are payments over and above costs for relocation; and there is the security, or at least the relief of major anxiety, associated with procedural sympathy for those involved in having to move. Of course there are also problems involved, and the supervisor should understand the negative benefits of moving.

Holidays and other time-off are important parts of the reward package; but it is rare that staff can accurately relay the full rules of entitlement. It is one's immediate superior's responsibility to make sure that one receives the entitlement, and therefore any supervisor's responsibility to know the rules, including, for example, extra days for length of service, and the rules for carry-over to the next year, and the complex problems which arrive at the turn of the year around Christmas and New Year – and their solution!

Before going on to the final set of benefits which can enhance life outside the workplace, we will pay attention to the *working conditions* and the supervisor's responsibility for ensuring that the working environment is pleasant.

Finally there are perks concerning access to the company product or service – in the case of banks, to money – in the form of subsidised loans. Bank staff have valuable additions to their reward package in cheap or free loans, for anything from houses to short-term overdraft. We shall look at the supervisors' responsibility for information and, where applicable, conduct and control.

■ THE REWARDS PACKAGE

In Chapter 4 we showed that people come to work for more than just the money. But even the money is more complex a package than just the salary notified on your salary slip at the end of the week or month, especially in banking. As you have seen from the introductory paragraphs of this chapter, there is a whole list of money-related or valuable rewards for working, and these are often referred to as the *rewards package*.

Once again, a complete and detailed account of all these will be found in your own bank's procedural documentation, which you should attempt to obtain, noting first how easy it is to do this, and second how clear it is to anyone reading it. Compare and contrast what you find in this chapter with your procedures material; and think all the time as you study, in terms of explaining each element to someone else.

Working for a bank will provide you with an excellent rewards package. But do not fall into the trap of believing, as many do in examinations, that it far outstrips the rewards of every other occupation! If this were the case, why on earth would people want to go into retailing, manufacturing, education, the arts, travel or insurance? When you consider this matter, especially for examination purposes, you need to have an understanding of the total rewards package, but it is worth concentrating on those elements of it which are either peculiar to banking or particularly advantageous to bankers.

ACTIVITY 9.1
We have not actually defined the term 'rewards package' but the meaning seems self-evident. List all the elements you can think of which you consider to be included in the package of rewards you receive for working for your organisation.

■ WAGES AND SALARIES

Whatever else there is in a rewards package, the salary is still, of course, the central and basic pillar of it. A good salary system will be:

1 *fair compared with outside bodies,* and therefore sufficient to keep the staff from leaving;
2 *consistent internally,* so that higher-valued jobs attract a higher salary, and similar jobs the same salary;
3 *flexible* enough to handle unusual or unique jobs;
4 *subject to negotiation* by the staff body, or by individuals, or on appeal against injustices;
5 *consistent with the economic environment,* so that it allows for inflation or changing economic circumstances.

In other words, the system must line up jobs so that there is equal pay for equal work and higher pay for more important work; and then it must ensure that the pay at each level compares with what is happening outside. You will have spotted immediately that, if this is the case, there must be an accurate way of measuring levels and importance of jobs, and indeed there is.

■ JOB EVALUATION

In fact for a salary system to fulfil all of these requirements, it must be carefully constructed, and there must be systems and bodies of vigilant review to keep it up to date. The way in which they are set up in the first place is also vital, and the method used by banks and other sophisticated organisations is *job evaluation*.

The clearing banks had a long-standing system, designed in the early 1970s, covering clerical tasks up to the level below that of the Bank Official or Assistant Manager; and the salary of the Branch Manager on first appointment to that level.

For all other jobs, each bank had its own system, but in all cases salaries were evaluated by reference to these central jobs; and even the most highly specialised jobs were fitted into the system as well as they could be, for the sake of consistency. In this increasingly complex age, all sorts of technical specialists must now be employed, and to attract them, in a free enterprise economy the organisation must pay the going rate.

In the 1990s banks have increasingly moved towards independent job-evaluation schemes but the *principles* which we discuss below still apply.

We shall concentrate here on clerical salaries.

The clerical job-evaluation system

Your bank will probably operate a job evaluation system which sets up a number of bench-mark jobs, or standard evaluations, such as filing clerk, cashier, senior clerk, and so on, based on a points system for elements of job-content. While it was designed some time ago, as we have said, it is subject to review and senior personnel staff are allocated almost exclusively to the task of job-evaluation and its updating.

The points are allocated to the jobs in six areas, as follows:

1 accuracy needed to avoid loss;
2 amount of knowledge and skill required to do the job;
3 how much judgement is needed related to the importance of decisions;
4 how much content in terms of recommendations and advice to be made;
5 extent and importance of the outside contacts;
6 value of assets in the custody of the job-holder.

The system then sets three clerical grades (2–3–4) and the banks line up all the clerical jobs into those grades (Grade 1 for people in their probationary period, or very near the start of their career).

It is vital for you to note, in the whole of this discussion, that it is the job, and not the job-holder which is evaluated. You are not a Grade 3 but you occupy a Grade 3 job.

Given all the above, why do certain people occupying Grade 3 jobs have a higher salary than some in Grade 4 jobs, and lower than some in Grade 2 jobs? Well, there is an explanation, and it may now be interesting for you to find out what it is.

■ THE GRADING SYSTEM

Any fair and manageable system must allow for three ways of advancing people's remuneration:

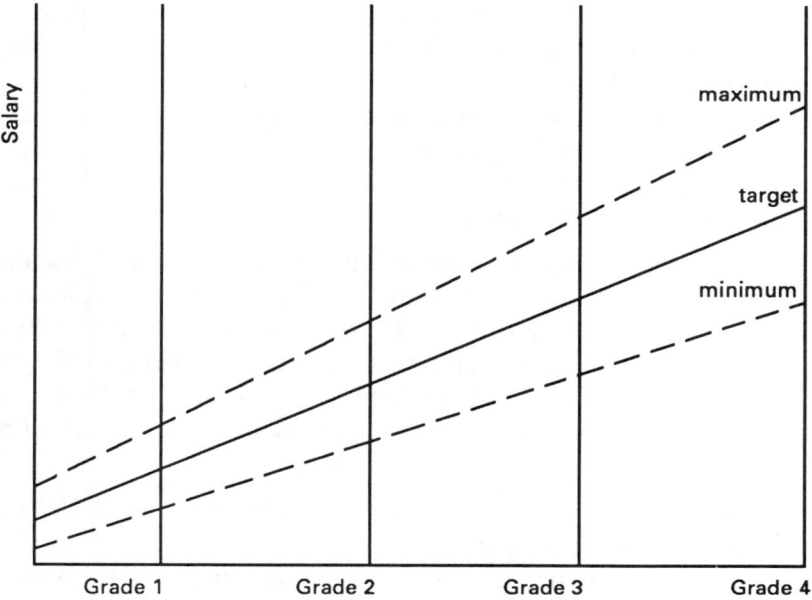

Fig 8.1

1 by relation with outside general rates, so as not to fall behind;
2 for excellent or outstanding performance in a particular grade or set of tasks, without actually promoting them to the next senior job;
3 by promoting them to a higher-paid, more senior job.

To do this it is not sufficient to have a set single salary for each grade. For each grade there must be a *band of remuneration*, with a minimum, a target and a maximum salary. This can be illustrated with a diagram (*see* Fig. 8.1), which shows why someone in a Grade 2 job can in some circumstances be better paid than a person in a Grade 3 post:

As you can see, since there is a range of salaries at, say, Grade 2, you can increasingly reward people for ever better work on Grade 2 jobs until they reach the maximum – which is higher than the minimum Grade 3. What happens at the top of Grade 2? The answer is that unless they are capable of promotion to the different, higher evaluated work in Grade 3, unfortunately they are being paid the top rate for the job they are doing, but nothing more.

ACTIVITY 9.2

Discuss with colleagues from another bank examples of differences in the salary system between your bank and theirs. Note these differences.

■ MANAGER'S SALARIES

It is not a good idea to believe the myths about why managers receive the generous salaries they do. Some of these strange myths are as follows.

- They are very clever people.
- They are old and experienced.
- They lead a very hard life.
- They have to go through a lot to get there.
- They are all fully qualified.
- They are very important.
- Their decisions are crucial.

But in fact managers' salaries are determined by job evaluation, exactly as everyone else's are, in a somewhat similar but more complex manner, and they do differ from bank to bank. In some banks they are based on a well-known managerial evaluation system known by the name of the consultants who designed it, namely, Hay/MSL. The system is based on three main components subdivided into more detailed elements. The three main components are:

1 know-how: what experience and knowledge and skills are needed to perform the job properly;
2 problem-solving: the intellectual challenge and thinking and reasoning processes necessary;
3 accountability: the decision-making element, responsibility, amount of resources commanded, the ability to take action.

Just to make sure that any problems or anomalies are sorted out, there will be a committee which deals with this sort of matter, and which evaluates the unusual or highly specialist jobs which do not easily fit into the system.

In the 1990s a new element has been introduced into managers' salaries in many banks, and it's spreading, not only to most banks but eventually downwards in managerial level. This is called 'performance related pay', and it adds a bonus element for meeting agreed targets in a specified period. This isn't a switch to a commission basis, but a bonus additional element! In most systems, the basic salary is the same as it ever was, but above that high level anything from zero up to, say, 15% more can be earned by meeting these agreed targets.

■ SALARIES AND THE SUPERVISOR

Banking salaries are normally fair and adequate; but there are often small measures of temporary dissatisfaction, and even more often confusion. The people who should deal with the technicalities of salaries are located in personnel departments, and it is useful for the supervisor to have a personal contact there who can be consulted.

As to the general principles, good supervisors have a good grasp of these. It is also their duty to ensure that their staff are fairly remunerated, that is, are correctly graded for the work that they do in the first place, and second, are paid at a point on the scales in that grade which is correct for their experience, or excellence, or on whatever other criteria used to determine that point.

ACTIVITY 9.3

Take as an example anybody in your section (or yourself) and write notes on *exactly* why they receive precisely the salary they do receive.

■ OVERTIME

Directly related to, and indeed part of, salary are overtime payments. These are not paid above a certain organisational level, because it is traditionally expected that people of management rank might be expected to donate extra time freely, in the expectation of having some long-term reward, like eventual promotion.

Lower mortals, however, are paid overtime! Quite rightly, of course, as the bargain you have with your employer is a commercial one: they hire your time, you offer it for payment.

In order to claim for overtime and, as supervisor, to ensure that staff claim correctly, you must know the precise rules:

1 to what extent overtime can be demanded;
2 the rules for minimum overtime before payment must be made;
3 the overtime rates;
4 the procedure for recording and claiming overtime.

You must then make sure that they are applied.

■ FINANCIALLY BENEFICIAL SCHEMES

Under this heading we will discuss the schemes that such organisations as banks have, to offer the staff either cash or share benefits other than their salary. These could be in the form of annual bonus, or profit-sharing schemes, of share options or allocations. Once again, while details of these will be made available from time to time from central locations, most staff look to their immediate superiors to explain and clarify the schemes to them.

In every case you should at least know the answers to:

1 Who is eligible for the benefit: everyone, or certain grades, or people with a certain length of service?
2 What if any is the qualifying period: do you have to have been in the bank's service for, say, a year before qualifying?
3 What are the principles on which allocation is based, that is, by percentage of salary, or so much per person, or by length of service?
4 What are the methods of access: how do you apply for them?
5 What are the benefits to you of the schemes? Short- or long-term benefits? Security? Retirement benefits?

Bonus payments

In recent years there has been a bonus payment to bank staff (at least in the

UK clearing banks) of some 2.5% of annual salary, paid before Christmas. This was at one time discretionary and based on bank performance – indeed it used to be called the Productivity Bonus – and it originated as a way of easing the severity of wage-freeze. It has itself become frozen into a sort of tradition. You will need to check some of the above questions of eligibility, especially what if any proportion your new staff are entitled to depending on when they joined the bank.

ACTIVITY 9.4

Taking your organisation's system of bonus payments, apply the questions in the section on 'Financially Beneficial Schemes' and write down the answers.

Profit-sharing

Here each bank will have a totally separate scheme, although most banks do go along with the idea that staff should share in such increases in profit that they have contributed to producing (one wonders if there are any schemes in which staff contribute to their bank in the case of annual loss?).

It will most likely be a payment based on a formula relating the annual bank profit with the bank's assets and your current salary; and you might like to investigate what that formula is.

You do not need to know exactly how it is calculated, or technicalities about whether profit means before or after tax, before or after provisions, before or after the payment of dividends, unless these things interest you. You will not really need to check up on whether you or your staff are getting a correct payment as the likelihood of mistake – or fraud – are fairly remote! But you really should understand the principles.

The payment may be in the form of cash, or you may be able to opt for bank shares. The benefit in taking shares in your own company, to start with, will be longer term, of course. But there are also financial benefits first of all from the expectation of the growth in the value of the shares, and second in the form of tax advantages. These change from time to time: but whatever they are, your bank should accompany the notice of the profit share with:

(a) the amount of the payment;
(b) the basis of the allocation;
(c) the options available;
(d) the benefits of choice between cash and shares;
(e) the conditions and methods of application.

If the details are too complicated or difficult for you to understand, the same will apply to your staff. As supervisor you ought to obtain clarification, and wrangle with the difficulties, so as to be able to explain them to your staff.

ACTIVITY 9.5

Imagine explaining your bank's profit-sharing scheme and its options to your staff. Consult your personnel-manual documentation, make notes on it carefully, and practice giving this explanation to members of your junior staff.

Share options and allocations

From time to time banks make some of their shares available for purchase by their staff, at advantageous rates. In a similar manner to the share option as part of the annual profit share scheme, you should be familiar with the terms and conditions and benefits.

Purchasing shares, of course, does indicate a certain commitment to your organisation and its future, although there is no pressure or obligation implied in the offer (or its refusal). Any share purchase should be decided on a purely financial basis and, having taken all the preferential treatment into consideration, buying bank shares must stand comparison with any other investment: if you will be better off from the returns on your deposit account, don't buy the shares!

■ CAR, CAR LOAN AND LEASING SCHEMES

Most banks introduce 'the company car' as a perk at very high levels compared with other organisations; indeed there are few bank schemes for a free or nearly free car below quite senior management. The only exceptions are for those who need a car for their work, and there are very few of those.

On the other hand, there are sometimes car leasing facilities, though again at fairly high levels, but down to senior official grades. In a typical scheme of this type, the participant may lease a car from the bank, and for a monthly payment, obtain a new vehicle and all running costs paid except petrol and oil. One way of estimating the benefit is to say that the candidate can get a new car for about the same annual cost as the three-year old second-hand car otherwise available to anyone at that level of income.

Find out whether your bank has a car loan or lease scheme for senior staff, and what the conditions and provisions are, if only for interest; after all, one of the tangible benefits of bank employment is hope of advancement!

■ LOCATION ALLOWANCE

Organisations have to make some form of differential to allow for the extremely different financial cost of living in London (and incidentally, for banks with Scottish connections, in Aberdeen, the oil town). There is, therefore, the *London allowance*.

In the London areas, to live at a standard of living and a style commensurate with the suburbs of even quite large towns outside London you have to live a good way out from the City; this entails considerable travel costs, as well as incurring high house purchase prices, and recreation costs, traditionally to be paid in the London area. If you choose the alternative, i.e. to live closer in to the centre, housing costs become very high indeed.

Costs of living aside, salaries are higher in London than in the provinces, and employment rates are also higher; therefore, employing organisations are in competition for skilled and competent staff. For all these reasons there must be a differential payment certainly to retain staff, and even more so to attract able staff from areas outside London, to alleviate the costs of moving to the capital.

In the late 1980s, deregulation of the banking industry caused salaries in London, and especially in the square mile of the City of London, to escalate; and companies had to scramble to attract new staff and keep the staff they had. The London allowance had to be increased, even backdated, by banks worried about staff turnover, and even this was not enough to stem all of the tide of moves, especially from the clearing banks.

As supervisor, you or your staff may be asked to move. Whether you are in London or outside, you should know where to find details of the London allowance, and its scope and amount, so as to make sensible decisions for yourself, or give advice to your staff, concerning the benefits and costs package of moving to and from what is the banking centre of the UK.

ACTIVITY 9.6

Find out whether your bank has special provision for working in London or any other high-cost area and note exactly what that provision is.

Relocation

Much of what there is to be said about relocation has been pointed out in the previous chapter. It is included for a passing mention here because though not a benefit, it should not be, and commonly is not, a cost: when banks move staff, they do not expect them to make a profit, but they equally do not expect them to be out of pocket, and you will find few people who have been moved complaining about the direct financial cost. Within the rules, which needless to say must be strictly observed, you will find enough flexibility: but you must, again, know the basics of the rules in principle, and know how and where to obtain the detail when necessary.

■ HOLIDAYS AS A BENEFIT

Well within the working lifetime of some of your senior colleagues, paid holidays were a privilege offered to professional people only. The standard length of time for an annual holiday for most people then was two working weeks. Banks, and in particular branches, all opened on Saturday mornings and your ordinary working week included this Saturday morning (nowadays 'volunteers' staff branches at the weekend).

'Bank Holidays' were introduced so that the few days they apply to would be given to staff by law, otherwise there would have been no compulsion on employers to give (paid) holidays at all. Nowadays, however, with increasing emphasis on leisure in our society, holidays are a natural and increasing part of working life, certainly in the UK. As evidence of this, look at the minor wrangling every year about how much time you will be allowed off over the Christmas/New Year period: it normally concerns more than just the three statutory Bank Holidays as in the past!

For interest, work out a rate for your weekly pay by dividing your annual salary plus bonus plus average profit share, by 52, and multiply that by the number of weeks of your annual holiday, plus a week's worth of the collection of Bank Holidays. That is the basic cost to your organisation of your holidays (what it is paying you while you are not there). You will see that it is quite a valuable benefit.

It is now, of course, regarded as an entitlement and most people know how much holiday they may take, even if they have not worked out, as you have just done, how much it is worth to them in salary terms.

Holiday entitlement

The actual amount of holiday entitlement is a little more complex than it initially appears to be. There are several matters to consider:

1 The *basic entitlement* will be a minimum to which everybody will have a right to claim.

Do you know what the basic holidays are for you and your staff? Where in your bank personnel documentation will you find it? Try your contract of service, your terms and conditions of employment, your staff manual.

2 Increased *entitlement for seniority* in the sense that the higher you are up the management hierarchy, the more holidays you may get.

Check this out for yourself and your staff. Inspectors, who check this among many other items, sometimes find that people who are promoted are not told about, or omit to notice, increased holiday entitlement.

3 Additional *entitlement for age*, and the odd extra day you get for passing such landmarks as your thirtieth birthday, or tenth year with the bank.

Once again, and even more so in this case, people either do not know of these benefits, or do not notice that they could be entitled to extra days after, say, five years – in fact they hardly notice reaching the five year landmark! Does your bank have a system of recording and reminding? Do you get any such extra holidays?

4 *Pro-rata variation rules*, for people who join (or leave) within a holiday year.

You will frequently come across this problem for your newly-joined juniors, and you will need to know how it is calculated. The formula, which you will undoubtedly find if you look for it, will be very precise. Try to imagine what you think it will be, write this down; then look it up. How accurate were you?

5 *Permitted periods* when you can and cannot take holidays, and who has priority of choice.

There will be overall bank rules as to how many people may be out of the office; procedures for relief staff; principles of priority (usually by rank, then within rank either by age or length of service or salary level). Check your rules, and any others, including local rules, which say when you must or may not take holidays.

You may also find that there is a rule about having to take a minimum number of consecutive days as a main holiday. It was once said that this was so that in case of suspicion, you would have to be away from accounts and finances you handled, for long enough for irregularities to show up. These days if it still exists it is more likely to be simply traditional, or for your own good!

6 *Miscellaneous minor rules*, such as for part-time or cleaning staff, and illness during holidays.

If you are the supervisor of anyone in any of these categories, do check the rules out. In any case, note a few of them for interest.

ACTIVITY 9.7

After each of the numbered points, we suggested a topic for personal research. Do this research now and make notes on the answers to the questions posed.

■ WORKING CONDITIONS

Are your working conditions a benefit? The answer must be 'yes' if only because of those who would say that they prefer to work in a decent office with reasonably pleasant surroundings, furniture, decorations, lighting and so on, to the kind of factory or even department-store conditions in which the majority of workers spend their lives.

Of course there are less-than-elegant conditions in certain operating departments of the bank, and even branch offices are not exactly the Savoy Hotel. The provision of decent working conditions can be affected by the supervisor's attitude and behaviour.

Referring back to people's motivations, they do need a certain amount of physical comfort, otherwise the higher-level motivational factors will not work, e.g. if Michelle is cold or in pain or discomfort, it is difficult for her to concentrate on problem-solving or giving a good service to customers. Second, while the removal of that pain or cold or discomfort does not positively motivate Michelle, it does remove the dissatisfaction which gets in the way of her positive motivation.

What can supervisors do? They can certainly monitor the conditions of work, and check, by asking the staff or responding positively to complaints, that the working conditions are as good as they can be. They can represent the group in negotiations to get improved facilities, in the interests of their staff. They can make sure that work in special conditions, such as work at a video monitor or VDU screen, is done under proper conditions.

It might be of interest to you to look at the conditions of work if your office. Do one specific 'patrol'. Is everything excellent? Is it all appalling? Have things drifted to where we put up with poor conditions because we are resigned to them, or it never occurred to us that it was not good enough? Make a list of possible improvement areas. See if you can get anything changed; and record your experience in the attempt.

■ USE OF THE COMPANY 'PRODUCT'

From the very early days of UK industry and commerce, workers have been offered the company product or service at reduced, concessionary rates, or even free of charge, under certain circumstances, such as coalminers's families being given an allowance of coal for their own use.

If you work for a detergent manufacturer, you would probably be encouraged to use the company product by being allowed to buy the soaps and detergents and washing-up liquids at bargain prices. People who are employed in public transport get free or cheap travel; clothes-manufacturer's workers can shop in the factory shop, and retail employees get discount in their stores.

Bank staff also receive this sort of benefit in the way of free or cheap use of the company services, namely financial: cheap loans on the one hand, and the free or cheap operation of accounts on the other. We shall go on to look at these benefits in a little more detail; but here we should note that they are not without penalty.

In return for financial concessions, bank staff suffer far more stringent conditions than their customers. For example, while nobody would encourage customers to 'anticipate salary', it happens; and in most ordinary circumstances, on an occasional and non-increasing basis, the bank will allow it: not for bank staff, for whom any tiny overdraft must be asked for and sanctioned, often by your boss of all people. And as we have mentioned previously, no customer has the inspection staff interrogate them about where the credit of £25 came from last month.

Still, these irritations must be tolerated, first because there is good reason for the bank to check that staff accounts are kept in order, both for the sake of the bank and its customers, and of the staff themselves; and second because, as we shall see, the benefits can be very great. We will look first at the house purchase loan, then at other loans and concessionary aspects of bank accounts.

■ HOUSE PURCHASE LOANS

Since the detailed rules for house purchase loans (let us call them HPLs) change from time to time, and differ from bank to bank, we shall look only at the benefit in general principle. But before we do, write down some of the most important rules and conditions of your own bank's scheme.

How much did you get down? Whatever information you did know, and what you need to know, should answer these questions, at least. They are put in the form of questions so as to enable you to complete your knowledge by answering them with reference to your own schemes:

1 *Purpose:* house purchase, of course; but what about flats? Shares in a house or housing association accommodation; or condominiums; or leasehold properties? And must it be for the borrower only? What about immediate family?

2 *Eligibility:* this is a crucial question: under what circumstances are you entitled to a bank HPL? There will be restrictions according to:
(a) age;
(b) marital status;
(c) income;
(d) length of service.

3 *Amount:* regulations will depend basically on income, a multiple of annual income or on a measured proportion of monthly income. It will be carefully calculated to ensure no excessive commitment by staff members (you should know what this is).

What proportion/percentage of the house-cost to be lent may also be the subject of bank rules, possibly put in the way of what deposit will be required. There will also be regulations as to whether the income of others may be taken into account. For example, you may or may not be able to share the loan with wife or husband.

4 *Location:* there could be variations on how much may be lent with relation to the location of the house (more in high-cost areas such as London or Aberdeen).

5 The *interest rate* will be stated, and although the standard rate does not change much, it can alter from time to time. But you should know what it is at present; and whether your bank's HPL interest rates are fixed at the outset, or variable like overdraft rates.

6 *Repayment:* in your staff manuals you will find details of repayment. These details will cover:
(a) length of term: to age 60? 65? Retirement?
(b) monthly repayment tables for different sizes of loan.

7 *Repayment method:* you may find you can use a *capital repayment* method, where you pay a little of the capital and a little of the interest off each month; or an *endowment insurance* method, in which each month you pay a little of the interest plus the premiums policy, the maturing proceeds of which pay off the whole loan at the end. The latter is less popular these days than when it was more tax efficient.

8 The *retention of profit* on the house you are selling, if the loan is not your first house: there may be rules as to how much 'equity' you may retain, either in absolute terms or as a proportion of the selling price (this is a cost to bank staff of the privilege of the cheap loan: no such restrictions on customers!).

9 What *insurance* you must take out, to protect the house, the contents, your repayments, possibly your health or income. These are usually not voluntary but conditions of the loan.

10 *Bridging finance* will be available, at concessionary rates for ordinary house purchase, and probably free for those moving to a new location at the bank's request. The length of time for which bridging finance is available is a very important issue.

11 Finally, *procedures for application* will be detailed, including what details of the house are needed, as well as for the borrower. There will also be details of who

must countersign the application, such as bosses or banking managers, and through whose hands the application must go.

As supervisor, you do not need to be an expert, but you are once again the person to whom your staff have a right to come for advice. Be familiar with the contents of your procedures manual about house purchase, and where to locate it by reading it just once as an exercise here.

ACTIVITY 9.8

For any person in your office who is eligible for a house purchase loan, or for yourself if and when you are eligible, go through all of the matters discussed above and write down the specific details relating to a house purchase loan for that person.

■ OTHER LOANS

There are many other forms of loan, most of them similar to those offered to customers. Some of them are as listed below, and you should look up the terms of these, and list any others available to your staff, in your procedures manual. You may like, for absolute completeness, to compare them with the offerings to customers, by looking at the customer leaflets. This would have the side-effect of making you more familiar, as you should be, with your bank's services!

1 *Home improvement:* this is a longer-term loan, usually subject to a minimum monthly repayment, and it may therefore be sensible to put together more than one item of home improvement under one loan, rather than having more than one loan and paying the minimum repayment twice or more.

Similarly with HPLs, the specific purposes which these loans may be put to, are likely to be closely specified by the bank, and for fixed rather than moveable home-improvement items.

2 *Season ticket loans* offer very low or no interest, to help people to pay for the costs of travel to work and are very valuable in large town offices. Of course there are savings to be made by long-term season ticket purchase, over the day-to-day payment for travel.

3 *Education loans* to send children to fee-paying schools, or to pay any fees associated with children's education, including further or higher education, are available.

4 *Study loans* are available to help staff pay for the expenses of gaining professional qualifications, principally those of the Chartered Institute of Bankers. There are also gratuities associated with passing the exams, with different sums for different stages and levels.

5 *Personal loans* can be granted, for specific items of value, just as for customers; and more than one can also be given at any time, although there is a belief that you must pay off one before another is granted. However, as long as the total repayments are not burdensome, this is not the case.

6 *Overdrafts* may be asked for, and are usually granted, for all the purposes for which customers might also need them. Naturally bank staff are examined very

carefully about the reasons for loans; and it is not expected that any overdraft loans will be given on a regular basis. However, everyone has the odd unexpected expense or the need for an extraordinary purchase, bank staff included, and bank overdrafts will be granted.

7   Other *bank staff loan schemes* may feature in your own organisation's packages of offerings, depending on the kind of bank, or its staff's special situation, or other special factors. Look them up and compare them with those of colleagues or friends on other banks.

Above all, no supervisor should allow staff to get themselves into financial problems, or to miss out on available enjoyments in life, for ignorance of staff loan facilities. They can easily and tactfully become the topic of conversation without having to probe the staff financial position too deeply, and this kind of help and counsel certainly cements good working relationships.

■ BANK ACCOUNTS

Bank staff have access to the same range of bank accounts as their customers, and usually at concessionary rates or free of charge.

It will not be worth our while to go into detail about the variety of accounts, although the main ones will be:

1   *Current account* (sole or joint) for everyday transactions, which must be kept in credit, and on which there is in some cases interest on credit balances;
2   *Bank revolving credit facilities* in which, on payment of a fixed monthly sum, you may borrow up to a multiple of that sum, similar to many high street store credit facilities (though banks discourage 'hard-core' borrowing, i.e. getting up to the limit and staying there);
3   *Access/Barclaycard/Visa* and the like, which are also revolving credit facilities but with a variable minimum, not a fixed, monthly payment. There are banks which do not allow staff to borrow on Access or Barclaycard, only to use them as a charge card and pay the entire bill at the end of the month;
4   *Budget accounts* for paying bills (gas, electricity, car, rates, even holidays), divide them by 12 and credit this account with the resultant sum, and pay bills as they arrive. There is a charge when this account is in debit, but it smooths the path of paying bills, and should balance out at the end of the year.

There will be rules about which branch the accounts must be held at ('domiciled'), and about offsetting balances in accounts, and about which accounts may be the source of credit facilities for the staff. You and all bank staff should know what these rules are.

■ PENSIONS

We end this chapter as we end our careers: with the pension.

You need hardly be reminded that this is a very complex matter because bank circulars about pension schemes are extremely difficult to understand! Have pity for those who must write them; they do try to explain them all by means of specially produced booklets which may use diagrams or cartoons to show how much gets paid by whom, to whom, under what circumstances and when. A feature of most bank schemes is that the pension is non-contributory, that is, the employee does not have a premium deducted from their salary as in the majority of other occupations.

ACTIVITY 9.9
(a) Obtain an explanatory booklet concerning your pension.
(b) Contact a colleague in a different organisation and ask them to obtain a similar document.
(c) Go through the points below checking the details with your documentation.

1 *Eligibility* and probation periods before you join the scheme, which would include sections on part-time and casual staff.
2 *Premiums* and payments into the fund: usually based on a percentage of salary, and sometimes with an adjustment to salary to pay the premiums; and usually deducted from monthly pay.
3 *Voluntary payments:* in certain cases you may want to pay extra into your pension fund for eventual extra benefits. It is a way of saving which (up to a point) is tax efficient, especially if you joined the organisation or started work later in life than at leaving school.
Either your booklet will show you how beneficial it will be, or the people who run it will advise you.
4 *Late joiners,* to take up the above point, can have previous years of work outside the bank credited to them, or they can 'transport' in, pension payments they made to their previous employer into the bank's pension scheme ('buying' a share in it).
5 *Leavers,* conversely, do not lose what they put in: provision is always made for transfer to the pension arrangements of their new employer or to their private scheme. Alternatively they can have their current share of the pension fund 'frozen', and receive proportional payments at retirement date.
Temporary leavers (mostly women who take maternity leave – either the minimum or on the new longer-term basis) will also have provision made for them concerning pension premium payment and adjustments to the eventual payout.
6 *Benefits:* there are a number of subheads to this section, the main point, for the members, of the whole exercise!
(a) The *pension* will usually be calculated as a proportion of the last salary earned before retirement, or an average of the last few years. This proportion will be varied according to the years contributed to the fund. Find out exactly what this is for your own pension, at least as an exercise.
(b) The *lump sum* which in some schemes may be taken out at retirement date. It reduces the regular pension, and is usually optional: you can choose between lump sum and reduced pension, or no lump sum and full pension.

(c) The *state benefits* which in many cases reduce the amount paid out by the fund: that is, you get your state benefits and the fund makes up the sum referred to in (a).

(d) *Death in service:* you should be able to find details of who will get how much of the accumulated fund if you die while in the service of the bank. The payment is quite generous. Without wishing to be morbid, but practical, again as an example calculate exactly what your beneficiaries would get if you were to be the subject of these clauses.

(e) *Death as a pensioner:* pension scheme documentation indicates who gets what and for how long. Check out whether there is any difference between the benefits male staff leave to their wives and female staff leave to their husbands.

(f) *Adjustments* are sometimes made to the rate of payment according to variations in the cost of living: pensioners can get a 'raise', depending on the fund rules.

ACTIVITY 9.10

Find out the precise details of what will happen financially to your beneficiaries if you:

(a) die in service;
(b) retire;
(c) leave the bank;
(d) die as a pensioner.

Compare and contrast the benefits of your bank pension scheme with others inside and outside your bank. You should as supervisor at least be able to explain the whole system to any member of your staff who wants to know why they should pay premiums for some distantly later event.

■ BENEFITS AND THE SUPERVISOR

The last point is the simplest: people come to work for a series of benefits which satisfy their needs, and they look to their immediate superior, their supervisor, for help and advice in gaining the maximum benefit from their labours. This means that the supervisor has a duty to be knowledgeable, or to know of sources of knowledge, about the rewards package. Supervisors are the people who make sure that staff do a fair day's work; equally it is their duty to ensure that they get their fair day's pay.

■ SUMMARY

In this chapter we have discussed, the following aspects of benefits:

1 Wages and salaries, and the requirements for a sensible system.

2 Job-evaluation, the foundation for salary determination in banks: the points system and the benchmark jobs; and the evaluation of job rather than job-holder.

3. The grading system: maximum, target and minimum ranges at each grade. Reward for excellent work in one grade, contrasted with reward by promotion to the next; and why it is possible to be paid less in higher grades than in lower ones.

4. Manager's salaries and the different basis for evaluating their content.

5. Overtime: its necessity, the rates, the entitlement to overtime pay.

6. Bonus payments: a matter of productivity or an entrenched right?

7. Profit sharing and the need for basic information concerning:

   (a) the amount of the payment;
   (b) the basis for the allocation;
   (c) the options (cash or shares?);
   (d) the benefits of the options;
   (e) the conditions.

8. Cars, car loans and leasing schemes: what each bank offers, and the levels of management at which they are offered.

9. Location allowances: the reasons for a London (or other exceptional location) allowance and the conditions of its application.

10. Relocation and the reimbursement of the costs thereof.

11. Holidays: i.e. paid holidays and their value in rough cash terms as a benefit to employees.

12. Holiday entitlements:

    (a) the basic entitlements;
    (b) additional entitlements for seniority in rank;
    (c) additional entitlements for seniority in age;
    (d) pro-rata entitlements for joiners;
    (e) permitted holiday periods, and staff priority of choice;
    (f) miscellaneous rules.

13. Working conditions as a benefit: how pleasant and amenable the office and its facilities are for work, and the supervisor's responsibility for the decency of working surroundings.

14. House purchase loans: bank rules concerning eligibility, amount, location, repayment, method and interest, the retention of profit, insurance and procedures for application.

15. Other loans available at cheap/reduced rates or free to staff:

    (a) home improvement loans;
    (b) season ticket loans;
    (c) education loans;
    (d) study loans;
    (e) other personal loans;
    (f) overdraft facilities;
    (g) other staff loan schemes.

16 Bank accounts: current, deposit, revolving credit, budget accounts, credit card accounts; and the rules for staff.

17 Pensions: eligibility, premiums, voluntary payments, late joiners and leavers; benefits: the pension, the lump sum, the State benefits, death in service, death as a pensioners, cost-of-living adjustments.

■ SELF-ASSESSMENT QUESTIONS

Try to answer these questions to remind you of the content of this chapter:

1 List as many items as you can which can be said to be part of your rewards package.

2 Write down some of the six areas in which points are allocated to grade the bench-mark jobs in branch banking.

3 What is wrong with the statement 'Hugh is a Grade 3'?

4 Explain in writing or with a diagram how someone in a Grade 3 job can be more highly paid than someone in a Grade 4 job.

5 On what basis are managerial jobs evaluated, i.e. what are the three main components measured?

6 What are the duties of a supervisor with relation to the salary of staff in their group?

7 By what process do staff in your office claim overtime? Detail each point as if explaining it to a newcomer.

8 In general terms, how is your share in the profit of your organisation calculated?

9 What are the rules, if any, of taking cash or shares in your profit-sharing scheme?

10 How much of the 2.5 per cent bonus payable just before Christmas is due to someone who joined the bank on August 1st?

11 How much is the current London allowance?

12 What are the basic holiday entitlements of your specific staff?

13 Is there anything in your physical conditions of work, such as decor or furniture or ambience (heating, draughts, noise) which is less than satisfactory? What is the procedure for improving it?

14 Exactly who is eligible for your bank's staff house purchase loan scheme?

15 What is the difference between the capital repayment and the endowment insurance repayment method? Are both permitted in your staff house purchase loan scheme?

16 What are the general rules for taking out a home improvement loan, for staff?

17 What charges are made on your staff current accounts? What is the bank's policy on interest on credit balances?

18 What exactly are the rules for conduct of staff credit card accounts?

19 What is your pension scheme's system for voluntary extra payments into the pension fund?

20 What are the rules for taking or not taking a lump sum as part of your retirement benefits?

Appendix

■ EXAMINATIONS

You cannot pass the examination in Supervisory Skills without any preparation, or believe that naive or untutored homespun philosophy, with no shred of evidence of study, will do you any good.

You will get credit for personal observations: but only on the basis of prior study and after an exposition of principle or theory. 'Common sense' is certainly necessary, but simply insufficient, to pass Supervisory Skills.

There are a few pointers you may like to consider about the kind of question you will usually be asked:

- The syllabus is always widely covered: there will be questions from every part of it;
- The questions are usually structured in some way, often in more than one part, even if not always laid out that way;
- Questions often contain the words 'you' or 'your': you always get credit for knowing your bank and relating it to your studies;
- There is usually an 'angle': questions ask you not just to regurgitate your knowledge but to apply thought;
- You are often asked to explain things, not just list them; and to exemplify, using well-thought-out and relevant examples.

Most importantly, answer the question as it is asked: you can lose up to the entire marks by reading and answering an imaginary question you would prefer the examiners to have asked, rather than the one on the examination paper.

There are no model answers for this paper. Here we will give you some idea of how we would expect you to approach the questions on two recent examinations approached in the answers.

■ OCTOBER 1990

Question 1

You have been given the responsibility for helping new employees in your office. What will they need to know about the bank's and your office's organisational structure?

A good answer would draw in a brief background of theory, then concentrate on the important elements of structure which permit sensible and efficient workflow, a full and wide service to the customer, and a clear chain of command, authority and responsibility, in the office and in the bank, so as to help the new entrant to settle in and work effectively.

You should indicate that you have some knowledge of organisational theory: the question is clearly about organisational structure. You could, for example, select to describe Burn's and Stalker's model of Mechanistic or Organic structures facing their appropriate environments; or you could write about Weber's bureaucratic or legal/rational model.

But theory, though required, is not sufficient. The question does not ask for all you know about organisational structure, but it specifically asks about 'your office', not just any one: a good description of your own bank and office is essential.

Draw diagrams: only in the context of an exceptionally well-structured or sensitive answer is it sufficient to state 'I would draw up a chart of the office', and then not to draw a full and accurate diagram. You must also pay attention to the wider context of the bank, because staff ought to have some reasonable understanding of the total organisation in which they operate.

Preparing for this sort of question you really should familiarise yourself with the whole structure of your bank: it has corporate, international, personnel and other service divisions, and these form a major part of their operations.

Incidentally the question does not ask for a description of a general induction process. Some would look at the question cursorily and trot out all they know about induction, for which they would receive no credit whatsoever; marks would be given only for the part of the answer which dealt with structure. Good candidates would spot that cue word, give a good account of theoretical models structure, think carefully about the structure of the bank and the office, and set down what a new entrant might find helpful in orienting themselves to work in 'your office'.

Question 2

'The Supervisor is caught between the devil and the deep blue sea'. Comment on the role of the supervisor, with special reference to any problems arising out of conflicts involved in keeping relationships with superiors and subordinates in balance.

The inclusion of a question on the role of supervisor can be reasonably foreseen, and examiners expect some preparation. You will notice that the questions always require some thought in the examination room, calling on you to apply what you know to the particular question asked. Notice here the particular angle, of relationships both with superiors and subordinates.

The question does ask you to comment on the role of the supervisor, so you could briefly list and explain the elements of that, either using the list of roles based on the organisational functions (production/operations, finance, marketing etc.), or the managerial functions (forecasting, planning, organising, control etc.), before you go on to deal with the part of the question concerning relationships with superiors and subordinates.

As to superiors, you could select out from what you may have read such elements in the supervisor's role as multi-way communication, planning, organising, the interpretation of objectives, and the role of intermediary. You might like also to select appropriate roles from the Belbin list (Chairperson,

Shaper, Plant and so on) or Mintzberg (Decisional, Motivational) to describe the managerial duties with which the supervisor must connect.

As to subordinates, a good answer would debate matters of delegation, control, counselling and the like; and again use roles from the Belbin list (Monitor-Evaluator, Finisher and so on) or Mintzberg (Informational) to describe the supervisory duties with which the manager must deal.

The examiners might expect some heartfelt comments on the position of the supervisor as first line management, taking the brunt of the day-to-day problems of both superior and subordinate; but this would need to be in the context of discussion of the problems of balance. Read the question again: you could certainly develop ideas as the need occasionally to defend unpopular management decisions to the staff, or to defend staff from over zealous management, or to handle conflict in general.

Question 3

Pamela is a supervisor in your office who always just succeeds in avoiding disasters. She can solve problems and handle a crisis well – she has to, because they are usually her fault. She rarely looks beyond tomorrow, and indeed she rarely has time to do so because she is handling the difficult situations her lack of foresight causes.

You are Pamela's manager: what advice would you give her on forecasting, planning and organising her work?

This question is helpful because of its specific division into forecasting, planning and organising: take advantage of that structuring to produce a systematic answer. The sensible candidate will realise that the question is really in the last sentence, and what is expected, first at least, is an outline of what is meant by those three elements of the supervisor's role.

Distinguish clearly between forecasting, planning and organising, but note the connections between them: forecasting is spending time considering likely future events, planning is instituting systems and intentions to handle them, and organising is allocating present resources with an eye to present and future.

It would be a good idea to divide future events into short, medium and long term, and prioritising tasks under 'Must be done', 'Should be done', 'Would like to be done' or a similar classification. But do demonstrate that you know what they mean, and that you have applied forethought to these matters, by giving examples of these various kinds of event or task: many questions on this paper use the words 'you' and 'your' because personal examples, which have been well thought through, are always welcomed.

You can now cast your answer in the form of advice addressed directly to Pamela, and you should remember to give her due credit for her problem-solving and crisis-handling abilities. These are important, but insufficient, and she must be advised to break the negative planning cycle into which she is trapped. Her behaviour affects not only her but her staff, and she needs to have this pointed out. You would also get marks for suggesting and making practical proposals for delegation. Pamela would also need to communicate such forecasts and plans that are made.

Question 4

Clearly outline the steps through which your bank's appraisal passes. What qualities does the system have which make it effective? If you were given the power to implement one single improvement to it, what would you suggest, and why?

When examiners read answers to this kind of question they know the wide range of variations there can be between bank systems, and they have to compare candidates' descriptions with a form of reasonable reality. Sometimes they get descriptions of appraisal systems so mediaeval as to be quite unbelievable, giving evidence more of the local misuse of a system than of a bad system: good candidates would distinguish between the system and its use.

They would also be genuinely familiar with their own system. We have pointed out in this book, and it is clear in the syllabus, that procedures manuals and other such instructions are required reading for this topic, and such details are freely and comprehensively covered in these publications. This question proves that specific description is essential, since it asks about 'your bank's appraisal system' and it asks for the stages it passes through.

You should start with the objectives of appraisal, of the filling and exchange of forms, of self appraisal, of the inclusion of immediate superiors in the process even where these are not of appointed grades, and of the fate of the forms and the actions to be taken when the appraisal interview is finished. While you are admittedly asked about your own bank's system, you would be given a good deal of credit if you contrast it with others you may know of.

When commenting on the qualities of the system, which is what the question asks next, you should give examples of the elements which work well. Be specific about how marks are allocated; don't say that marks are given over 'a range of categories' without listing them and discussing whether they are the right ones for the job.

Finally, the question asks for suggested improvements. You must be realistic to satisfy the examiners, all of whom are familiar with the practicalities of organisational life. Grizzles about personal injustices will attract no marks, nor will recommendations such as promotion for all after completion of certain training, or rises above the top limit of a grade simply on continued excellent performance.

Organisations might be able to make improvements, for example, in more frequent regular appraisal; or a check on the style and level of marking by particular managers, to minimise variation; or a new stage, after the interview between the local management, with head office personnel. This sort of suggestion, with some comment on its implementation, would have rounded off a good answer.

Question 5

What evidence do you have from the office you work in that your bank is abreast of modern office technology? What improvements could be made to the efficiency of the supervisor's work by the use of more modern information technology?

Just occasionally the examiners will come up with a question which is on, but not in the mainstream of, the syllabus, like this one. There is little in the way of formal theory to be applied: what is required is sensible structuring, informed observation and objective debate.

Your experience of modern information technology will be as wide and varied as the different offices you work in. Banks may have made a slow start in widespread use of personal information technology in the early 1980s, but have in recent years begun to join the leaders in what might be described as service technology designed to make life easier at the interface with the customer.

The question required reasonable non-technical explanation of what is available to the supervisor; and what should be available, and how it would render supervisory tasks more effective. It specified office technology (PCs with wordprocessor, spreadsheet, graphics, databases, facsimile, telephones with sophisticated exchange switching facilities and answer-machines, laser printers, advanced photocopying and so on); but you could also legitimately mention ATMs, EFTPOS and debit card systems, and customer account handling and enquiry technology, because it did ask how the supervisor's work could be improved, and all this adds to general efficiency.

Again there are two parts. You should answer the first part by observation of your own office and the computers, word-processors and customer-oriented technology, and you could contrast that with what you have seen of other offices, branches and banks.

In the second part you should connect what you have available, and what you would like to see available, with the various tasks or role elements of the supervisor in your office, and how improvements could be effected by the use of information technology. However, you would here, as always, be expected to be reasonably realistic in the costs of your suggestions, with some sense of what it would take to equip everyone with expensive pieces of electronic hardware!

Question 6

As part of a work experience scheme, Rachel, a fifth former from a local school, has spent a day in your office. At the end of the day you are surprised to hear her first reaction:

'I'm not so keen: it seems so dangerous. There's so much paper and furniture that a fire could easily break out, and there's all that electrical stuff: I don't think I would feel safe.'

Outline for Rachel the general precautions you are supposed to take to ensure that risks to health are minimised. Include any criticisms you may have of systems or practices in your office, and recommendations for improvement.

If you have studied, you would begin with a mention of the Health and Safety at Work Act 1974; your preparation would have included practice in summarising the main points of the act. The question asks for an outline in general terms, and you need not provide intricate detail. However, you would prove that you had prepared by mentioning the various responsibilities of employer, supplier, and employee.

Whether there is an Act of Parliament or not, sensible provision should be made for the health and safety of staff. Examiners read in answers to this kind of question, with horror, some believable (and some unbelievable) observations on local lapses in safety procedure.

Don't think that the examiners are just looking for sensational or scandalous breaches of proper provision: it is at least equally acceptable to say that procedures are meticulously carried out locally, and you should give evidence of your close inspection of this. If, however, there are criticisms of actual shortcomings in local office procedure, describe them carefully and express them objectively, even if you feel strongly about them. You may allow your concern to show through, but maintain a managerial attitude.

Recommendations for improvement are asked for in the final part of this multiple question. Marks will be given both for corrective suggestions to right a wrong practice and for innovative ones to advance safety from an already reasonable situation, provided that all are practical and economically feasible. The examiners would hope that what you say will be acted on, so as to preserve the supply of candidates!

Question 7

'Banks are equal opportunities employers'. Explain what is meant by this statement, and comment on it, supporting what you say with evidence from your own observations.

This is a sensitive topic, and you have to beware of treating it insensitively because of lack of preparation.

A good answer would suggest that there are laws or Acts of Parliament relating to this matter, and better ones would specifically quote these laws. The question specifically asks what is meant by the statement, and the initial sections of the answer would mention bank policies and their statements in terms of race, creed, and gender.

Banks are in the forefront of organisations which officially strive for equal opportunity, and cannot be criticised for their policy and practical attempts to achieve it. Sufficient credit should be given to the banks for specific actions to correct past and present discrimination: return-to-work plans, creches, accelerated training programmes, counselling and training for those trapped by their upbringing into prejudicial attitudes, equal opportunity managers: whatever your bank does or provides should be described, with just sufficient detail to show that you have considered this matter.

You may feel that these policies are indeed successful in your bank, and if so you should say so, backing your contention with evidence. However, it would not be unusual for your bank to have problems in implementation, and you might have clear evidence of a failure to treat all equally either on the grounds of sex or of race. You should give accounts of personal observations backed by some statistical enquiry and research done by questioning managers and personnel staff, which is recommended in this book as preparation for your examinations.

As to sex equality, UK banks are still top heavy with males. Look for example at the officially published photographs of banking conferences, indicating an extremely low proportion of female delegates. Make statements with statistical backing and not unsubstantiated grizzles about personal impedance. Examiners don't like the famous sexist myths about all women really wanting babies rather than careers, or acting on their emotions rather than logic.

As to race, managerial staff who are other than white are very rare, and it will be interesting to see if that changes as we advance towards the year 2000. Don't, by the way, use the term 'English' to refer to white staff and 'foreigner' for others (yes, people do that in examinations, believe it or not). Currently 'black', 'of Asian origin' or 'Afro-Caribbean' are acceptable in the context of sensitive discussion.

The question permits you also to comment on the success or failure of your own and other banking organisations to attract and to facilitate the careers of disabled people. You would obtain good marks for practical suggestions to right any wrongs you see about you, so that the bank's policies and top-level schemes are aided in achieving their objectives of true equality.

Question 8

How does your bank attempt to make sure its rewards package is fair to all? To what extent does it succeed in its attempts?

Questions are quite often asked about benefits. Please remember that a trot-out of a list of every single benefit available to bank staff almost invariably fails, however comprehensive and accurate. Depending on the question, pages of such lists may not even be counted as part of your answer. There is always an angle; always the need for you to apply what you know of the benefits to, for instance, comparisons with other occupations, or the various stages of your career, or specific rewards for specific excellence, or fairness.

Benefits questions also sort the studied from the casual: in this case, the former would know that the 'rewards package' refers to all that you get for going to work, and many of the latter would consider it to refer to an 'awards' package or performance incentive scheme, which will not only demonstrate their failure to study, but also their inability to read the question. It was in fact clearly about fairness in principle and in practice.

In answering, you should use the grading system to demonstrate that equity is aimed for by banks: advancing ability in the same job is rewarded by allowing progress within a grade, and increasing responsibilities by progressing a staff member from grade to grade. There is the 'fair' possibility of earning more as a very experienced and expert person in a lower grade than as a new and untried, but senior, person in a higher one; and equally, it is 'fair' that in the higher grade there is a greater earning potential.

You might also quote an appraisal system as evidence of fairness, so that nobody drifts for years at salary levels which under- or over-estimate their worth just for lack of attention to the matter; and there is usually some form of supervision of managerial judgement to prevent rewards being too dependent on local management prejudices. In banking, furthermore, the structure of rewards is such that as the career progresses the rewards are richer, and justly so. You also must point out that banks will ensure fairness by comparisons with outside organisations (and if the management don't do that, the staff representative bodies certainly will!).

There are lapses in fairness, and the question specifically permits you to demonstrate, if true in your case, that you have evidence of problems involved in the application of the bank's systems. However, the rewards package in the UK clearing banks and in most similar institutions is generally fair, and you may say so as a conclusion to a discussion such as is suggested here.

■ MAY 1991

Question 1

You have just been promoted to be supervisor of a section of your office. Your manager has asked you to put forward some objectives to improve the section's performance.

(a) What do good objectives have in common?
(b) With a specific section in mind
   (i) describe the work of the section;
   (ii) set out some of the more important objectives you would set for it;
   (iii) show how achieving those objectives would benefit your bank.

Essentially the candidate who has studied would understand the nature and characteristics of objectives, which should be:

- derived from higher goals;
- agreed by those who must attain them;
- visible and communicated to those people;
- realistic and within reach; but
- challenging and inspiring; and
- rewarded if attained.

After a brief description of the office in question, the good answer would specify objectives which complied with the characteristics.

Do please note the distinction between objectives – measurable targets for advancing achievement – and the simple requirements of the job. There is a danger of setting an objective to be accurate, or to provide an efficient service, or to be friendly to customers, or to work as a team, or to keep the office tidy, or complete the work of the day. These are not objectives but what you might reasonably expect in any case. Equally, objectives of absolute perfection are not sensible, such as; no mistakes, all customers seen immediately, all work completed every day and every complaint settled within 24 hours.

You should give reasonably realistic objectives stated in the form of targets, with a measurable or quantified element, the achievement of which would

would advance the work or the attainments of the office or section. And they could relate directly to your own department: there would be no harm in using real objectives or targets to answer this question, if you have any.

If the objectives are sensibly set, the benefits implied are easy to relate, and having succeeded in the first parts of the question, you will not find it difficult answering the last, preferably with quantified results.

Question 2

Is there a type of personality which is especially suited to bank work? What is the relevance of this to success in banking?

The examiners never give any marks for cosy fireside chat, in this case about the characteristics possessed by some sort of ideally virtuous bank clerk, who is friendly, smart, tidy, outgoing, service oriented and honest. You are required to select one or more (theoretical) model of personality, and the question does call for a little ingenuity in the selection.

You should give explanations of such models as that of Eysenck, distinguishing between extravert and introvert, stable and unstable; or Belbin's team roles (Chairperson, Shaper, Plant, Resource Investigator etc.) and the idea that a team would comprise many different personalities matching the team roles; or McClelland's model of people fitting achievement, affiliation and power types.

In particular, you might concentrate on the NOOP Seven Point Plan, used in recruitment and selection, to answer this question, discussing acceptable features under the headings of:

- physical make-up
- attainments
- general intelligence
- special aptitudes
- interests
- disposition
- circumstances

If properly done, and by that is meant adopting a contingency approach to the bank work described, this is a very sensible way to answer this question.

But don't forget to answer the last part of the question: bank work is so varied that there can be no one type of personality which is or is not suitable. It depends on whether you are talking about the night security guard, the receptionist or the executive director and there are a variety of personalities which would help a person to succeed in progressing from the position of first two to the last.

Question 3

You have overheard a conversation between two senior people in your bank. One has said that there is no problem about leadership: people do as they are told by managers just because they are managers, and the bank's rules mean that people automatically

obey those who are in authority. The other was of the belief that it is only good leadership practices that led to effective working, not just a manager's title.

What are the merits, if any, of each of these arguments?

In answering this question on leadership, start by being realistic and admit that those in authority do indeed have to be obeyed. You would obtain marks for discussion of Weber's theory or ideal type of bureaucracy, and the idea of lines of top-down authority.

The question gives a clear and obvious cue for the exposition of leadership models. Discussion (and rejection, largely) of trait theories might be followed by the exposition of management style ranges such as those of Tannenbaum and Schmidt, Likert, Blake & Mouton, and the like; and you will recognise that an authoritarian style, while effective ad hoc and in the short term, is not calculated to provide long term motivation for the staff.

Good management practices, in this case relating to leadership, are well characterised in John Adair's Action Centred Leadership model, for example, and you could explain what a good leader would do to satisfy task, team and individual needs. This and the other models would first of all have to be explained, then possibly applied to imaginary or real examples, or debated in terms of the question.

Little or no sympathy will be offered to those who are expansive concerning their managerial philosophies of life, with leaders being friends and advisers, running tight ships but happy teams. Just as with every other question on this paper, and every paper in this subject, you should give studied models and not personal aphorisms.

Question 4

What are the most important elements of the role of the supervisor?

This question may seem basic but in fact provides a possible pitfall, even for the prepared. What is required is to answer the question set and not the one hoped for. It asks for elements of the role, not the characteristics, of a good supervisor; but it would be all too easy to present either a set of supposed characteristics for the personality of a supervisor, or a set of skills which you believed a supervisor should have, or a mixture of qualities, skills and duties.

The answer should be constructed by means of a list of the various aspects of the role of supervisor as junior manager. There is a choice of such lists: an adapted form of those suggested by classical theorists, for example, including forecasting, planning, organising, motivating, controlling and monitoring; or those associated with managing the functions of an organisation, namely operations, finance, personnel, marketing and administration; or that of Mintzberg, the familiar roles under the headings of informational, motivational and decisional.

A good answer would define the role of supervisor, then make a systematic attempt to structure the contention in terms of the variety of managerial tasks the supervisor should undertake, as outlined above; better answers will use well-chosen examples from personal experience to illustrate individual points.

Question 5

'To be decisive means to make decisions instinctively'. Comment on the validity of this statement, using examples related to supervision in banking.

If you have a tendency to fail to read questions properly, you are likely to fail in particular to read the second half of this one: 'using examples related to supervision in banking': and you'll duly attract fail marks for the question. It is worth repeating as a general point that personal examples, if recounted in an objective and relevant way, are welcomed throughout this paper.

The model of decision making used in this book is as follows:

- Discern the need for a decision
- Set criteria for a good decision
- Gather facts and opinions
- Analyse the facts
- Set out a range of possible courses of action
- Calculate the utility of the outcomes of each
- Compare them with the criteria
- Make the decision
- Implement and monitor

People who can reproduce this in exams do so all too frequently bare and without explanation of each step; just expand each with a sentence which proves you know what they mean.

Now it is eminently obvious that some managerial decisions have to be made quickly, even instinctively. But there is often enough time to take a careful and considered approach; and answers taking an example of a specific decision through the above steps, either as they are described or subsequently, will be given sound marks. Strangely, in questions like this some candidates give answers which proceed well in terms of the theoretical steps and then founder by relating an example which simply does not fit, or even ignores, the model.

You would gain extra marks by referring to and giving an example of group decision-making techniques and the involvement of others in supervisors' decisions, which by definition eliminates the instinctive approach.

Question 6

'Training can be considered as a human right'. What do you suggest that trainees in a bank have a right to expect:

(a) from their training in general, and
(b) from their supervisor as far as training is concerned?

Yet again you can easily be trapped into giving prepared answers to a question you would like to have been asked, rather than thoughtful answers to the one which was asked. You are not asked for the advantages and disadvantages of on- and off-the-job training, which would only pass if the discussion is of what trainees have the right to expect from each. The question is also not about the location of responsibility for training.

The first part of the question actually asks what trainees have a right to expect in general from training, and a good answer would discuss this in terms of present needs to fill immediate training gaps in the job they are currently doing, and longer term training for the purposes of career advancement or for the fulfilment of their potential. On the other hand, you simply cannot expect promotion or tangible rewards simply for having completed a training regime.

The second part of the question, concerning what one might expect from the supervisor, should be divided into expectations before, during, and after the training. Supervisors have more to do than supervise staff training and keep an exclusive and constant eye on the development of staff, by the way: don't express unrealistic expectation of the training role of the supervisor. But whatever is the case in practice, trainees can expect briefing and orientation before training, support by ensuring job-cover during training, and debriefing and the supervisor's best effort to have the newly-acquired skills and knowledge put into practice after the training.

Question 7
It has been reported to you that a clerk on your staff has been overheard talking on more than one occasion about a specific customer's accounts in the bar of a local hotel. What would you do immediately to correct this situation, and what further steps are available to discipline the staff member if the offence is repeated?

This hypothetical case-style question is of course intended to have you demonstrate knowledge of your bank's disciplinary procedure. Anyone truly familiar with one would know that if the facts were established, the staff member in question here should have been subject immediately to the formal disciplinary procedure as the clerk is guilty of a serious offence (of misconduct or gross misconduct, via the breach of the Declaration of Secrecy and of bank disciplinary rules, not of breach of contract). The Chartered Institute of Bankers examiners will take a serious view, incidentally, if the answer suggested a course of action so incorrect as to plunge the bank into even deeper problems.

However, for the purposes of this examination the suggestion of initial informal steps would be accepted, provided that they are firm enough. Answers that suggest pussyfooting, skirting round the problem, or a kindly friendly initial chat on general subjects, creeping gradually towards the matter in question, would not be so well received. The issue should be honestly, firmly and straighforwardly – if confidentially – confronted, first of all to establish the facts as best you can.

The initial discussion over, simply lay out the formal steps to be taken in your disciplinary procedure. Transfer to another office would not solve the problem, just shift its location – this seems to be some candidates' solution to disciplinary problems! Don't say that the final responsibility for dismissal lies in the supervisors' hands, or that ultimately you would 'ask the clerk to resign', neither of which is appropriate.

You can go for higher marks by expanding on the issue, for example by quoting the ACAS Code of Practice on Disciplinary and Dismissal Procedures, or by discussing the fairness of your procedure, or debating the divided loyalties of the supervisor whose responsibility includes the protection of staff and ensuring a fair process. Where relevant personal examples are available and sensibly related, they will also be welcomed. By the way, brief mention of the basic elements of Tournier, the Prevention of Terrorism Act and drug-trafficking legislation would also score marks.

Question 8

'I don't know why I stay in banking – the benefits are not much different from any other employment'

To what extent is this statement true? What are the particular benefits of working for a bank?

Whenever this sort of question is asked, the examiners fear a trot-out of a list of every single benefit available to bank staff: and every such answer will simply fail, even if as an afterthought it occurs to you to admit that some of these benefits (such as salary, paid holidays and pensions) are also available outside banking.

When 'benefits' questions are asked there is always an angle. In this case, the clue was 'the particular benefits' of working for a bank: comparisons with other occupations are clearly requested. It isn't expected that you know exactly what is offered by other occupations: but you could first concede a short account of what all reasonable employment might offer in common; and then take benefits clearly exclusive to bank staff, and for each item, to show how it might be better than what is offered outside.

Good answers will concentrate on the concessions made for the use of 'the company product', namely finance, such as cheaper house-purchase and other loans, concessions on bank account charges and extra deposit interest, the non-contributory nature of bank pensions, profit sharing in a profitable business. But in other occupations cheap or free product is not the only non-salary benefit: paid holidays, maternity leave, annual bonuses, share option schemes, holiday savings clubs, sickness benefits, or relocation packages are not confined to banking, nor even particularly favourable in their generosity in banking.

You could certainly mention intangible benefits such as a higher probability of a progressive career, job security, status and prestige, decent working conditions, and declared equal opportunity policies. Better answers would point to elements of reward packages which might even be better in non-bank occupations, such as higher salaries, more flexible incentive and commission schemes, cars at earlier career stages, longer holidays, cheaper travel, as well as heavily discounted product.

You would also gain good marks by drawing tabulated comparisons between banking benefits and those of one or more outside occupations. In all cases specific examples are welcomed and rewarded, and accuracy in quoting rates and amounts is expected.

Index

ACAS 145, 168
Advice 86
Appraisal 163-7
   elements 164
   forms 165
   objectives 163
   problems 166
   and supervisor 166
Assertiveness 125-9
   and aggression 126
   techniques 128
Authority 9

Bank accounts (staff) 151, 194
Branch security 141, 149
Briefing 61
Budgets 13
Bureaucracy 3

Communication 52-62
   barriers to 59
   definition 52
   language 59
   media 56
   model 53
Classical Theory 3
Contingency 4, 5
Composition 60
Consultation 161
Control 51, 52
Corporate Plan 13
Counselling 86

Decision-making 43
   by group 44
Delegation 45-51
   benefits 48
   complex 47
   planning 50
   reasons for 47
   risks 49
   simple 46
Discipline 167-9
Dominant aggressor 127

Ego states 85, 122
Employment 143-9
   contract 143
   protection 145
Equal opportunity 147
   and supervisor 149

Environment 5
Expectations 78

Forecasting 39

Getting organised 117
Grading 183
Grievance 167-9
Groups 93-102
   conformity in 100
   definition 93
   development 97, 98
   formal and informal 95
   norms 98, 99
   sanctions 101
   and teams 106, 109

Hawthorne experiments 94, 99
Health and safety 136-41
   committees 140
   Health and Safety at Work Act 137
   need for 136
   and supervisor 140
History 2
Holidays 188-90
   entitlement 189

Information technology 62
Inspectors 141, 151-3
Interviewing 87-9
Introvert and extrovert 68, 124

Job evaluation 181-4

Leadership 102-9
   action-centred 104
   and group needs 104, 109
   qualities 102
   situational 103
Learning 75
Line and staff 9
Loans 187, 191
   house purchase 191
   other loans 194

Management 24
   functions 24
   roles 24
   style 27
Manager 24-8
   supervisor as 26

MBWA (Management by walking about) 111
Mechanistic 5
Mobility 174
    location allowance 187
Monitoring 51
Motivation 48, 78–84
    and reward 80
    internal 81

Needs 81, 104–9
    individual 81, 107
    task 105
    team 106

Objectives 12–16, 37
    and behaviour 14
    and expectations 30
    in interviewing 87
    management by 30
    setting 37
    statements 12
    and supervisor 15
Office representatives 159–60
Organisations 1–18
    charts 8
    depicting 8
    functions 6
    organic 5
    structure 4
Organising 25, 40
Overtime 185

Pensions 194
Personality 68–9
Personnel 7, 23
Planning 25, 39
    interviews 87
Private life 120
Problem solving 41–3
Problems
    my/your 129
Profit sharing 186

Relationships 31–3

Respect 31
    gaining 32
Reward 80, 180
    package 180
Role 1, 10
    conflict 11
    learning 11
    requirements 11
    separation 11
    signs 12

Satisfaction 83–4
    and dissatisfaction 84
    and motivation 84
Selection 70–2
Self-knowledge 122–5
Seven-Point Plan 70–2
Supervisor 19–33
    definition 21
    self-development 130
    title 21
Systems thinking 4
    socio-technical 5

Targets 12–16
    and behaviour 14
    displaying 14, 16
    specification 15
Teams 109
Things to do list 118
Time management 117–22
    equipment 119
Training 74–8, 169–74
    and learning 74
    gap 74
    on-and-off the job 75
    planning 76
    procedures 169
Transactional analysis 84–6

Unions 157–60
    officials 159

Wages and salaries 181–5
Working conditions 190